POLITICS AND SOCIETY IN WALES

The Pit and the Pendulum

POLITICS AND SOCIETY IN WALES SERIES
Series editor: Ralph Fevre

Previous volumes in the series:

Paul Chaney, Tom Hall and Andrew Pithouse (eds), *New Governance – New Democracy? Post-Devolution Wales*

Neil Selwyn and Stephen Gorard, *The Information Age: Technology, Learning and Exclusion in Wales*

Graham Day, *Making Sense of Wales: A Sociological Perspective*

Richard Rawlings, *Delineating Wales: Constitutional, Legal and Administrative Aspects of National Devolution*

The Politics and Society in Wales Series examines issues of politics and government, and particularly the effects of devolution on policy-making and implementation, and the way in which Wales is governed as the National Assembly gains in maturity. It will also increase our knowledge and understanding of Welsh society and analyse the most important aspects of social and economic change in Wales. Where necessary, studies in the series will incorporate strong comparative elements which will allow a more fully informed appraisal of the condition of Wales.

The Pit and the Pendulum

A COOPERATIVE FUTURE FOR WORK IN THE WELSH VALLEYS

By

MOLLY SCOTT CATO

*Published on behalf of the Social Science Committee
of the Board of Celtic Studies of the University of Wales*

UNIVERSITY OF WALES PRESS
CARDIFF
2004

© Molly Scott Cato, 2004

British Library Cataloguing-in-Publication Data.
A catalogue record for this book is available from the British Library.

ISBN 0–7083–1869–X

Typeset by Bryan Turnbull
Printed in Wales by Dinefwr Press, Llandybïe

For the people of the Welsh Valleys

'Lord', said he, 'we have risked our lives, and would do it again, but the country and the people for whom we slave ought to think a little more about us.'

Comment by one of the rescuers at the Tynewydd mining disaster reported in *Buried Alive! A Narrative of Suffering and Heroism, Being the Tale of the Rhondda Colliers as Related by Themselves* (London, 1877).

Contents

Figures

Photographs

Tables

Series Editor's Foreword

It must be blindingly obvious to the most casual observers that the Valleys of south Wales have economic problems but it takes courage and imagination to argue that we will not find the solutions to these problems in economics. Molly Scott Cato is an economist by training but she brings to her work the convictions of a social critic and it is on the basis of these convictions that she is able to map out the uses and limitations of economic analyses. Indeed, it is the way in which Scott Cato manages the creative tension between her values and her knowledge of economics that gives her book its distinctive character and purpose.

This book makes a contribution to the social science of economic behaviour, a field which is undergoing something of a renaissance characterized by a return to the intentions of the classical critiques of Durkheim, Marx, Simmel and Polanyi which judged economic behaviour according to clearly declared values.[1] Of course it is not enough to declare one's values in order to mount such a critique. A way has to be found to make values count in the analysis and, when this is done successfully, it amounts to a remarkable achievement. In spite of the promise of a classical renaissance, this field of social science is still dominated by the approach epitomized by economics in which only economic values – efficiency, growth, cost reduction – count. In order to build a critique these economic values have to be cut down to size before other non-economic values can be brought into account. Molly Scott Cato proves herself equal to this task. She shows how the familiar economic arguments and ways of accounting for costs, profits and loss are not all that they seem and in this way she is able to begin to put economic values on a par with non-economic ones.

The most important example of this achievement lies in the manner in which this book deals with the historical problem of the dearth of Welsh entrepreneurship. Throughout the last century, the leitmotif of any story about economic development in Wales was the absence of entrepreneurs and the consequences of this absence for wealth generation and job creation. This book looks very hard for new evidence of home-grown entrepreneurship that will be committed to Wales in a way that FDI, or foreign direct investment, has not been. FDI was at the heart of the economic development strategy for Wales after the age of coal and steel. In this book we search for signs of an alternative kind of entrepreneurship which will continue to create jobs and wealth in Wales even as markets and technology change. To do this the entrepreneurs will need to judge themselves by something other than just the bottom line.

Let us be clear that Molly Scott Cato is proposing that non-economic values are put on a par with economic ones but not, as some have argued, as a kind of golden key to growth. Any reader can readily understand that Scott Cato hopes that new indigenous enterprise will succeed but social science offers no guarantees. She is in a position to undermine the economic logic of FDI, and make us sceptical of the credo that 'uneconomic' jobs should not be supported, but she knows that she cannot claim that co-operative enterprises or sustainable development are the best ways to make Wales more prosperous. The important point that we must grasp is rather that, once the economic logic of the old strategies is put in question, we can begin to see how other things than simple accounting can be made to matter, things such as creating enterprises that persist because they have the will to reinvent their purpose as the years go by, creating work that people value, and even work that carries some sense of social responsibility.

In *The Pit and the Pendulum*, Molly Scott Cato sees such a sense of social responsibility as the flip side of the Welsh dislike of the profit-orientated entrepreneurial culture. In the south Wales valleys she describes, people are more likely to live by non-economic values such as cooperation, altruism and equality and do not wish to have to betray these values in the way they do their jobs and even when they choose what work they want to do. As in many working-class localities, these values and the experience of industrial work and culture have been mutually reinforcing but when the jobs go, and prospects dim, reinforcement is no longer possible. The acquisitive and competitive culture of capitalism, so familiar to the middle class, is adopted amongst the younger generations. The old cooperation and altruism connotes nothing but failure to young men and women. Yet when they acquire the needs of a consumer culture without the necessary jobs the result is dependence on benefits, and rising drug use and crime which threaten social cohesion. A Welsh route to jobs, perhaps as envisaged in this book, might go some way to address this demoralization over the longer term, but in the short-to-medium term, Scott Cato knows that we cannot rely on job creation alone. With her convictions given equal prominence alongside the values of economics, she argues for additional ways of supporting demoralized communities, for example by using citizens' incomes to give renewed meaning to social responsibility.

Many of the non-economic values that are championed here are familiar from studies of working-class culture in the UK and elsewhere and in this sense they are not peculiarly Welsh. Yet devolution has created a more favourable climate for the embodiment of these values in an economic strategy which has the stamp of a peculiarly Welsh experiment. Economic values are still central to UK government thinking on the economy and regional development; indeed much of this thinking bears the hallmark of an even more narrow obsession with the supply side of the economy. Little real thought is given to the way the demand for labour is generated, and still less to the sort of jobs that are created, but this need not be the case in Wales.

Evidence of Welsh experimentation in widening democratic participation is an example of the elevation of non-economic values in a post-devolution Wales. The expensive equal-pay deals recently agreed for the Assembly civil service and other groups of workers could hardly be justified on conventional economic grounds alone. The results of such experimentation include a reduction of the pay gap between men and women and the highest percentage of women in parliament anywhere. There was certainly nothing inevitable about these innovations and space had to be made for them to happen. Thirty years ago anyone might have scoffed at the idea of a uniquely Welsh approach to gender and diversity. Perhaps twenty or thirty years from now the success of socially responsible indigenous enterprise in Wales can be celebrated in the same way, but it is not necessary to argue that there is a rich, Welsh cultural resource from which growth and prosperity has simply to be drawn. It is just as plausible to argue that there is a rich culture of dependency which will handicap any attempt to grow and prosper.

Instead of romanticizing a tenuous link between culture and economy, we can agree that, largely because of devolution and the decline of traditional patterns of making a living, there is now the space to make new links between values and the economy in Wales. Here we have a promising direction for public policy, and a new doctrine for the Welsh Development Agency and other public bodies charged with promoting economic development. This book is about the development of a new strategy for Wales's areas of deprivation and decline which represents a more morally conscious alternative to the flawed doctrine of FDI.

Ralph Fevre
Cardiff
January 2004

Note

[1] For a recent discussion of the classical renaissance see R. Fevre, *The New Sociology of Economic Behaviour* (London: Sage, 2003).

Preface

In 1996, in conjunction with a Green Party campaign called *Why Work?*, I published a book called *Seven Myths about Work*. In it I attempted to examine what it is about work that is important in people's lives. Clearly, most people work to earn money, yet there is much more to it than that. Work is a way of establishing identity, of interacting with others, of finding one's place within a society. Good work adds meaning to life; bad work leads to demoralization for people and their communities.

I was fascinated by the concept of 'creating jobs' and was interested in the motivation behind this policy. I was also interested at an early stage in the government's favourite make-work policy: attracting foreign companies to invest in depressed areas of the UK. I could see how such a policy, supported as it was by the transfer of large amounts of public money, was attractive to the companies who invested. I was less clear about whether it served the interests of the workers in those economies and whether it represented good value for money for us all.

These were my theoretical interests and to explore their practical relevance I decided to carry out a piece of social research in a specific local economy. My reasons for choosing Rhondda Cynon Taff are discussed in the book itself. The romantic appeal of the area in terms of the history of work are obvious enough. Everybody knows the triumph of the Valleys during the Age of Steam and yet, I found, people were far less comfortable in dealing with the reality of the area today, in the 'post-industrial' era, which is, of course, not an era without industry, but an era when we pay people in other parts of the world to do our industrial work for us.

The findings of my research are offered in this book. I have tried to make them as rich as possible without straying too far outside the bounds of acceptable academic discourse. But there is so much I could not include that was both striking and troubling. I have failed to convey adequately in pictures or words the immense power of the landscape of the area, with its horizontal and vertical extremes. I would like to be able to share with you a conversation with any number of former miners I met, and the way their words are forced out past years' worth of coal-dust, emerging as though through an antique squeeze-box. I would like to be able to sum up the warm atmosphere in the many smoky, steamy cafés where I enjoyed lunch, or the sadness I felt when watching a couple of eleven-year-olds buying their Rizlas along with their sweets.

I am sure that before you can set out to invent policies for an area you must first understand the area in human as well as statistical terms. I have done my best to convey my understanding of Rhondda Cynon Taff. I invite you to share my insights. Perhaps I may even tempt some of those who do not yet know it for themselves to visit the Welsh Valleys.

Molly Scott Cato
Aberystwyth
December 2003

Acknowledgements

I should like to express my gratitude to Sue Charles and Andy Henley, my Ph.D. supervisors for their support, encouragement and interest throughout the course of this research. I must also thank Jane Black, without whose encouragement I would not have found myself back at University. Professor L. J. Williams was a source of kindness while I was writing my thesis and also supported my decision to write the findings into a book. I am grateful to the University of Aberystwyth for a research studentship that enabled me to conduct the research reported here.

Richard Wyn Jones, editor of *Contemporary Wales*, kindly encouraged me to submit a paper for publication there that is similar in content to Chapter 3 of this book. I would also thank Ralph Fevre for his help in ensuring that these findings would be published. My thanks also go to the librarians at the Hugh Owen Library, the National Library and RCT's many local libraries, without whose help this research would not have been possible – in particular Meirion Derrick, who gave me much assistance in finding data sources. The statisticians at the Welsh Assembly's Statistics Directorate have also been patient and helpful. I have recently had supportive collaboration in further work into the cooperative sector in Wales from colleagues at the Welsh Institute for Research into Cooperatives at the UWIC Business School: thanks for Len Arthur, Russell Smith and Tom Keenoy.

I am grateful for the support of the Social Science Committee of the Board of Celtic Studies of the University of Wales for ensuring that this book would see the light of day, and to Ceinwen Jones, Liz Powell and the staff of the University of Wales Press for their expertise.

I have had my fair share of crises of confidence during the production of this book, which were borne bravely by my partner Chris. My children Ralph, Josh and Rosa should also be thanked for tolerating my frequent headaches and need for peace and quiet.

Lastly, I would like to thank the people of Rhondda Cynon Taff. It is a social researcher's dream to meet people who are not only open and interested, but also opinionated and eloquent. Their courage and good humour in the face of the economic battering they have taken over such a lengthy period has been an inspiration.

Molly Scott Cato
Aberystwyth
December 2003

A Note on Data Sources and Language

A research study such as this always relies heavily on published data. The production of social and economic data follows its own schedule, focusing on the censuses that are conducted every ten years. It is only during the census that research at the ward level is gathered. (The ward is the lowest level of aggregation, corresponding to the area represented by a local councillor.) It is unfortunate for researchers who carry out their own research towards the end of a census period that the secondary sources they rely on are always going to be rather out of date. Since the censuses are conducted in years ending in the digit 1, the latest available data at ward level when this research was conducted was for 1991, although some basic data from the 2001 census have been included. The publication of this book is likely to coincide with the publication of the next round of census data drawn from the 2001 research, although it takes several years for the ward-level data to be published.

A researcher must adopt a strategy for dealing with this issue and I have chosen the following. Since my own research study was conducted in 1999 I have used data for that year whenever it was possible (in some cases the data itself was only published after I conducted the research). When it is important to present data at a lower level of aggregation – for example unemployment or poverty figures for actual wards – I have used data from the 1991 census. Data are drawn mainly from Welsh sources, especially the publications of the Wales Statistical Directorate and the Welsh Assembly online statistical resource, supplemented by data from the government's Nomis website.

As far as language goes, a choice had to be made between Welsh spellings of local place-names and choosing the English-language equivalents. In view of the sense I developed of the spiritual unity of Wales – which underlies the artificial economic and political divisions into north, mid- and south Wales – the first course would have been preferred. Readers visiting the Valleys for the first time would, I think, be surprised by the prevalence of Welsh place-names in an area where Welsh is not the standard medium of communication. However, since this is a book written in English, and with a predominantly English-medium readership, the decision was taken to choose the commonly accepted English-language forms or spellings for place-names where the two versions differ.

Abbreviations

CCC	Coalfields Communities Campaign
CI	Citizens' Income
FDI	foreign direct investment
GDP	gross domestic product
ILO	International Labour Organization
LQ	Location Quotient
MGCC	Mid Glamorgan County Council
R&D	research and development
RCT	Rhondda Cynon Taff
RSA	Regional Selective Assistance
SME	small and medium-sized enterprise
TNC	transnational corporation
UA	unitary authority
WDA	Welsh Development Agency

1

Welcome to the World of Work

Their mark on this land is still seen and still laid
The way for a commerce where vast fortunes were made,
The supply of an empire where the sun never set
Which is now deep in darkness, but the railway's there yet.
P. Gaston, 'Navigator'

If you had travelled a mere half-century ago by train in India or Kenya or any part of what was the British Empire, the chances are you would have been travelling along rails forged in Dowlais, Merthyr Tydfil.[1] And the coal that powered the trains and the ships that operated the trading system of the empire was hacked out of narrow seams by men in Treherbert or Porth or Trehafod.[2] In a most fundamental sense the empire of which the English were, and in some cases are, so proud was made by the work of the men of south Wales.

Yet, just as the 'navvie' who dug by hand most of the cuttings and tunnels our railways still use today has been mythologized as a drunken waster, so the workers of Wales have been denigrated and then discarded. They received little acknowledgement during the 'British' boom, but at least they were relatively well paid for their labours. Industrial culture has since moved on, strong men are now superfluous, and the workers of the Valleys are forgotten. The image of the scrap-heap that emerges so frequently in discussions of regions that have suffered from what economists euphemistically describe as 'industrial restructuring' is apt. Like exhausted or broken machine parts that no longer fit, men are cast aside. Because they have no use to the machine they are accorded no value.

It is because the Valleys of south Wales played such an interesting and important role in the history of industry in the UK that they offer such attraction to the student of employment policy. But the very strength of the historical tradition is also a potential pitfall. It is so easy to fall into nostalgic reminiscence about the days when the Valleys worked: when they raised the red flag at Hirwaun, when Paul Robeson sang at the Miners' Eisteddfod, when the miners marched back to Maerdy after the strike . . .

But a history, however grand, can only feed a community for so long. The Hollywood imagery of mam in a shawl gnashing her teeth, so hilariously satirized by Christopher Meredith in *Shifts*, was drained of meaning before it ever reached the cinema screen. Once Max Boyce arrived, with his upmarket rugby songs and his unfeasibly large leek, the game was well and truly up. South Wales can no longer rely on its history, however creatively packaged and resold to tourists from the Welsh diaspora. It is time to walk outside the museum and start thinking honestly and creatively about the future of industrial south Wales, and specifically about the future of its work.

This was my focus when I began the research reported in this book. I was surprised to find how little attention this issue had received from other academics, and particularly from economists. Apart from the periodic, and often inconsistent, forays by policy-makers into the mysterious land that lies at the end of the M4, Rhondda Cynon Taff (RCT), along with other similar mining and steel-making areas of the UK, has been condemned as an industrial geriatric case and left to wither. But these are places where millions of people continue to live, where children are born and raised, and where the human spirit thrives as much as it does in the more prosperous parts of the country.

Having decided to investigate the present and future of work in the Valleys, my training in social research, as well as my inherent nosiness, led me to wonder what the people making up the labour force there might think of their situation. Again I was astonished to find that nobody had asked them. It appeared that for the most part policy was made in London, based on investment from South Korea or the USA, but without considering the needs and aspirations of the people for whom the 'jobs' were being created.[3]

It is easy to see the former industrial areas of the UK as failures. The economy has failed to develop in the exciting new industries of information technology and services. The local workers have failed to adapt to new employment opportunities. But this sort of judgement is unfair. In an area reliant on a single form of employment, as the pit villages were, the whole culture and style of life became adapted to fit that type of work, whether coal mining or steel-making. If you know you are going to find work in your local village your expectation is that you do not have to travel to work. The local infrastructure and transport system respond to this. When jobs appear in the next valley or in Cardiff it takes a major cultural and institutional change to enable you to fill those jobs. Getting on your bike is a particularly unhelpful response to unemployment in such an area, for practical as well as cultural reasons.

Similarly, if you know that you will earn your daily bread as all your male relatives have done, by using your muscle-power, you see little reason to develop dexterity, sensitivity or intellectual skills. Such skills might well be disadvantageous in your future workplace. In such a cultural setting it is not sufficient to build a factory that requires neat, disciplined, pernickety workers and expect people to appear to fill those posts. In most areas, but especially in single-employer areas, workers adapt to the employment available. The precise adaptation of miners in south Wales explains the huge success of their work during the Age of Coal, but it equally explains their failure now. According to evolutionary theory it is the very well-adapted species that become extinct when the ecosystem changes: it is their very success within the existing environment that guarantees their failure in the changed one. If, as the Coalfield Communities Campaign (2001) claims, 'Many of the towns and villages that grew up in the Valleys and in North East Wales had just one purpose – to serve the coal industry', it is not surprising that since the decline of this niche they have not flourished. There has been no attempt by policy-makers to address the fundamental reasons why areas such as south Wales have failed to thrive in the New Economy. Without an attempt to explore and understand the cultural and psychological situation in such areas, any top-down policy-making is bound to fail.

Another inadequacy of the current debate on employment policy is its exclusive concentration on the quantity of jobs created (see OECD, 1994a, 1994b; European Commission, 1997). The argument in this book attempts to widen this discussion by including considerations of the quality of those jobs. Information about workers' subjective responses to their jobs is derived and these responses are compared across different workplaces (in Chapters 5 and 6). As is discussed in the section on ethics below, the research conducted for this study has been based on a commitment to value the subjective response to the jobs created on the part of those who are expected to carry them out. This is important not only in terms of an ethical employment policy, which respects individual autonomy, but also, and more practically, in terms of the likely success of policies in encouraging participation rather than avoidance (with reference to the importance of finding labour institutions that 'fit', see Freeman, 1996).

This book focuses on one area of high unemployment, but its findings are relevant to the issue of unemployment in general, particularly in the European context. The continuing high rate of unemployment within developed economies is driven particularly by areas where unemployment remains high in spite of economic growth elsewhere in the economy, so-called unemployment blackspots (see Webster, 2000). Often these blackspots occur in areas that were once dependent on a single employer, and where industrial restructuring has caused the rapid decline or disappearance of this employer. For this reason, understanding the mechanisms causing unemployment to persist in the long term in such areas, and generating effective policies to counter this tendency, can have a disproportionately beneficial effect on unemployment within a whole economy. The Valleys of south Wales represent such a blackspot, following the demise of the coal-mining and steel-making industries, and the research results reported here may therefore offer guidance for policy-makers in such areas in other industrialized economies. The research focuses on the Valleys, but findings from research conducted in other high-unemployment areas of the UK, especially those that have experienced industrial restructuring, are provided for context and comparison.

This introduction has made clear that this book will be informed by my heart as well as my head. I shall not engage in the typical quest for objectivity of the academic author. I could argue this case (and do later in this chapter) on the basis of a postmodern critique of the status of truth. However, it is simpler and more honest to say that I find such objectivity phoney. Leaving aside the possibility that one has no emotional commit-ment to one's field of study (and would it be possible to tolerate the long hours of research without it?), it seems to me that there is a simple choice: to be heartless or to wear one's heart on one's sleeve. Of these two I choose the second course.

SETTING THE SCENE

The image of the colliery is dominant in the popular conception of south Wales. So it is surprising to learn that until a mere two centuries ago the Valleys were the same undeveloped, wild, spiritually resonant landscape that many parts of mid and north Wales are today. The veneer-like quality of the industrial backdrop becomes clear once the slag-heaps acquire a thick coating of grass and become almost indistinguishable to the un-trained eye from the surrounding hills, the flat-topped *moelion*, that are so typical of the ancient uplands of the country.

The historical unity of Wales was brought home to me during one of my research jaunts when I took a wrong turning in the upper Rhondda Fach Valley. For those who are unfamiliar with the territory I should explain that human habitation has extended in narrow strips alongside the river valleys, so that each settlement tends to have one road, wide enough for only one car to pass in safety, although local drivers seem to have developed particularly good whiskers as a consequence and pass each other breezily enough. How-ever, for a timid outsider in a hired car there are few possibilities for a change of direction if you take a wrong turning, and hence I found myself way up on the heights once I had missed the signpost for Tonypandy.

Photo 1.1: The village of Pontygwaith in the Rhondda Fach valley is named after the works bridge. Many Valleys settlements take the names of the local mine-owner, hence Williamstown, Tylorstown, Wattstown and the Welsh versions Treherbert and Treharris.

The signs told me that I was coming into a place that some of the world outside south Wales has heard of, but for all the wrong reasons. Penrhys – on a promontory overlooking the Rhondda Fawr Valley – has been called 'one of the most brutally stereotyped estates in Wales'. It attracts such interest because it was built with the objectives of the planner in mind rather than those of the people who live there – rather as the local employment policy has paid little attention to the aspirations of local workers. The resilience shown by local people cannot on its own overcome the estate's many problems. These problems are largely failures of planning and policy but the estate's residents are routinely expected to take responsibility for them.

This is the veneer. Because underneath Penrhys is a stunning promontory with spectacular views of the still beautiful surrounding country. Penrhys was an important pilgrimage site during the days of the flourishing Celtic Church, as was the commemorative shrine of Saint Tydfil a few valleys to the east. Pilgrims came to Penrhys to worship at the shrine of the Virgin Mary, and before her doubtless of the Goddess herself.[5] The statue certainly attracted the wrath of Thomas Cromwell's men when they sought out all remaining manifestations of the Old Religion following the

Photo 1.2: Two faces of Penrhys. On a promontory overlooking the Rhondda Fawr valley, Penrhys was visited as a pilgrimage site to the Virgin Mary until the destruction of her statue in 1536. It is now best known for the social housing estate pictured here behind the new statue.

Reformation. They ranked the statue in importance with some that are now more well known: 'She hath been the devil's instrument to bring many (I fear) to eternal fire; now she herself, with her old sister of Walsingham, her young sister of Ipswich, with their other two sisters of Doncaster and Penrhys, would make a jolly muster in Smithfield' (letter from Cromwell to Bishop Latimer, dated June 1536, quoted in Pride, 1975). Cromwell's emissaries were sent out to destroy these statues and instructed to act 'with quietness and secret manner as might be', but the people nonetheless defended their carved statue (Gray, 1996).

In an area which has adapted so perfectly to its industrial role, it seems paradoxical that Valleys people are still in close contact with the land. The description of pit 'villages' with their close community ties more typical of rural areas is one example of this. Another is the widespread love of the wild countryside (always referred to as 'mountains') and the large number of lovingly tended allotments. A recent survey of local people found that the environment was their highest priority, a finding which surprised the RCT economic planners who carried out the survey.

However, there is no question that 150 years of coal mining has left a deep mark on every aspect of the Valleys and its people and an understanding of the demographic, economic and cultural impact of coal mining in RCT is essential before any policy proposals for tackling unemployment can be made. The basic statistic underlying any consideration of employment in the former coal-mining areas of the UK is a simple one: 'during the 1980s and early 1990s the UK coal industry shed more than 90% of its workforce' (Beatty, Fothergill and Lawless, 1997: 2041). When you combine this with the understanding of the concept of a 'pit village', whose whole employment rationale revolved around that one form of employment, you begin to grasp how devastating the pit closures were. Some statistics indicating the impact of mining and its decline are presented in Chapter 2, and an exploration of the social consequences is offered in Chapter 4.

WELSH EMPLOYMENT POLICIES IN TRANSITION

The rapid change in the economic structure, particularly of industrial south Wales, is the background against which the study reported here was conducted, and against which future employment policy in Wales must be developed. These changes have come as a result of economic and political pressure and a largely laissez-faire attitude to economic development. This research study was carried out on the cusp of great changes for Wales as a whole and the Valleys in particular. The election of a Labour government for the UK was expected to spell the end of twenty years of neglect by local people. The movement in power over the Welsh economy from Westminster to Cardiff, following the establishment of the Welsh Assembly in 1999, meant that the future in Wales would surely involve an increased role for state planning in employment policy. This was acknowledged in a report compiled for Welsh MPs before the establishment of the Assembly itself: 'These are exciting times for Wales. The creation of the National Assembly gives us an opportunity to develop a regional economic policy distinctive to Wales and framed to meet our particular needs' (WAC, 1998: para. 2).

Given the major political and cultural changes currently taking place in Wales it may be illuminating to consider Wales as an economy in transition. In common with transitions from colonialism and from communism the future direction of change is unpredictable. While Wales, in contrast to emerging economies of the Second and Third Worlds, has all the institutions of a market economy in place, it shares with these economies an uncertainty as to its identity and a national culture which requires distinct forms of market and social institutions (for a discussion of these issues in eastern Europe see the collection edited by Tykkyläinen, 1995, particularly the chapters by Klemencic and Shteinbuka; see also Strömpl, 2000; Lauristin and Vihalemm, 1997; Summers, 1992).

It also shares with the former Eastern bloc countries a sense of 'learned helplessness' that results from a history of paternalist employment provision by nationalized industries and the public sector. This emerges strongly in the interview evidence presented in Chapter 6, and helps to explain the weakness of the small-business sector in the former industrial areas of Wales (see EAPSG, 1999: 7). Another shared problem is the existence of a majority class of male, industrial workers who have traditionally received the highest wages and who are reluctant to accept market wages appropriate to their skill levels. In industrial south Wales, as in the former Soviet Union, the male, industrial worker was idealized, and adjustment to work in the twenty-first-century setting is difficult for both groups of workers.

Meanwhile, some common threads can be found between the Welsh situation and that facing developing countries after independence: weaknesses such as the absence of a strong sense of independent economic identity, a large informal economy, and the lack of an indigenous entrepreneurial base are common to both (J. J. Thomas, 1992), combined with a desire to establish autochthonous economic models, possibly in opposition to an economic model that may be considered to have been 'imposed' by a perceived 'foreign' power. Rajan writes of the situation facing policy-makers in newly independent India:

> The modern bourgeoisie of a post-colonial country such as India are trapped by the Western 'Enlightenment' education they have received and the new homogenised culture of modern times. They seem destined to repeat the errors of the West, but from a position of dependence and inferiority, caught in a nightmare of trying to catch up, though they know they will never be able to do so. (Rajan, 1993: 13).

For many developing countries establishing authentic and appropriate economic models is a crucial stage of economic development which may be overlooked by economic planners trained by Western institutions (for a discussion of this issue in different national contexts see Marglin and Marglin 1990, 1996; Apffel-Marglin, 1998; Visvanathan, 1997; Ngugi, 1986; Said, 1994). As Wales begins to take control over its national economy it is important that the same process occurs here.

Evidence for the attempt to construct an authentic Welsh form of economic development in Wales is emerging from debates conducted in the Welsh Assembly, particularly, and predictably, from the Plaid Cymru AMs. Dafydd Wigley, Plaid Cymru AM for Caernarfon, made the point in a debate in the Assembly on its strategic plan 'A Better Wales' held on 10 October 1999:[6]

> Let us not mince words. We do have values in Wales that are different to those in England. They are not better or worse, but different. Those values include

the importance of community, the attachment we have to social justice, and a greater emphasis on public well-being rather than only on private profits . . . The Assembly must base its vision on those values.

Later in the same debate another Plaid Cymru AM, Cynog Dafis, acknowledged the importance of creating authentic Welsh models and policies:

I am extremely pleased to see the need for policy development tailored according to the needs and circumstances of Wales in the summary of responses . . . At the moment there is a tendency to copy slavishly the policy hand-me-downs from London . . . We must reject that sort of tendency . . . We will judge the strategic plan in the light of this question: to what extent will it reflect our national priorities in Wales, not ones that have been set in other places?

In summing up the debate the Welsh Secretary for Economic Affairs, the Labour politician Edwina Hart, acknowledged and supported this position: 'We have Welsh values and a community that must be part and parcel of this. We are different. We have certain community values, dreams and ambitions that bind us together. That must be reflected in the plan.'

It is also vital that planners deal with the specific problems of Wales's coalfields. The failure of the coalfield areas of England to achieve economic regeneration attracted the attention of the Labour government shortly after its election in 1997. But 'in the spirit of devolution' Wales's struggling coalfields communities were left out of this initiative, including considerable funding for local projects from the Coalfield Enterprise Fund. Some success has been achieved in England and there is a particular duty on Wales's politicians to match this in a framework of devolved power over economic development (see Coalfield Communities Campaign, 2001).

The Welsh worker, or at least the image of her/him, is also undergoing a transition. In Chapter 4 I describe in some detail the traditional image of the worker in Wales as a male, unionized worker in heavy industry, particularly coal and steel. As these industries have been restructured this image has hampered Wales's attempts to attract alternative forms of employment. In response to this employment pattern policy-makers in Wales have attempted to replace it with a new image:

So in an effort to enhance Wales as an investment location the WDA [Welsh Development Agency] has tried to eradicate the country's historically strong associations with coal and steel, because these are felt to be unattractive to potential high technology industry. Indeed the main emphases of its marketing campaign have been to project Wales as a rural idyll, with good communications (for instance, the celebrated M4 motorway in the South) and a 'flexible' workforce. (Morgan, 1987: 41)

Although this strategy may have been effective in attracting inward investors its potentially negative impact on the identity of former industrial workers, and on those who live in the depressed areas, has been overlooked. They may not recognize themselves in the 'flexible' worker of the WDA brochure, leading to their further demoralization and discouragement.

For younger workers in south Wales, however, the influence on the Welsh workforce of Japanese corporate values appears to be a lasting one (Munday, 1989). While this culture of strict discipline and management control may have positive effects in terms of productivity, it may also act to undermine Welsh workers' and business people's confidence in their own ability to undertake economic development along their own lines. This may be another reason for the apparent weakness of the small-business and self-employed sector in Wales, and the absence of entrepreneurship.

It is crucial that future employment policy is rooted in Welsh reality, hence the value of the example of Tower Colliery that I discuss in Chapter 7 as an instance of successful indigenous economic activity. While there has been no shortage of initiatives suggested to tackle Wales's economic problems, a model which derives from Welsh sources would seem to have more chance of success than any transplanted model.

METHODOLOGY AND THE PROBLEM OF OBJECTIVITY

The methods commonly favoured within the discipline of economics involve the development of theoretical models and, sometimes although not necessarily, their testing using the method of multiple regression. This methodology has been so successful in generating robust and generalizable results that it is now dominant within the discipline, so that methodology is a topic which is not frequently discussed by economists (see Lawson, 1994). While the regression methodology may be valid mathematically, interpretation is always problematic, since different real-world events may produce mathematically identical results. T. Lawson (1997) questions the capacity of such a methodology to explain complex social phenomena when it requires radical simplification and strict and sometimes implausible assumptions. For this reason the research reported below is based on a less strict, more ethnographic method, based on a detailed exploration of one local economy, using local publications, a small-scale survey, and unstructured interviewing. This has the risk of losing tightness and generalizability, but yields a depth of understanding that is simply impossible to achieve using quantitative analysis.

The method followed in the research reported in later chapters draws on ethnographic methods used more frequently in related social sciences such as social anthropology and sociology. The use of sociological insights to deepen economic analysis is by no means new. In his *Economic Sociology* (1996), Swedberg defines his subject as 'the sociological approach applied to economic phenomena'. He distinguishes this form of economics as one that views the economic actor as part of a group or society, and views the economic systems he operates within as based in an underlying social system. In an edited collection by economic sociologists Granovetter outlines a 'theoretical agenda for economic sociology'. He explains the role of the discipline: 'economic sociology can make a first contribution to understanding the economy by calling attention to the mixture of economic and social motives that people pursue while engaged in production, consumption or distribution' (Granovetter, 2001: 3). This conception of economics as socially based leads to the use of a variety of methods distinct from the formal model-building of conventional economics. While the present volume could not be said to be wholly within the tradition of economic sociology (and there is, of course, a vast literature concerned with work in the field of sociology), relevant insights from sociology are brought to bear on the problem of unemployment.

While economic analyses of unemployment have focused heavily on measurement and modelling, some characteristics of long-term unemployment have been admitted to have a psychological or cultural component, for example Friedman's (1975) exposition of the expectations-augmented Philips curve with reference to the theory of sticky wages and the idea of the 'work-shy subculture' (e.g. Lindbeck, 1996). Economists are also aware of the social and psychological costs of long-term unemployment – see, for example, the discussion of the 'psychic costs' of unemployment by Layard, Nickell and Jackman (1991: 1). These issues may indeed be important in terms of developing economic policies, but they have been inadequately addressed empirically.

The following sections explore some of the issues relevant to the choice of methodology for this research.

Philosophical problems

A primary requirement for research to be considered 'scientific' is that it should be objective. Following the tenets of logical positivism as originally developed by the philosophers of the Vienna Circle,[7] the prototype for all scientific study should be mathematics and its irrefutable analytic truths.

This ideal held sway in the sciences and to a lesser extent the social sciences from the early years of the twentieth century until it was challenged from the 1960s onwards. Its influence on the discipline of economics, where mathematical analysis is now dominant, is clear.

The scientific method, taken as based on experimentation with theory choice following a Popperian falsificationist pattern, has been undermined in recent years. Although the radical position on science adopted by Latour (1987, 1999) is often thought of as a new departure, it is in reality only an extension of the insights in Kuhn's 1962 work *The Structure of Scientific Revolutions*, where Kuhn challenged the accepted view about theory choice. According to W. C. Salmon,

> The choice between two fundamental theories (or paradigms), he maintains, raises issues that 'cannot be resolved by proof'. To see how they are resolved we must talk about 'techniques of persuasion', or about 'argument and counterargument in a situation in which there can be no proof'. Such choices involve the exercise of the kind of judgement that cannot be rendered logically explicit and precise. (W. C. Salmon, 1990: 257)

Kuhn suggested that, rather than having any claim to an independently existing 'objective' world, decisions made by a community of trained scientists constitute the best criterion of objectivity that we can have. He suggested that such scientists should choose their theories according to a number of characteristics: accuracy, consistency, scope, simplicity and fruitfulness.

Thus science's claim to objectivity has been radically undermined for the past forty years. Following Kuhn other philosophers of science extended his view of the ineligibility of claims to objectivity, in the case of Feyerabend in spite of his early determination to construct such a rational scientific model. He found that this was philosophically impossible and adopted instead a position characterized as 'naive falsificationism'. According to Feyerabend (as cited in Preston, 1997: 16):

> We should feel no embarrassment about constructing and pursuing theories, even the most highly metaphysical ones, which go well beyond the data. All theories are on the same footing in being *hypotheses*. But this does not mean that we are wrong to theorize.

While such an extreme denial of the need for objective or even factual foundations for our theories would lead to research that had very limited representativeness, it does indicate the extent to which scientific objectivity has been philosophically undermined.

This problem is exacerbated in disciplines falling within the social science faculty, whose subject matter is human beings. Even for those who are still prepared to accept the objectivity of experiments involving inanimate objects, research with people introduces additional problems related to both the unpredictability of the subject and the threat to scientific objectivity posed by the relationship between researcher and researched (this issue of relationship in research is addressed further in a later section).

Political problems

Science has faced a separate critique since the 1960s – one which is grounded in politics rather than philosophy and which is associated with philosophers of critical theory and postmodernism. The critical theorists (particularly the francophone philosophers Foucault, Lyotard and Derrida) focused on the importance of dialogue and the very language it is written in when accounts of phenomena are presented. Foucault's critical view of the image of the self radically undercuts the view of the scientist as an independent, objective observer of the research subject (see e.g. Foucault, 1969). Derrida's target is the language of philosophical debate itself: his method of deconstruction aims to show how the outcome of discussions is largely determined before we even begin speaking, since the words we are able to use already contain the assumptions of the existing power structure (see e.g. Derrida, 1967). Lyotard, whose work developed critical theory towards an interest in *The Postmodern Condition* (1967), rejected the possibility of a social consensus upon which a research project could be built, as well as questioning the ability of people to achieve successful communication at all.

The overall result of the intellectual activity of the critical theorists is to undercut the foundations of the Western scientific tradition; what was once considered solid intellectual ground has been demonstrated to be quicksand:

> [the] fate of science was finally sealed, on this account, by the Lyotard–Foucault–Derrida assault. The linguistic gap between description and reality and the interplay of power and discourse mean that science is suspect on more than one count: it is either sheer surface or mere power. (H. Lawson, 1989)

So fundamental is this critique to the contemporary intellectual project that Lawson himself characterizes the question of 'the status of truth' as 'the central question of our time' (1989: xiii).

The contribution of postmodernism, a philosophical position most closely identified with Baudrillard (1975, 1988), is an application of some central Marxist concepts to the present economic conditions. A key feature of postmodernity identified by Baudrillard is the trivialization of values: extending Lyotard's point about the breakdown of traditional consensual ideologies, Baudrillard suggests that these have been replaced with meaningless 'simulacra' which 'refer to nothing but themselves', TV adverts being the exemplar of such a form. In such a world the research project faces the problem of distinguishing the real from the image. (This is a salient problem in the research field studied here, as identified by J. Evans, 1994.)

For many postmodernists one of the key areas of life that has undergone change in the movement from the modern is that of work. Extending the old idea that our understanding of 'work' has always been subject to ideological pressure (as theorized in Weber, 1915), in the postmodern world our central role as workers is undermined and replaced by our role as consumers. For Bauman (1998) the most significant problem facing the 'workless' is that they no longer have a role or identity, not because they cannot work but because they cannot consume. A research project that focuses on work, and the lack of it, cannot therefore ignore the post-modernist conclusion that the 'axial principles' of society are becoming increasingly located in 'theoretical knowledge' rather than in 'capital and labour'. This has clear economic implications, in terms of job creation as well as the distribution of wealth. As identified by Lyon (1994: 40):

> an impression was given . . . that the information society is one in which the benefits of new technology will be distributed in a roughly equitable fashion . . . As a social reality, however, high levels of unemployment persist in an era of technological and economic restructuring, despite apparent growth . . . Productivity no longer spells job creation, it seems.
>
> Moreover, that uneven advantage is geographically accented . . . However much the potential of new technology may point to the possibilities for novel sites for 'informational' expansion, the reality is that traditional centres of manufacture and innovation tend still to offer benefits such as an existing financial, labour and transport infrastructure.

A specific discussion of postmodernism in the context of the south Wales Valleys has been provided by J. Evans (1994). He draws attention to the vast gulf between the image of the area as presented in films and novels and the real situation in the locality and deconstructs the political dialogue surrounding the pit closure programme:

> To isolate the miners and to win much needed public support, the Government used a partisan media to bring into play its key words, 'economic', 'un-economic', and 'law and order', while the miners countered with 'community', 'right to work' and 'right to manage' as their own. (Evans, 1994: 8)

This existence of two parallel discourses of reality, where the same word can have different meanings for different groups and in different contexts, emphasizes the difficulty of engaging in debate over the unemployment situation in south Wales, and the impossibility of simply applying a given methodology, with its accompanying definitions and assumptions, to such a complex and contested situation.

Psychological limitations

Although the issue of unemployment has attracted the attention of many economists, the subject of motivations towards work has attracted only a few. While labour-market theory accepts that the demand and supply sides of the labour market are equally important in establishing an equilibrium, consideration of workers' decision to 'supply' their labour tends to be limited to considerations of financial reward, plus the subjective value placed on leisure. More sophisticated consideration of the effect a certain employment situation might have in terms of status or psychological feedback has been absent, despite the acknowledged inability of conventional methods to explain 'persistence mechanisms' or workers' unwillingness to take up the available employment. The subject of motivations in employment, while still marginal to economics, is the bread and butter of several related disciplines. Psychology has already been identified, and plays a limited role in this book. However, insights gained from the anthropological and sociological literature are adduced in the following chapters when their contribution is considered helpful.

A related psychological problem attaching to a consideration of work from any perspective embedded in the intellectual community is that of cultural limitation. Social anthropologists have led the way in their developing awareness of how their own social and cultural situation affects their view of the object of their study (see Clifford and Marcus, 1986; James et al., 1997). However, such a problem also affects any consideration of work, particularly since it is a subject of such ubiquity. Since, in a broad sense, we nearly all work, most of us have considerable conceptual baggage surrounding what work is and should be, and this affects any theoretical analysis we undertake. The classic example of this within economics is the stereotype of the male breadwinner, which underlies much of the model-building in labour economics. The work of Becker illustrates this dilemma in spite, or perhaps because, of his willingness to address the motivational concerns sidestepped by other economists. His writings on the division of workplace and domestic responsibilities between men and women (1986 and 1991) epitomize the danger of viewing economic reality through spectacles of a certain hue – in this case that of a late twentieth-century, male US breadwinner – as illustrated in the following quotation:

> The advantage of a division of labour within families does not alone imply that women do the child-rearing and other household tasks. However, the gain from specialised investments implies the traditional sexual division of labour if women have a comparative advantage in childbearing and child rearing, or if women suffer discrimination in market activities. A sexual division of labour segregates the activities of men and women and segregation is an effective way to avoid discrimination. (Becker, 1986: 9–10)

More subtle cultural specifics result from the particular nature of academic work itself. As Hakim (1998) identifies (herself a rare example of an academic with lengthy experience of work outside academe), economists' comprehension of workers' attitudes towards monitoring and discipline are limited as a result of their particular experience of the flexible hours and low levels of supervision that have traditionally typified the life of a university lecturer.

Feminist concerns

The cultural limitations of conventional economic methodology, and social scientific methodology more generally, have also been the subject of analysis by feminist theorists and methodologists both within economics and in other disciplines. Feminists see one specific power structure, the patriarchy, as deeply embedded in both language and the scientific method. Thus a feminist methodology would seek to reveal the gender dimension that is implicit in all disciplines. Beyond this basic commitment, feminist methodology is committed to emancipation, in the sense of including within analysis and debate those whose perspective may have been neglected: 'Feminists embrace and legitimize the experiences of those who are traditionally objectified, injecting the subjective into the discourse and respecting plurality' (James, 1998: 5). A commitment to such plurality has also influenced the methods followed in this book.

The feminist critique of economics has focused particularly on its assumptions, for example the selfishness and individualism of economic actors which are based, according to England (1993), in 'a separative model of human nature' that reflects a masculinist view of reality. Nelson (1995a) identifies the four aspects of conventional economics that reflect patriarchal biases: the nature of the models it is based on; its methods of research; the topics that research focuses on; and the way the discipline is taught to students. She argues that 'a fuller range of tools to study and teach about a wider territory of economic activity would make economics a more productive discipline for both male and female practitioners' (1995a: 146). While there is insufficient space here to become embroiled in these debates, they have certainly influenced the methodology followed in this research, so that a more questioning perspective on economic action has been adopted.

Feminist methodology extends beyond casting a critical perspective on the subject matter itself; it also concerns itself with the way the research is conducted. In contrast to the objective, distant scientist as portrayed by masculinist methodology, within the feminist research tradition the importance of intuition, personal experience, and relationship in research are acknowledged. James, whose research in the field of international relations used the unusual method of unstructured interviewing (James, 1996), discusses the marginality assigned to this method within the social sciences:

> If we are to take social science seriously as a science, then data tends to be quantifiable, readily tabulated and compared . . . Unstructured interviews . . . can be criticised for providing data that relies on subjective judgements, and for being unable to give expression to or account for differences between private thought and actual, given comment. (James, 1996: 6)

She justifies the use of such a method on the basis that it allows the respondents themselves to set the agenda. This not only respects their autonomy as research subjects, but also reveals deeper dimensions than those revealed by a predetermined questionnaire.

In terms of the nature of the research relationship, feminists have extended the critique of scientific objectivity, pointing out that any research situation 'in the field' inevitably involves a relationship between two people. For example, Oakley (1981) considers that any such relationship is bound to involve not only personal and emotional contact, but also a subjective judgement of support or antipathy towards the research subject. Thus the distant objectivity suggested by classical social scientific methodology is impossible (see Fox Keller, 1985). Similarly, the commitment to 'neutrality' has been challenged: Nelson goes so far as to suggest that, in the field of economics, research without values may turn out to be research without value (Nelson, 1993). Taking issue with an artificial objectivity, which she terms 'objectivism', she suggests a pluralist alternative:

> Strong objectivity, or objectivity that does not degenerate into 'objectivism', is based not on an illusion of detachment, but rather on a recognition of one's own various attachments and on the partiality this location lends to one's views. The antidote to subjectivism and personal whim comes not from purity

in method, but from comparison and dialogue among various views within an open community of scholars. (Nelson, 1995b: 48)

This refusal to avoid emotional involvement may be strongly justified in research conducted in the Welsh context since, as identified by a US anthropologist, within the Welsh culture 'emotional engagement is the correct approach to people' and it is considered that 'intellectual detachment from other people is to some degree inhuman' (Trosset, 1993: 150, 155).

Ethical dilemmas

Consideration also needs to be given to the ethical basis of the methodology that is chosen. How research is conducted, which people are included and which excluded, for example, is a decision with strong moral implications. According to Preston:

> The kind of knowledge, science and society we have is up to us . . . because epistemology (and therefore philosophy of science) is normative and because our knowledge depends not on how things are in a world independent of our will but on our decisions, the decisions we make can and must be evaluated by reference to our ideals. Some of these ideals, perhaps the most important ones, will be ethical. (Preston, 1997: 21)

A strong ethical position implies that, particularly in a research project which aims to influence policy-making, it is a moral imperative to involve as much as possible the people for whom the policies are being recommended. For this reason the research reported here involved making contact with 'the field' and consulting the people who work in Rhondda Cynon Taff before suggesting future courses of action that may affect them deeply. While my contact with workers in RCT was far more limited than I would have wished, it does provide a snapshot of working life in the area from the perspective of those who carry out the work. Aside from any ethical position, the richness of understanding yielded by spending time in a certain area greatly enhances the knowledge derived on the basis of published data alone.

A related ethical issue concerns the autonomy of the research subject. Again this is a question addressed most fully by social anthropologists, who have expressed concern that they may be using the subjects of their research merely as 'research fodder' and that one form of economic colonialism may be being replaced by a more subtle form of intellectual colonialism (see, for example, Apffel-Marglin, 1998). One response to this is to change the nature of the research relationship:

To act responsibly, our engagements with people living lives different from our own must result first of all from a *mutual* desire for interaction. We must stop arriving uninvited in people's back yards . . . our commitment must shift from profession and career-building to mutual nurturance – and this requires the abandonment of the pursuit of knowledge for knowledge's sake. (Apffel-Marglin, 1998: 42)

While I may stand accused of arriving uninvited in Rhondda Cynon Taff with my tape recorder and notebook in hand, I have tried to give weight to the concerns of the people I met there and to respect their needs and perspectives.

Pragmatic problems

Aside from the ethical concerns expressed in the foregoing section, there is a far more pragmatic reason for developing a deep understanding of the area under study and the people who work there. This is quite simply that a policy is unlikely to be successful if it is wholly inappropriate to its setting. In the case of the research presented in this book a good example is the existence across the south Wales Valleys of a thriving informal economy. For obvious reasons, the true extent of this activity is unknown, but to ignore its existence entirely is to remove an important source of motivation towards or away from conventional employment for many of those towards the lower end of the earnings scale. Ignorance of the impact of the informal economy on employment decisions will inevitably reduce the effectiveness of employment-creation measures.

More generally, a failure to be sympathetic to the culture of an area will also reduce the effectiveness of policy measures (on a related point see Freeman, 1996). This issue is addressed in detail in Chapter 3 as part of a critique of the limited success of inward-investment job creation in south Wales. For the past two decades or so a style of work developed in East Asia has been introduced into an area with a completely alien work culture. This attempt to make the workers change to fit the jobs that are created, which I elsewhere refer to as 'Procrustean policy-making' (Cato, 2000a), has proved of only limited effectiveness. An alternative approach, and one which I attempt to follow in this book, is to start with the workers themselves, their personalities, attitudes, prejudices and aspirations, and to combine a knowledge of these with an understanding of the economic realities facing the area to build an employment policy which is appropriate. Merely from a pragmatic point of view it would seem that such a method of developing policy is more likely to meet with success.

Methodological conclusions

How far should concerns about the scientific underpinnings and cultural biases of research influence the choice of method? It seems that for many economists this is an area best avoided altogether. According to T. Lawson (1994: 106), Hahn's advice to young economists on the occasion of his retirement from Cambridge was to 'avoid discussion of "mathematics in economics" like the plague [and to] give no thought at all to methodology'. At the other extreme the conclusions of the philosophical and political critiques of positivism can lead to intellectual lassitude and methodological nihilism. Two suggested pragmatic responses are reflexivity and triangulation.

In response to the critical theorists' attack on discourse we need not throw out the baby with the bathwater. Rather than seeking to defend an unattainable objectivity, we can acknowledge the limitations of our perspective but turn its subjectivity to advantage by also presenting a 'reflexive account' of our personal ideological baggage. This allows readers of our research to judge for themselves the bias and the kinds of perspectives they are likely to find in it. This is a course rarely followed by economists, but for the importance of the recognition of personal baggage in anthropology see Nader (2001). In my case it seems central to my research concerns and the methodology I adopt that I am a woman; if I were a man I find it impossible to believe that the same issues would have attracted my attention. In addition, it seems important that readers should know of my own family links to the study area I have explored.[8]

Triangulation refers to the use of differing research methodologies to cast light on a research question from different perspectives (by analogy with the process of mapping land from three points). Since it seems impossible to prove the unassailability of any individual methodology, the use of several is likely to provide a firmer foundation on which to draw conclusions (for further details see Flick, 2002; and in the Welsh research context Trosset and Caulkins, 2001). Thus the work conducted in the study area and reported here uses two different methodologies: survey research and the quantitative analysis of its results, together with informal interviewing more similar to the ethnographic work of social anthropologists.

Throughout the book I also use a variety of sources including visual images and literature. The intention is to weave together insights from different disciplines and different parts of human experience to come to a deeper understanding of the whole.[9] This may present a challenge to readers who are more familiar with a straight-line way of thinking, one that ruthlessly separates wheat and chaff to arrive at the grain of truth, the essence of a parsimonious explanation. The reason for adopting an alternative method of accumulating evidence is that, as Oscar Wilde pointed out, the truth is rarely pure and never simple, so that an explanation that ignores the chaff may be merely simplistic. Mary Midgley addresses this point in her argument for the need to reunite science and poetry:

> Of course simplicity is one aim of explanation. Of course we need parsimony. But it is no use being parsimonious unless you are relevant. Explanations must be complex enough to do the particular work that they are there for, to answer the questions that are actually arising. There are always many alternative ways of simplifying things and we have to choose between them. The kind of parsimony that is too mean to deal with the points that really need explaining is not economy but futile miserliness. For any particular problem, we need a solution that sorts out the particular complications that puzzle us, not one that ignores them because they are untidy. (Midgley, 2001: 8)

Her use of the word 'untidy' has a particular resonance in Wales, where 'tidy' is a word that is used in a generally positive sense for issues as varied as a well-conditioned engine or a productive allotment. However, the life of workers in the Valleys is far from tidy, and hence studying it has been a messy process. I have concluded that it is more important to communicate what I have come to learn of the Valleys in all their untidiness than to comply with academic conventions.

STRUCTURE OF THE BOOK

As already mentioned, Chapter 2 presents an account of the recent employment history of Rhondda Cynon Taff to provide a framework for the discussion. The temptation to wallow in history has been avoided as far as possible; those who wish to learn more about how the area arrived at its current situation are recommended to read Chris Williams's account (1996) or the massive fifth volume of the *Glamorgan County History* (John, Williams and Williams, 1980). Chapter 3 addresses one feature of policy-making that has been followed with particular assiduity in the Valleys: the attraction of inward investment. An attempt is made to assess the quantitative and qualitative impact of this policy on the local labour market. Chapter 4 offers insights of a different kind, by providing the sort of social and cultural analysis of work in the Valleys that is often omitted from economic studies, but which is vital to understanding why employment policies have failed to take root and thrive there.

In Chapter 5 I begin to present the results of my own study, first by offering the data gleaned from a survey questionnaire completed by employees in various workplaces in RCT. This is supplemented in Chapter 6 by the findings of a series of semi-structured interviews I conducted with a smaller sample of local employees. Some of the respondents to both surveys were employed at Tower Colliery, and this workplace is the subject of a case study presented in Chapter 7. Finally, in Chapter 8, I draw together the findings of the study as a whole and use the conclusions to make recommendations for the future of employment policy in Rhondda Cynon Taff.

2

Living on Songs and Hope: An Employment Profile of the Rhondda Cynon Taff County Borough

Everybody has given statistics about the economics of pits or about the steel industry, but nobody has weighed up the social costs to the communities in these areas, and the unhappiness caused by the unemployment situation. And how can you weigh up the social costs to a community against the economic costs to a pit?

Miner at Cwm Colliery reported in M. Thomas, 1991

In Chapter 1 I explained my decision to choose the County Borough of Rhondda Cynon Taff as the setting for a study of work motivations and employment policy. It should be emphasized that it has its own history and culture, which means that results found for such a specific area can only be generalized to a limited extent. While some of the factors that have created unemployment will be common to all areas that have experienced major industrial restructuring, some aspects of the economy and culture of the south Wales Valleys are unusual or unique. The purpose of this chapter is to give an overview of the economy of the study area to provide a background against which the findings presented in later chapters can be judged. This profile will also alert researchers to peculiarities of the area that should allow them to judge how much caution is necessary when comparisons with the area are made. To set this overview in context, the first section provides background information on the process of industrial restructuring as it has affected other parts of the UK, especially the coalfields. Much of the chapter is based on the presentation of statistics; in order to balance this rather cold, objective data, the first section lays more emphasis on the human consequences of industrial restructuring.

THE PAIN OF INDUSTRIAL RESTRUCTURING

Industrial restructuring is frequently only addressed as an economic phenomenon. The economy moves on; certain industries are left behind and move into decline or disappear altogether. To an economist this features as an increase in local rates of unemployment, a fall in the rate of local investment or GDP, or perhaps, for more radical economists, a rise in other forms of hidden unemployment such as sickness rates. Often the human cost remains uncounted. This has not been the case with the coalfields communities, whose decline and regeneration have been documented by many academics, primarily those working with the Coalfields Communities Campaign.[1] This particular focus of attention is unsurprising given the scale of the issue. According to the government's own figures (DETR, 1998) 3.7 million people, or more than 6 per cent of the total population of the UK, live in coalfield areas, with 1.4 million of those living in 'pit villages'. For all these people, and especially those living in the villages whose only *raison d'être* is the local pit, the decline in the coalfields has been devastating. In Wales the impact has been even greater, since the coalfield areas represent a much greater proportion of the country's economy, particularly in terms of population. Wales has also failed to attract a share of regeneration money proportionate to its greater need. During the period of the most intensive pit closures 15.2 per cent of the jobs lost were in the coalfields of north and south Wales. Yet only 2.57 per cent of the money provided by the Coalfields Regeneration Trust (set up in 1999 as a result of the election of the Labour government in 1997, and, crucially, after the devolution decision had been taken) was made available for regeneration in coalfields communities in Wales.[2]

The immediate impact of pit closure is serious enough for those who lose their jobs and those who depend on them for their financial support. But the redundancies also have much wider effects on the community and the local economy through multiplier effects:

> For every colliery that closes and every job that is lost, further jobs are lost elsewhere in the locality. The most immediate impact is on the industry's suppliers – engineering and haulage firms, and contractors, for example. Local shops and other consumer services also lose business because of loss of income in the community, even if in the short run the blow is eased by redundancy payments. In the longer term, areas that lose jobs suffer from out-migration, and as people leave to find work elsewhere, they add a further downward twist to local spending and the health of the local economy. Eventually, if population falls enough, even employment in public services (for example, schools and hospitals) adjusts downwards. (Fothergill and Witt, 1990: 11)

In the Welsh context the redundancy of 5,000 workers at BSC Port Talbot under the Slimline Programme was the focus of considerable research interest. Fevre (1987) explored the effect of EEC assistance payments, and found that they enabled the general lowering of wages, since ex-steel-workers were able to boost their low wage rates with redundancy payments. This forced others out of the labour market and led to a permanent reduction of wages which Fevre compared with the effects of the Speenhamland system of poor relief in nineteenth-century England. Harris (1987) chronicled the devastating psychological consequences for those made unemployed and found, in support of what is presented in Chapter 5 for the case of redundant miners, that two-thirds of those made redundant considered job security to be more important than wage rates.

Westergaard and colleagues (1989) studied 600 people made redundant from a steel company in Sheffield in the late 1980s. In line with other studies, they found that the men and women became discouraged workers or economically inactive. They make the general point that 'redundancy signifies a crucial change in social identity for those who experience it, and one which exposes them to powerful pressure' (p. 81). The consequence of the experience was an attitude of helplessness and resignation. Even the 'lucky ones' who became re-employed did so on lower grades with less pay, poorer conditions, and less job security.

Waddington, Dicks and Critcher (1992) studied the effects of the pit closures in South Yorkshire on the miners themselves, their families and their communities. The most damaging effects were in terms of individual self-respect. They were 'frequently told of ex-workmates, once proud and apparently resilient, now prescribed valium because they could not cope with their loss of self-respect'. Their conclusion was that 'unemployment in pit communities brings a sense of despair, a lack of self-worth, social isolation and family conflict, as well as inevitable financial problems'. Marital relationships were put under great strain, especially in cases where women became the main breadwinners, further undermining their husbands' self-esteem. Beyond this individual setting the consequences for the community at large were equally severe:

> The demoralising effects of pit closure on the wider mining communities are evident in the deterioration of the physical environment, control over young people and participation in community life. The closure of a mine and the redundancy or transfer of its employees fragment the sense of cohesion and identity engendered when people live and work in such close proximity. (M. Thomas, 1991).

The loss of confidence in such communities has been exacerbated by the insecurity engendered by changing targets and timescales and the failure of strategic planning by government. The Selby coalfield provides an excellent reminder that even 'an example of a highly technological, flexible modern industry' which is reckoned as 'the jewel in the crown of the UK coal industry' can become economically unviable within a mere twenty years (Leeds Metropolitan University, 2002). The Selby mines face closure because the complex has become a loss-maker, in spite of the fact that its production costs are less than half those in Germany; it would be profitable if the price of coal had not fallen as a result of the 'dash for gas' in the electricity generation industry. With no long-term government support for the sector it will now be closed, with the loss of the enormous investment made in creating such a modern, state-of-the-art mining complex.

There has also been a focus in the redundancy literature on the psychological and social consequences of insecure employment in an era of 'downsizing'. 'Headcount reduction', a euphemism for making workers redundant, can be an attractive option for managers who are keen to cut costs, in spite of the recognition that it has adverse effects on morale, motivation and productivity and works against a stable and committed workforce (Turnbull and Wass, 1999). Economists have identified a 'paradox' since, as shown by a 1996 survey, two-thirds of British workers felt their job was not secure, in spite of no evidence of a genuine reduction in employment security (OECD, 1997). It may be that the data had yet to catch up with the perception, since by 1999 researchers were reporting that for three-quarters of the workforce job insecurity had increased over the previous ten years (Gregg, Knight and Wadsworth, 1999).

Lee viewed the widespread redundancies caused by industrial restructuring from the perspective of sociology, in an analysis that has some relevance to the situation in south Wales (Lee, 1987). His focus was on how such severe social change can be accommodated without the creation of violent social unrest. He finds an answer in the work of Erving Goffman and his description of the 'cooling out' process that takes place during the pulling of a confidence trick, whereby a person is assisted to accept their loss of face and status as the victim of the trick. As Lee writes:

That article [Goffman, 1952] repays careful study by anyone interested in the sociology of redundancy. It seems that policies designed to cope with redundancies frequently function to cool workers out of employment in ways which help to minimize resistance. One hypothesis is that different kinds of workers may be dealt with in different ways; some being provided with a basis upon which they can construct an alternative or compensatory identity, while others, those with relatively low amounts of power (e.g. women workers or immigrants), are not judged worthy of the effort. To the extent that workers *are* successfully cooled out of employment, however, or remain relatively powerless in the face of redundancy, then the less surprising it becomes that a rising tide of social protest has not accompanied increasing levels of redundancy. (Lee, 1987: 18)

However, it seems that any such attempt to manage the discontent caused by the large-scale redundancies in coal-mining areas of south Wales would be unsuccessful because of the high levels of political awareness and class-consciousness that still exist there. This is obvious in accounts of the closures presented in works by former and current miners (e.g. M. Thomas, 1991; Francis, 1997; O'Sullivan, Eve and Edworthy, 2001), as well as from the accounts of miners I interviewed myself. Because any such social management is impossible, the psychological impact of the redundancies is likely to have been that much more severe, although the awareness of 'struggle' and the representation of the closures as a 'defeat of working people by Thatcherism' does provide those who have lost their jobs with a narrative that offers them some comfort.

More effective in 'softening the blow' of redundancy were the generous redundancy payments that were offered. These were a particularly strong incentive to many miners in the period of the late 1980s, who still had large debts incurred during the 1984/5 strike (M. Thomas, 1991). O'Sullivan, Eve, and Edworthy (2001) present an account of how extra redundancy offers with a limited window for accepting them were used to put pressure on miners to accept 'voluntary' redundancy.

This introduction has provided a general background to the economic and social consequences of redundancy. We turn now to a detailed analysis of one of the areas of the UK to be hardest hit by industrial restructuring: Rhondda Cynon Taff.

OVERVIEW OF THE RCT AREA

History

The Rhondda Cynon Taff County Borough was formed as part of the reorganization of local government in Wales which took place in 1996. It has a population of 231,952 people, 112,454 male and 119,498 female; the population is divided between the three constituencies of Rhondda (34 per cent), Cynon (28 per cent) and Pontypridd (38 per cent) (population figures are from the first release of the 2001 census; the proportions are based on the intercensal survey of 1996, published in Welsh Office, 1998a: table 1.2). The borough covers an area of some 44,000 hectares stretching from the Brecon Beacons in the north to the outskirts of Cardiff in the south. It includes large areas of what is anecdotally referred to as the Valleys and, as its name implies, the valleys of the Taff, Cynon, Rhondda Fach and Rhondda Fawr rivers are entirely included within the borough. The historical settlement patterns of this part of southern Wales have led to very high population densities within these river valleys, which are

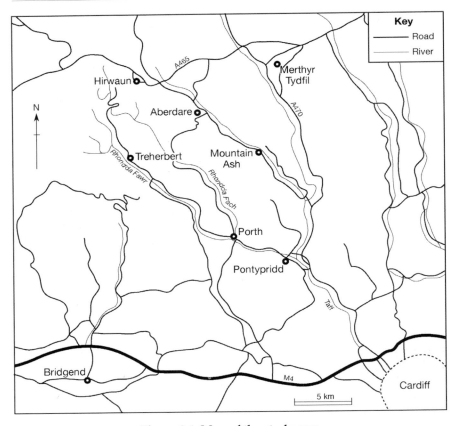

Figure 2.1: Map of the study area

surrounded by areas of high ground that cannot be used for domestic or industrial development. This lends the area an unusual demographic profile. The largest settlements in the RCT Borough are: Pontypridd, which lies at the confluence of the area's four rivers and has a population of 39,193; Aberdare, at the head of the Cynon Valley with a population of 29,980; Porth ('gate' in Welsh), which forms the entrance of the Rhondda valleys and has a population of 16,300; and Mountain Ash, at the southern end of the Cynon valley with a population of 14,200 (figures from MGCC, 1995;[3] see also the map presented as figure 2.1).

Any introduction to the area of south Wales known as 'the Valleys'[4] needs to take account of both the history and the geography of the area. It is superfluous to point out that the reason for the density of population in the south Wales Valleys is the discovery in the region of valuable natural resources, specifically coal and iron. In terms of the study area as defined here, the earliest development was in the Cynon Valley, where coal and ironstone outcropped on the hillsides around Aberdare and so could be obtained relatively cheaply. This resource was exploited at Aberdare from around 1750, and also at Hirwaun, at the top of the Cynon Valley, where an iron furnace was established in 1757 (Boyns, Thomas and Baber, 1980; Grant, 1991). The most significant expansion in population occurred in the second half of the nineteenth century, after the discovery of steam coal at Cwmsaerbren near Treherbert in the upper Rhondda Fawr and the growth of the coal-export trade (Lewis, 1959). There followed the most rapid period of expansion for the coal industry in the area, with the opening of twenty-three new collieries between 1872 and 1888 (J. Williams, 1980: 183). However, the development of the coal industry was subsidiary to that of metal smelting, with the ironmasters initially moving into coal production to guarantee supplies for their own works (Williams, 1980). The exploit-ation of these resources caused a steady growth in the population of the area from the last decade of the eighteenth century onwards. Between 1851 and 1911, 366,000 men and women flooded into south Wales from the surrounding rural counties of Wales and other nearby areas of the south-western UK (D. Jones, 1995: 110; Lewis, 1959: 228ff.).

While the geography and geology of the Valleys were ideal for this form of employment they offer few alternative opportunities, and the decline of employment in the area follows exactly the decline of the 'Age of Steam'. From the last decade of the nineteenth century onwards a range of factors undermined demand for coal: a preference for alternative fuels (especially oil for shipping); more efficient use in secondary production; the growth of coal-mining industries in countries which had been importers; and the adverse effects of British monetary policy (Baber and Thomas, 1980). A temporary boom in coal production in south Wales during the First World War was followed by a 'catastrophic collapse' at the end of the 1920s, with annual sales reduced by some 25 per cent (Baber and Thomas, 1980: 521). According to the RCT *Profile* (MGCC, 1995), a specific problem posed by the geography of the area is the shortage of flat land for the construction of factory units. Because the area is so mountainous much of the terrain is steeply sloped and unsuitable for the development of manufacturing industry. This is particularly true of the Rhondda area. As the *Profile* notes 'the area of the Rhondda because of the poor topography has difficulty in assembling good quality sites for industrial development' (p. 2).

Although the area has a mixed profile in terms of development sites, its communication links are good. The M4 runs along the southern part of the county borough, which provides links to the heartland of the UK economy. The A470 (which follows the route of the canal that once served as the main transport artery in a NW-SE direction to the east of RCT) is a good-quality

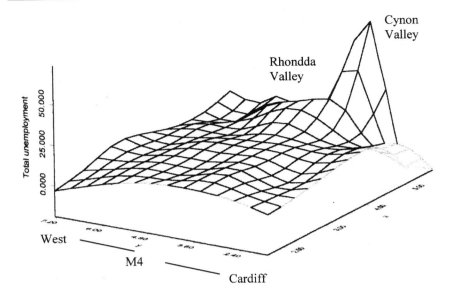

Figure 2.2: Percentage unemployed of the working population, by ward
Source: 1991 Census.

major trunk road which provides access to Merthyr Tydfil from Cardiff. The other major route in the area is the A465, known as the 'Heads of the Valleys' road, running parallel to the M4 but along the tops of the valleys. Because of the nature of the terrain, with a string of populated river valleys running in a rough north-west to south-east direction, direct links between the major settlements are poor and access is generally via one of the major roads at north and south, that is, the M4 or the A465. This has undoubtedly restricted the prospects for industrial growth, the Valleys being considered 'inaccessible and incommodious' by industrialists seeking to invest in new industries (Baber and Thomas, 1980: 545). The importance of access to the M4 in terms of employment opportunities is illustrated in figure 2.2, which is a three-dimensional plot of unemployment rates across the study area at the 1991 census. The perspective provided is approximately that facing a person standing towards the Cardiff end of the M4, so that rates of unemployment increase in both directions as you move away from that point. The figure shows clearly that the areas of less height, and therefore lowest unemployment, are mainly towards the southern end of the borough, close to the M4. The peak on the figure represents the very high rates of unemployment in some of the wards in the upper Cynon Valley.

Demographic profile

Table 2.1 gives population rates for the RCT Borough by age and gender. According to projections made in the last Mid Glamorgan Structure Plan published before the formation of RCT in 1996, the number of households is expected to increase by 12 per cent by the year 2006 (MGCC, 1995). The

Table 2.1: Population rates in Rhondda Cynon Taff, 1996 and 2001

Area	*Persons*	*Male (%)*	*Female (%)*	*0–15 (%)*	*15–59/64 (%)*	*60/65+ (%)*
Pontypridd	87,000	50	50	21	59	20
Rhondda	76,700	49	51	22	58	21
Cynon	64,700	49	51	22	58	20
Total RCT	228,400	49	51	22	58	20
	231,952	*48.5*	*51.5*	*19.5*	*61.7*	*18.8*
Wales	2,921,100	49	51	21	59	20
	2,903,085	*48.4*	*51.6*	*18.9*	*61.0*	*20.0*

Note: Figures in italics are for 2001 (only available for all RCT and Wales).
Sources: Welsh Office, 1998c, table 1.2; census first release figures from ONS website.

table shows that RCT has a slightly younger age-profile than the whole of Wales, although interestingly the number of young people relative to old people fell between 1991 and 2001. The recent furore caused by census findings that we now have more people above retirement age than below age sixteen is true for Wales as a whole but not true for the study area. This is likely to be due to the poor health and early death of older people in the area (see below). Predictions of out-migration from the Valleys to find work in more prosperous areas in Cardiff and elsewhere would show up in a reduction in the relative size of the working-age group, the opposite of what is seen here, where this segment has grown since the last census.

RCT is one of the poorest boroughs in the United Kingdom. There are two factors which cause the area's poverty: the high level of unemployment and lack of other economic activity, and the low levels of earnings of those who are employed. Average gross weekly earnings in RCT were £292.42 in 1999, compared with averages of £299.12 for Wales as a whole and £336.63 for the UK. The disparities are even more striking if we take the case of men, who in the UK earn on average £420.15 per week, but in Wales only £367.35 per week, with an even lower rate of £352.38 in Rhondda Cynon Taff. This is some 15 per cent lower, on average, than UK rates. The hourly rates of pay, presented in table 2.2, are more revealing.

They show that men in Wales earn nearly £2 less per hour than the UK average, with the disparity for women being closer to 50p.

Table 2.2: Hourly rates of pay in RCT, Wales and UK, 1999 (£)

	RCT	UK	Wales
Male	8.69	10.64	9.16
Female	7.61	8.14	7.45
All	8.26	9.60	8.46

Source: Nomis.

The discussion about how much the economic development strategy followed is responsible for low earnings is taken up in the following chapter but one aspect is worth mentioning here: the growth of part-time employment. The part-time nature of many of the employment opportunities created in Wales during the last decade as a result of the job-creation strategy has unquestionably affected household income levels. According to one study, the part-time jobs created by multinationals are low-skilled jobs, mainly for women, and deliver only part-time wages (Mainwaring, 1995: 23). The shift from male, full-time, well-paid positions to female, part-time, low-paid positions has therefore had an inevitably negative impact on local income levels and the wider local economy.

A general explanation for low earnings could be the low level of skills, which are discussed further in a later section. However, it is worth noting that the human-capital theory that associates higher levels of education with higher earnings breaks down at least at the aggregate level in Wales, where there is no statistical correlation within Wales's twenty-one boroughs between either GCSE results or percentage of the population with degrees and the average level of earnings in the borough. For interest, and to indicate the poor levels of educational qualifications in RCT, data for GCSE results in that and other Welsh boroughs are presented in figure 2.3.

As a first indication of the level of poverty in the area, table 2.3 presents the historic trend in the level of GDP in the whole of Mid Glamorgan as an index of the all-Wales level. It should be borne in mind that the Welsh rate is already substantially lower than that of the UK as a whole. The table makes it clear that the period of significant relative decline was the early 1980s, the period of the initial pit closures. These figures indicate that, although the employment situation has since improved, because of the low-skill, low-pay nature of many of the new jobs, income levels remain severely depressed. Due to the potential effect of the large black economy

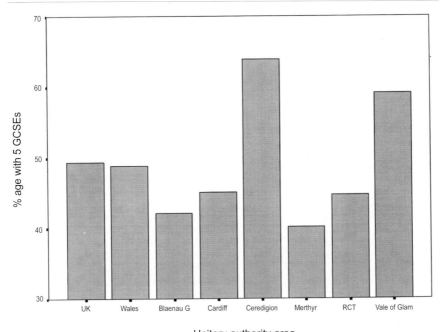

Unitary authority area

Figure 2.3: Levels of educational achievement in various Welsh local authority areas: percentage of school leavers achieving five or more GCSE grades A*–C, 2001
Source: Welsh Assembly Statistics Directorate.

Table 2.3: Historical GDP index for Mid Glamorgan/RCT, 1981–1998 using all Wales as a base

Year	1981	1984	1991	1995	1998
Mid Glamorgan/RCT	92.2	84.2	81.2	79.8	*67.0*

Note: The figure for 1998 is printed in italics because it relates solely to RCT.
Source: J. J. Williams, 1998: table 2.3; RCT website.

in the area (see the discussion below), it is possible that these bald income figures distort the true picture, and more complex measures are required to provide a clearer indication of deprived standards of living, rather than merely low income levels.

The RCT Borough is also disadvantaged in terms of housing stock, although this can be concealed by the high levels of owner occupation (some two-thirds), which is often used as an indicator of housing wealth. In RCT, however, the historic pattern of homeownership is a handicap,

Table 2.4: RCT wards in top 100 most deprived Welsh boroughs

Electoral division name	Index of multiple deprivation score	Rank of index of multiple deprivation	Income domain score[a]	Rank of income domain	Employment domain score[b]	Rank of employment domain
Pen-y-waun	73.34	2	59.68	9	35.75	4
Maerdy	68.43	5	46.04	35	34.77	6
Tylorstown	64.66	11	45.95	36	32.03	13
Glyncoch	57.71	26	52.62	17	29.61	32
Llwynypia	55.3	29	40.75	74	30.84	22
Penrhiwceiber	54.01	31	45.20	41	25.49	77
Treherbert	53.84	33	39.66	85	31.03	20
Cwm Clydach	53.56	36	37.99	107	30.38	26
Rhydfelen Central/ Ilan	52.94	38	52.64	16	27.05	59
Gilfach Goch	52.46	39	38.09	105	27.70	53
Mountain Ash West	51.67	42	43.64	52	28.58	41
Cymmer	47.33	56	41.28	66	27.02	60
Ynyshir	47.05	59	37.35	119	28.11	46
Trealaw	46.99	60	37.46	115	28.89	40
Aberaman South	46.95	61	40.21	79	28.04	48
Tonyrefail West	46.22	67	36.11	143	28.10	47
Pen-y-graig	45.57	71	36.23	140	28.01	49

[a]Rate of population (including children) reliant on means-tested benefits.
[b]Those unemployed or on certain schemes and those on Incapacity Benefit/Severe Disablement Allowance as a proportion of those economically active plus those sick.
Source: Welsh Assembly website.

since many homeowners do not have the income to keep their houses in good condition. The housing stock is also old, with half of all houses built before 1919 (two-thirds in Rhondda; MGCC, 1989: para. 3.7). Some idea of the poor value of the housing stock can be derived from data on the comparative rates of houses in different Council Tax bands in 1998–9 (Welsh Office, 1999: table 5.8). The median band in RCT is B, whereas outside the Valleys the median bands are C or D.

Morris and Wilkinson (1995) produced an analysis of wealth differentials across the county boroughs of Wales, comparing the social and economic situation at the 1981 census with that in the same areas ten years later at the 1991 census. This period coincided with the most rapid period of pit closures. The authors used eight separate indicators of prosperity at the micro-level, including unemployment rate and rate of long-term sickness, which are particularly relevant in the study area. In terms of amalgamated index scores the two poorest areas in Wales both fell within the study area: Rhondda and the Cynon Valley. The third part of the study area – Taff Ely – comes approximately halfway down the ranking, in eighteenth place out

Table 2.5: Selected deprivation indicators for the ten most deprived RCT boroughs, 1991

Borough	Unemployment	Car non-ownership	Non-earning families (%)	Deprivation z-score[a]
Tylorstown	16.1	55.9	50.0	12.9
Maerdy	14.5	54.7	40.4	10.3
Ilan	18.6	58.2	55.6	10.0
Penrhiwceiber	14.2	49.1	34.3	9.9
Cwm Clydach	9.8	43.4	29.5	9.1
Aberaman South	11.6	45.8	25.8	8.9
Pen-y-waun	15.8	59.4	51.0	8.8
Glyncoch	14.0	53.6	42.2	8.6
Llwynypia	–	48.0	28.3	8.6
Treherbert	12.2	49.7	31.7	7.7

[a]The z-score is based on the following eight factors: unemployment, percentage of population economically active, low socio-economic groups, population loss in 20–59 age group, permanent sickness, overcrowding in housing, basic housing amenities, Standard Mortality Rate.
Source: MGCC 1995: pp. 11, 18–19, 26.d

of thirty-seven. These scores are based on a number of different indicators of deprivation, and hence present a picture of a general situation of poverty.

Following the establishment of the Welsh Assembly an updated study was commissioned to develop a Welsh Index of Multiple Deprivation, again based on a range of indicators (available from the Assembly website). The index shows that of the 100 most deprived boroughs in Wales, seventeen are found within the RCT unitary authority (these are listed in table 2.4). This represents 17 per cent of the most deprived boroughs, whereas only 6.4 per cent (55) of all Wales's 865 boroughs are in RCT.[5] The index also shows that the highest levels of deprivation are found in the Rhondda wards, with a lower level of deprivation in the wards to the south, in the old Taff Ely borough.

The most recent analysis providing data to the lowest level of aggregation (the ward level) on a range of other items is provided by a survey of the borough carried out by the Mid Glamorgan Council (MGCC, 1995). It shows a similar picture, although it offers more fine-grained analysis of particular poverty blackspots. Some figures from selected wards for levels of unemployment, car non-ownership, and non-earning families, plus a socio-economic z-score, are presented in table 2.5. The figures were rather dated by the time this research was carried out, since they relate to the 1991 census, but they are still the latest data of this sort currently available.

EMPLOYMENT IN RHONDDA CYNON TAFF

Pit closures and the decline of heavy industry

No account of employment in the Valleys of south Wales can avoid the obvious starting-point of the decline of the mining industry. In fact, any researcher visiting the area must be immediately struck by the frequent emergence of the topic of mining once the subject of work is raised. For many men of middle age in the Valleys the obvious source of employment was the colliery, and any jobs that have been created since the decline of coal are inevitably compared with mining, in terms of the satisfaction derived from the work, the nature of the relationship between employees, and the rates of pay. The centrality of the history of mining to the present situation in this part of Wales is expressed in the introduction to Mid Glamorgan's planning report *Issues for the 1990s*:

> Mid Glamorgan's current social and economic characteristics are almost entirely the result of a century of dependence on coalmining and its long-term decline. The coal industry has shaped virtually every aspect of life in Mid Glamorgan, from the creation of its towns and villages, the construction of its housing and the appearance of its landscape, to its economy, its people's health and of course community, political and cultural life. Although the coal industry has now virtually disappeared – fewer than 1,000 jobs remain at just two collieries – it has left a powerful legacy, both positive and negative. (MGCC 1989: para. 2.1)

A publication from Mid Glamorgan's Economic Policy and Research Unit, written in June 1988 as a lobbying document for local MPs, provides a snapshot of the rapidly changing employment situation in the coalfields towards the end of the period of most precipitate decline. The report states that during the 1979–88 period some 10,400 jobs had been lost in the coal industry, out of a total workforce of 15,500 (Mortimer and Davies, 1988). Figures cited in the report for losses of jobs in the collieries are presented in table 2.6, together with employment figures for 1960, for historical comparison. By 1988, when this report was written, all mines in the Rhondda Valleys had been closed; three mines in the Cynon Valley were still operational, although all were to face government closure within five years.

The figures show that 70 per cent of jobs in the collieries of the study area vanished in these eight years. They represent the final stage of the

**Photo 2.1: Signs of the Valleys' past reliance on coal-
mining are to be found everywhere: The Colliers,
Trealaw**

extended death of mining in these valleys, which was already a moribund
industry in the years following the First World War, largely as a result of
the replacement of coal with oil as the main fuel for international shipping:
by 1939 coal production in Rhondda pits was one-third of its 1913 level (C.
Williams, 1996: 25). Declining employment opportunities and wage cuts
led to a long period of economic depression which has continued to the
present. There was some respite for the industry following coal national-
ization in 1947 and a government energy policy in the 1960s and 1970s
which guaranteed the use of coal in the generation of electricity by the
nationalized CEGB, as well as similar guarantees of supply to the

Table 2.6: Number of employees in the mining industry in the three parts of the study area, 1979 and 1987 compared

	1960	1979	Reduction 1960–1979		1987	Reduction 1979–1987	
			N	%		N	%
Cynon Valley	6,712	3,804	2,908	43.3	2,259	1,545	40.6
Rhondda	8,752	1,576	7,176	82.0	0	1,576	100
Taff Ely	6,207	2,925	3,282	52.8	223	2,702	92.4
TOTAL	21,671	8,305	13,366	61.7	2,482	5,823	70.1

Source: Mortimer and Davies, 1988: para. 2.1; Mortimer, 1989, p. 14.

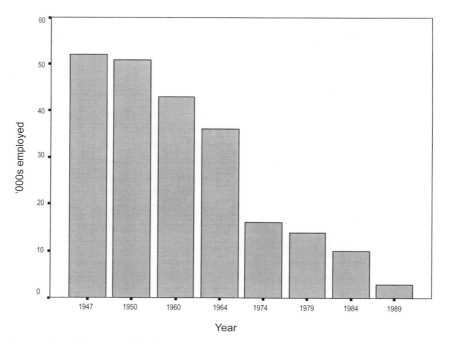

Figure 2.4: Decline in employment in mining since 1947
Source: Mortimer, 1989.

nationalized steel industry. The trends in manpower levels in the whole of Mid Glamorgan since 1947 are shown in figure 2.4.

The change of political climate following the election of a Conservative government in 1979 was the final blow to the coal industry in south Wales and the closure programme was accelerated following the 1984–5 Miners' Strike (Wass and Mainwaring, 1989: 162; Mainwaring and Wass, 1989). The

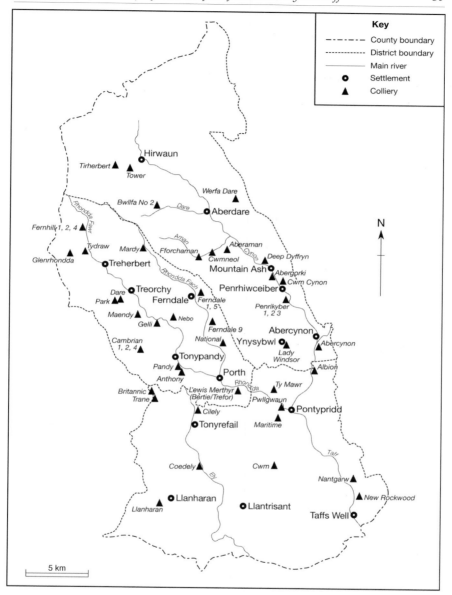

Figure 2.5: Mines in the Rhondda and Cynon Valleys and Taff Ely that are now closed

Source: Mortimer, 1989.

privatization of the electricity industry had serious implications, since a large proportion of the steam-coal produced in Mid Glamorgan had been guaranteed purchase by Aberthaw Power Station, which would now be free to seek cheaper imported supplies from subsidized European competitors (Wass and Mainwaring, 1989: 181–2).[6] The impact of half a century of decline is illustrated in figure 2.5, which shows the working pits in the Rhondda, Cynon and Taff Valleys at the time of privatization in 1947; the only colliery now remaining is the worker-owned Tower at the top of the Cynon Valley (discussed in more detail in Chapter 7).

Current employment profile

The traditional employment pattern in the mining areas of south Wales was for men to work and live in the same community; women's work was unusual and culturally discouraged (see John, 1995). Throughout the Valleys houses were built around the pits, and these communities were closely identified with the mine which provided the livelihood to all the residents (C. Williams, 1996). This tradition of proximity of home and workplace has broken down since the decline of mining, with many workers now travelling longer distances to find employment along the M4 corridor, either in Cardiff or Bridgend, where British and foreign companies, such as Ford and Sony, have developed major production sites. Access to the M4 is relatively easy for all parts of the RCT borough, and the development along this major trunk road has been encouraged by the availability of workers from the valley areas.

On a smaller scale a similar pattern has emerged within Rhondda Cynon Taff itself, with male employment now provided at industrial estates on the edge of the community (see the following chapter for a fuller discussion of this development), often by foreign companies or companies that have been attracted to RCT by the grants offered by the Welsh Development Agency. The overwhelming majority of those employed now travel to work, usually by car. In the borough as a whole 69.7 per cent of workers drove to work in the mid-1990s, ranging from 44.4 per cent in Ilan in the lower Cynon Valley to 83.5 per cent in Brynna, a ward at the south-western corner of the borough. In addition, an average of 10.9 per cent of workers travelled to work by public transport (MGCC, 1995: 20). In Mid Glamorgan as a whole, one in five of the residents travelled outside the county for work (Mid Glamorgan Careers, 1996: 5).

The employment structure of the borough has diversified rapidly over the past twenty years, although its weak service sector was a concern to planners in 1995, who estimated that it provided just 59 per cent of employment in RCT, compared with 69 per cent in Wales as a whole and 71

Table 2.7: Sectors of employment: RCT, Wales and GB compared, 1999 (%)

Sector	RCT	Wales	GB
Manufacturing	31.3	19.9	17.6
Construction	7.1	7.7	7.0
Distribution/hotels and catering	13.0	18.6	19.8
Transport and communications	n.a.	5.4	6.9
Banking and finance	6.5	10.0	15.5
Public administration	30.8	29.0	24.6
Other services	6.2	5.1	5.9

Source: Nomis.

Table 2.8: Rates of commuting in south Wales boroughs, 2001

Area of residence	% of residents working in area	Out-commuters ('000s)	In-commuters ('000s)
Blaenau Gwent	61	10.4	5.2
Bridgend	75	14.5	13.1
Cardiff	81	27.1	71.2
Merthyr Tydfil	63	7.3	8.3
Neath Port Talbot	60	20.4	10.3
Newport	71	17.7	29.4
RCT	62	36.3	16.3
Swansea	83	16.6	23.1
Torfaen	61	14.9	11.1
Vale of Glamorgan	77	13.1	15.7

Source: Wales Statistical Directorate, *Statistical Bulletin* 21/2003, March 2003.

per cent in the UK (all these figures relate to 1991 census figures, published in MGCC, 1995). At 59 per cent of total employment the service sector was still the largest provider of employment, accounting for 40,800 employees. Table 2.7 gives the breakdown of more recent figures for employment by industry. The table makes clear the contrast between the economy of RCT and that of Great Britain: the former's economy has a much larger proportion of employees in manufacturing, a sector that has long been under pressure. The figure of 31.3 per cent employed in that sector is nearly twice the proportion in Great Britain as a whole. The corollary is that a much smaller proportion of the workforce is employed in the retail and hostelry sector, in banking and finance and in transport and com- munications – the last figure being too small for the Nomis statisticians to consider it statistically reliable. The table also shows the heavy reliance on the public sector to provide jobs, both in RCT and in Wales as a whole. Table 2.8 offers further evidence of the low level of economic opportunity within the borough by comparing the rates of commuting into and out of RCT and other comparable boroughs. RCT has the highest rate of out-commuting in Wales, although the high rate of in-commuting suggests that the situation may be worse in neighbouring Valleys boroughs.

Unemployment

Unemployment has been a persistent trend in the study area, as indicated by figure 2.6, which gives the focus rate for unemployment in RCT over the period 1975–2001, a technique which involves plotting this year's unemployment against last year's, thus producing a plot which 'focuses' around the average rate of unemployment in a particular period. The figure makes clear that the rate of unemployment in the Mid Glamorgan area moved sharply outwards in the early 1980s, first as a result of the

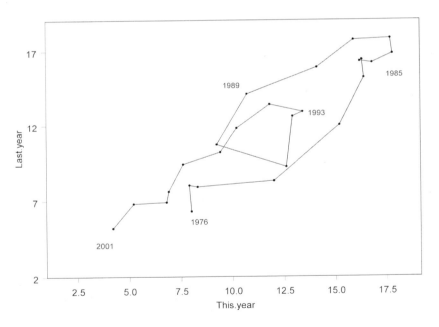

Figure 2.6: Focus rate of unemployment in Rhondda Cynon Taff
Note: The data from which this figure was plotted are claimant counts and thus subject to change consequent upon administrative changes. This is particularly noticeable in the more recent period, following the introduction of the Job Seekers' Allowance in 1997.
Source: Welsh Office 1998a; author's calculations based on Nomis data.

Table 2.9: Unemployment rates in RCT travel-to-work areas, 1996 and 1999 (%)

Travel-to-work area	1996	1999
Cardiff	7.6	4.1
Merthyr	11.5	7.8
Pontypridd and Aberdare	9.4	6.8

Source: Wales Statistics Directorate website.

Table 2.10: Unemployment by age in RCT wards, April 1998 (%)

	Under 25	25–44	45+	All
Pontypridd	32.5	43.6	23.9	1,879
Rhondda	33.4	45.6	21.0	2,168
Cynon	32.8	46.7	20.5	1,938
Wales	28.8	46.3	24.9	70,793

Source: Welsh Office, 1998a: table 2.11.

general recession in the UK economy, which was then exacerbated locally by the pit-closure programme. During the years from 1983 to 1987 the focus rate was around 16 to 17 per cent. During the 1990s it declined, with a focus rate of around 11 to 12 per cent in the early 1990s, falling rapidly to the low single-figure values we see today. These are claimant rates and do not take account of other people who are outside the labour force, either the long-term disabled or partners whose spouses are working.

Table 2.9 shows the rates of unemployment in the two travel-to-work areas into which RCT is divided for the purposes of compiling employment statistics, compared with the rate for Wales's most successful TTWA – Cardiff. Unemployment is unevenly distributed by age, as indicated by the figures in table 2.10, with the highest levels concentrated in the middle-aged group. The levels fall off in the older age groups, presumably because of the higher rates of chronic, long-term sickness in this age group. Comparing the rates for the three boroughs in the study area with the all-Wales rate indicates that unemployment is more prevalent amongst people in the youngest age group, roughly comparable amongst middle-aged men, and lower amongst men in the oldest age group.

Unemployment duration also varies significantly by age, as shown in table 2.11. For all age groups the long-term unemployed are the most numerous; in the case of men aged over fifty, half of those who are unemployed have not worked for more than a year. It is also interesting to note that in the young group the rates are very similar between the sexes but

Table 2.11: Unemployment duration by age in RCT, 1999 (%)

Sex and age	< 6 months	6–12 mo.	Over 12 mo.
Men			
16–24	28.0	35.2	36.8
25–49	22.8	31.7	45.5
50+	20.2	29.8	50.0
Women			
16–24	27.8	35.4	36.8
25–49	24.9	33.4	41.7
50+	24.2	31.7	44.1
All			
16–24	27.9	35.3	36.8
25–49	23.2	32.0	44.8
50+	21.1	30.3	48.6

Source: Author's calculations based on Nomis data.

they diverge as the age increases. This suggests that the pattern of employment between the sexes is becoming more similar, perhaps as the male
breadwinner model declines, although it is impossible to tell from the data
whether this is a generational or a cohort effect, that is, whether younger
women are more likely to register as unemployed in their own right, or
whether they have not yet reached an age in their own lives when they
would expect their male partner to register as unemployed on their behalf.

The unemployment profile of RCT seems to fit that identified in the
literature as being found in areas formerly dominated by heavy industry.
According to Glyn (1996: 3):

> Traditionally in the OECD countries this has been relatively well paid, mainly
> [industrial work] carried out by men, working full-time with skills that are
> specific to industrial work and requiring only basic education as a prerequisite.
> Major declines in industrial employment result in large-scale geographically
> concentrated redundancies which flood local labour markets with less-
> educated labour. It is difficult for service employment to take up the slack.

In all the OECD countries, the average rate of industrial employment fell
by 13 per cent between 1980 and 1985, while employment in services rose
by nearly 8 per cent (Glyn, 1996). The impact of this shift is seen in the
Rhondda Cynon Taff area, where, as identified above, the service sector is
weak and accounts for a smaller percentage of total unemployment than in

national averages. It indicates that during the 1980s the predominant cause of unemployment in RCT was industrial restructuring.

Qualifications and skills levels

One explanation offered for the poor rates of employment in RCT is the low levels of skills amongst school-leavers, as well as older workers. Levels of qualifications in Mid Glamorgan are low when compared with averages for Wales: the proportion of men with higher-level qualifications in 1991 was only 11.3 per cent compared with an average for Wales as a whole of 14.1 per cent. For women the level was even lower at 9.7 per cent, compared with a Wales average of 13 per cent (Mid Glamorgan Careers Ltd, 1996: 8). A report from the Coalfields Communities Campaign (2001) indicates that the situation is not improving amongst school-leavers, only 42 per cent of whom attained five or more GCSEs at grade C or above in 1998/9, compared with the UK average of 47 per cent. League tables for Mid Glamorgan schools for 2001 show that very few schools in the area (less than 5 per cent) have half or more of the fifteen-year-olds obtaining five GCSEs at grades A to C, compared with 30 per cent of schools in Wales as a whole.

Levels of skills in the areas likely to generate employment are also low: the local training council's report for Mid Glamorgan suggests that there are skill shortages, particularly in the distribution, hotel and catering, and financial and business services sectors (Mid Glamorgan tec, 1996: 17). Employers show a low level of commitment to training, as indicated by a survey conducted by Welsh employers which found that 56 per cent of employers had not trained their workforce (Mid Glamorgan Careers Ltd, 1997: 4). Commitment to training amongst unemployed young people is also weak, with 65 per cent of participants on a local Training Credit scheme leaving before the end of the course (ibid.).

The discussion of the low level of skills amongst the workforce of Mid Glamorgan must be seen against the background of the work history of the area. The best-paid and most common jobs (for male workers) in the area have always been jobs that required no qualifications, and with skills which were completely job-specific, that is, mining work. Since in the local labour market this work represented the best opportunity of maximizing lifetime earnings, the return on an investment in education was greatly reduced. But the low level of skills and qualifications, and the weak culture of education in the area, make the local workers highly vulnerable in a globalized economy:

> Both technological developments that raise the productivity of the skilled relative to the unskilled workers, as well as rising trade with countries that

have a comparative advantage in producing goods which are relatively intensive in unskilled labour, pull in the same direction, in that they reduce the demand for unskilled labour relative to the demand for skilled labour. (Snower, 1996: 120)

A related problem is the differential out-migration from the study area of the younger and more skilled workers. Within the study area the drift of population has been away from the old Valleys communities of Rhondda and Cynon and towards the Taff Ely borough in the south, which is providing more service jobs and is also within commuting distance of Cardiff or further afield. More serious is the migration of younger people outside the area altogether: between 1981 and 1990, 16,600 people left Mid Glamorgan as a whole (MGCC, 1989: para. 2.3) The concern for economic planners was that the majority of these out-migrants were under forty-five years old and moved outside Wales, leaving behind older and less skilled members of society, who are less able to contribute to a thriving economy. Recent data show that the trend continues with 5,600 people leaving RCT for other parts of Wales and the UK in the single year of 1999/2000, 3,700, some two-thirds of them, aged between sixteen and forty-four (Welsh Statistics Directorate website).

Economic inactivity

A worrying trend in depressed economic areas of the UK is the growth in economic inactivity, particularly amongst male workers. At the national level, about 28 per cent of men older than fifty are now economically inactive; in 1975 this rate was only 7 per cent. The rate of inactivity for men as a whole is 8 per cent, compared with only 1 per cent in 1975. These national averages also act to conceal the fact that such inactivity is heavily concentrated in economically depressed areas such as RCT, and particularly amongst less skilled workers (Dickens, Gregg and Wadsworth, 2000). The same researchers found that most of those now economically inactive had passed through a period of unemployment before arriving at that status. They hypothesized that a failure of incentives, due to the poor quality of available employment, might explain some of this increase.

It has long been suggested that claimant counts are an unhelpful measure of real unemployment, particularly in depressed areas. The movement towards the ILO search-based unemployment measure allows for regional and national comparison across Europe. However, it may not be the best measure in economically depressed areas. Researchers continue to suggest that it underestimates the true level of unemployment, since, particularly in depressed local economies like RCT, discouraged workers

Table 2.12: Economic inactivity rates in RCT, Wales and UK, 1999

	Males	*Females*	*All*	*50+*
RCT	31.1	26.4	35.9	53.0
Wales	26.2	21.3	31.7	40.8
UK	21.5	15.8	27.7	30.9

Note: The 50+ column includes men and women up to their respective retirement ages.
Source: Nomis.

are unlikely to be included in such a measure. Researchers at Sheffield Hallam University (Beatty et al., 2002) have attempted to develop a true measure of unemployment to supplement the ILO measure. The growth in the numbers on government schemes, some of which they describe as 'make-work' and 'benefit-plus' schemes rather than true employment, has reduced the number in registered unemployment, as has the large number signing on for sickness benefits. Beatty et al. (2002) estimate the true rate of unemployment for Mid Glamorgan in January 2002 as 16.2 per cent, compared with an official rate of 3.9 per cent; rates for male unemployment increase from 5.2 to 14.6 per cent. In their figures rates for female unemployment rise from 2.1 to 18.4 per cent, reflecting the fact that signing-based rates grossly under-represent women who would work if their husbands were earning, but whose sole earnings could not make the household better off than it would be when signing on for state benefits. This is a clear indication of the huge levels of untapped resources in depressed local economies that are not communicated by standard unemployment figures.

Table 2.12 gives official rates of economic inactivity in the study area, compared with those for Wales as a whole and the UK. The rates for both men and women are considerably higher in RCT than in the UK, with the Welsh average falling in between. This reflects the low level of economic activity in Wales, on the one hand, with poor opportunities for finding or creating employment, and on the other the failure of incentives to attract such large proportions of the population into work. The most striking figure is that for all workers aged between fifty years and retirement age, more than half of whom are economically inactive in RCT.

In RCT the majority of this economic inactivity is reflected in high rates of long-term sickness and invalidity. Partly as a consequence of migration, but also because of the unhealthy nature of mining work, the south Wales Valleys demonstrate very poor levels of health. Merthyr Tydfil has the highest rate of men on permanent sickness benefit in the country, as shown

Table 2.13: Male sickness claimants, August 2001, top twenty districts: percentage of 16–64-year-old men claiming sickness benefit

Rank	District	%
1	Merthyr Tydfil	26.9
2	Easington	26.2
3	Glasgow	20.7
4	Blaenau Gwent	19.8
5	Liverpool	18.9
6	Neath Port Talbot	18.9
7	Rhondda Cynon Taff	18.2
8	Caerphilly	18.0
9	Knowsley	17.8
10	Inverclyde	17.4

Source: Beatty et al., 2002.

Table 2.14: Standardized mortality ratios in Rhondda Cynon Taff, 1995–1999

	Persons	*Males*	*Females*
RCT	116	146	90
Merthyr Tydfil	129	164	99
Blaenau Gwent	120	147	96
Caerphilly	110	133	89
Torfaen	106	134	82

Note: SMRs are calculated as the number of actual deaths in each authority in a given year as a percentage of deaths expected if the local population had the same sex- and age-specific mortality rates as Wales as a whole.
Source: Welsh Assembly.

Table 2.15: Percentage of household members with a limiting long-term illness, by sex and age, 1997

	Male					Female				
	0–15	16–44	45–64	65+	All	0–15	16–44	45–64	65+	All
Pontypridd	2.9	6.9	30.1	51.1	16.2	2.5	6.6	22.6	46.3	16.6
Rhondda	3.7	11.7	46.9	63.3	25.4	2.9	13.5	36.5	54.9	26.1
Cynon	3.6	9.0	41.1	57.3	21.9	2.7	9.1	27.1	49.2	20.7
Wales	2.8	6.8	28.3	45.5	16.4	2.3	6.4	20.0	40.9	16.4

Source: RCT, 1995.

in table 2.13. Four of the ten unitary authorities with the highest rates of sickness claimants in the country are found in the south Wales Valleys. Rates of early death, as indicated by the standardized mortality ratios presented in table 2.14, are a good illustration of the general poor health outlook for local residents. The table shows extreme rates of early mortality especially for men, who in the study area are nearly 50 per cent more likely to have died at any given age than those of the same age in Wales as a whole.

As well as this poor life expectancy for men (women actually have much better health expectations than the national average), the quality of life of the residents of the various parts of the study area is significantly worse than that of inhabitants elsewhere in Wales, as demonstrated by rates of long-term illness. This is the case for all age groups and both sexes, as shown in table 2.15, although the rates of chronic illness amongst older men in Cynon and Rhondda are particularly serious.

There is considerable discussion in the academic literature, as well as in the more popular media, seeking to establish whether these levels of chronic sickness and disability are genuine or represent a form of hidden unemployment. Holmes, Lynch and Molho (1991) conducted an econometric analysis which found that higher levels of unemployment in a local area did affect the rate of claiming invalidity benefit, although not the duration of claims. They conclude that 'the findings relating to age and unemployment rates do suggest that being in receipt of IVB may be being used as a form of early retirement and hidden unemployment, respectively'. Disney and Webb (1991) conducted a similar analysis and confirmed that the local male unemployment rate has a significant influence on the level of invalidity benefit. Surveys conducted locally in former mining areas including Merthyr in south Wales suggest that some 30 per cent of redundant miners went on to claim sickness benefits in 1993, confirming the econometric suggestion of hidden unemployment in these areas (Fieldhouse and Hollywood, 1999).

In a study which focused specifically on the post-redundancy careers of miners, including a sample from south Wales, Fieldhouse and Hollywood (1999) found that 25.4 per cent of those who were employed as miners in 1981 and were still aged under sixty-five were retired by 1991, with 14.3 per cent signed on as permanently sick, and a further 1 per cent in other inactive statuses, which includes education. Levels of permanent sickness are particularly high amongst those aged 45 to 54 at 20 per cent, compared with 8.2 per cent amongst 35 to 44-year-olds. The miners from south Wales who formed part of the sample faced the highest level of economic inactivity of all the areas studied: 39.1 per cent of miners who had been employed in 1981 were in one of the 'other unemployed' categories by 1991. These figures

Photo 2.2: View of the Rhondda Fawr valley from Penrhys: note the terraced appearance of the higher hills indicating repeated dumping of spoil

suggest that levels of true unemployment are particularly poorly measured in former mining areas, where redundant miners who see no prospect of obtaining employment they consider acceptable are finding statuses other than 'unemployed' which will guarantee them an adequate income.

While the 'hidden unemployment' thesis may be part of the explanation, the nature of work that many men have previously undertaken (see e.g. Beatty and Fothergill, 1996; Beatty, Fothergill and Lawless, 1997; Coalfields Taskforce Report, 1998), as well as the poor quality of housing and unhealthy lifestyles, provide other reasons for arguing that the levels of ill health are genuine (see Welsh Office, 1999). In addition, there is likely to be a confounding of the two explanations, since the areas where unemployment was high during the period analysed (the 1980s) were areas of industrial restructuring where levels of occupational injury and illness are also likely to have been high. In the study area it may be suggested that the high rate of invalidity may be in part a response by local health and social security professionals to a situation where, for many men over the age of forty, the realistic chances of finding a full-time job are minimal. In this situation, it is argued, doctors may feel it is unreasonable for them to have to justify their need for income support on the basis of job-search activity, and may sign them off for a condition that is not really serious enough to prevent employment.

The black economy

A final issue that cannot be ignored in a discussion of the labour market in the RCT area is the undoubted existence of a thriving unofficial or black economy, which may be seen as another consequence of the problem of economic inactivity addressed in the previous section. The difficulty of identifying, still less measuring, activity that takes place outside the formal economy is acknowledged by the government, and its significance as an economic concern is indicated by the commissioning of Lord Grabiner to produce a report into ways of tackling it. The Grabiner Report estimated that 'Every year billions of pounds are lost to the informal economy' and estimates that some 120,000 people are working while signing on for the dole (Grabiner, 2000).

The black economy tends to thrive in depressed economic areas, and its existence in Rhondda Cynon Taff has been acknowledged during debates in the Welsh Assembly.[7] According to J. J. Thomas's (1992: 6) typology of informal economic activity it would appear that most of such work taking place in RCT is either irregular or criminal. In the first category falls the work that is done in the area in legitimate occupations that is undeclared, thus avoiding the need to pay taxes. Some of this work is undertaken by people who are also claiming unemployment benefit or invalidity benefit (see anecdotal evidence in Chapter 6). In terms of the criminal sector of the economy, it appears that there is a considerable criminal labour market centring around the sale of prohibited drugs. According to a recent journalistic investigation, one death occurs every week as a result of drugs in RCT. This is a higher rate per head of population than in Manchester, which of all UK areas usually attracts the most attention for violent, drug-related crime. The area has the cheapest drugs in the UK, while 70 per cent of crime in the area is drug-related; £130m per year is spent on crack cocaine and heroin alone (BBC *Wales Today*, 3 April 2002). During a particularly bad fortnight in June 2002 there were five drug-related deaths in the Valleys as a whole (*Western Mail*, 10 June 2002). For obvious reasons, official data in this area are sparse. While personal accounts must, of course, always be treated with caution, it is important not to neglect the existence of a large black economy, particularly because of its impact on other aspects of the labour market.

The fact that many basic service and maintenance functions are carried out by unregistered unofficial workers may help to explain the weakness of the service sector that is apparent in official figures. For example, if washing-machine repair and childcare are tasks that in RCT are performed unofficially, but in return for payment, then these parts of the official economic statistics appear to be smaller than they are in reality. The fact that a large proportion of the income of a sector of residents in RCT is obtained unofficially also casts some doubt on the validity of official statistics for regional GDP, and regional poverty levels. For this reason it is important when assessing the standard of living of people in the area to take into account the presence of goods and services in the home rather than merely considering the official income level. The presence of an informal economy is not unique to RCT, but anecdotal accounts suggest that the rate is particularly high there. Given the scarcity of published data in this area, the interviews conducted for this study can provide some information which, though unsupported by statistical evidence, may help to elucidate the nature and extent of this form of economic activity.

The existence of a thriving unofficial economy may also impact on the effectiveness of job-creation policies in the area. According to supply-side explanations of unemployment, both low income levels on benefits and the social unacceptability of unemployment act as spurs to encourage the unemployed to seek work, and perhaps to accept work at lower levels of remuneration than they previously enjoyed. The existence of opportunities in the black economy in RCT could help explain the wage stickiness which may prevent the expansion of the low-wage sector. In the literature it is argued that a high and persistent level of unemployment may influence social conditions so that unemployment becomes more acceptable:

> A more 'sociological' version of these mechanisms is that habits and social norms in favor of work ('work ethic') may be weakened when major macroeconomic shocks hit societies with generous benefit systems . . . Such shocks tend to throw more individuals onto various safety nets, and the hesitation to live on various types of benefits would be expected to fall by the number of individuals who are financed this way. Induced changes in habits and social norms will then contribute to persistent unemployment and non-employment, and perhaps also to a higher equilibrium employment rate.
>
> Habits and social norms among individuals may often be connected more with the values of subgroups in society than with the values of the population as a whole. This means that 'unemployment cultures' may develop within groups of interacting individuals who share similar unemployment experiences. (Lindbeck, 1996: 624)

If this theorizing about 'cultures of unemployment' is justified, then the RCT area is a prime example of a fertile breeding ground for such a culture. However, its existence is clearly difficult to demonstrate with any certainty, as is the existence and magnitude of the unofficial economy which financially protects those who no longer seek employment in the formal economy.

Economic inactivity is a major problem in the study area. It is clearly a loss of energy to a local economy which is already seriously depressed. As identified in *Pathway to Prosperity* (Welsh Office, 1998d) local policy-makers face a major challenge to bring that lost energy back into the local labour market so that it can stimulate economic activity, rather than operating as a drain on that activity.

THE CHANGING NATURE OF EMPLOYMENT

An increasing rate of female participation

An analysis of the employment situation of the Rhondda Cynon Taff area needs to take account of the significant gender aspect to employment in the area. The sexual division of labour has traditionally been strongly upheld in this area, with the predominant feeling that the man should provide and that it was a shame on him if his wife had to go to work. It was considered evidence of his inadequacy and even his 'unmanliness'; while the woman's responsibility to maintain the home spotless and 'tidy' was equally strongly reinforced (see discussion in D. Jones, 1995; Beddoe, 1995). Feminist historians have argued that the division between the public world of employment and the private, domestic world has been particularly clear-cut in Wales, and is underpinned by cultural peculiarities such as the strength of Nonconformity, the macho tradition associated with coal mining, and the demand for women to work as maidservants outside Wales (John, 1995; C. Williams, 1996). As the most recent history of industrial Rhondda makes clear, 'This mono-industrial society was also a society where women enjoyed few opportunities for waged work . . . At its economic and social peak in the early years of the twentieth century . . . Rhondda was both a coal society and a man's world' (C. Williams, 1996: 16–17).

It seems that some of this traditional opposition to female employment has persisted, since Mid Glamorgan as whole has the lowest female economic activity rate amongst all counties in England and Wales, with only 59.9 per cent of working-age women in Mid Glamorgan being economically active (MGCC, 1995: 8). The prevalence of the male-breadwinner model of domestic economic arrangement has proved an impediment to the tackling of unemployment when most of the jobs being created are either specifically intended for women or are in sectors that would be considered to be 'women's work', particularly in the service sector. The gender issue may be one factor that explains the weakness of the service sector in RCT.

However, the precipitate decline in traditional 'male' employment sectors has provided an impetus for women to leave the home in greater numbers, and has undermined the cultural prejudice against women's employment in the area. It is hard to distinguish between the push factors relating to poor male employment opportunities and pull factors relating to women's greater opportunities, but the figures, as shown in table 2.16, are clear. They show the relative increases and decreases in the number of male and female jobs in various different industrial sectors (measured in terms of SIC – standard industrial classification) during the period of most

Table 2.16: Percentage change in male–female employment rates 1984–1991 by SIC (%)

SIC		Males	Females
0	Agriculture, forestry and fishing	−99.7	−40.0
1	Energy/water supply industry	−82.1	−66.5
2	Extraction of minerals/metals	−1.4	1.1
3	Construction of metals goods/vehicles etc.	+29.5	+20.7
4	Other manufacturing industry	+9.2	+13.4
5	Construction	+0.9	+53.0
6	Distribution/hotels and catering	+29.5	+29.9
7	Transport and communications	−12.6	+0.9
8	Banking, finance, insurance, etc.	+16.8	+28.1
9	Other services	+1.0	+33.3

Source: MGCC, 1995: table 4.

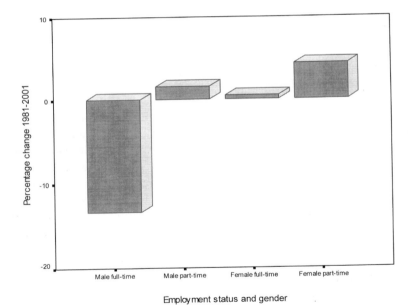

Figure 2.7: Increases and decreases in male and female full-time and part-time employment in the study area, 1981–2001
Source: Author's calculations based on data from the Welsh Assembly Statistics Directorate.

Table 2.17: Sex segregation in choice of jobs/training opportunities and further education courses in RCT, 1994/1995

Sector	Jobs/training entered[a]			
	Girls		Boys	
	N	%	N	%
Science/engineering	3	2.1	104	28.8
Motor vehicle	3	2.1	110	30.5
Skilled construction	3	2.1	100	27.7
Clerical/secretarial	86	59.7	46	12.7
Hairdressing	49	34.0	1	0.3
Total	144	100	361	100
	Further education places[b]			
	Girls		Boys	
	N	%	N	%
Engineering	2	0.6	137	46.0
Construction	4	1.2	115	38.6
Business/secretarial	105	30.2	35	11.7
Health/caring	237	68.1	11	3.7
Total	348	100	298	100

Sources: [a] MGCC Update, winter 1994; [b] EOC Wales, n.d.

intensive pit closures. In eight of the ten major SIC categories, job opportunities for women increased during the period of rapidly rising unemployment, with the largest overall increase occurring in the 'distribution, hotels, and catering' and 'other services' sectors, the latter including public administration, education, medical and other health services, personal services, and recreational services.

The figures (see figure 2.7, above) indicate that while rates of male full-time employment declined more rapidly in RCT than in Wales and the UK as a whole between 1984 and 1991, female full-time work in the area expanded at a similar rate and female part-time work at a faster rate than the national averages. The overall impact of this in terms of women's employment has been dramatic, with more women than men now being employed in Wales as a whole (Welsh Office, 1998c).

The division of jobs into 'male' and 'female' that underlies this discussion is itself artificial, although it pervades documents published by the local authorities in Mid Glamorgan. This is unsurprising once note is taken of the unusually high levels of sex segregation in employment patterns in this area, a source of continuing concern to the local careers service. Mid

Glamorgan Careers Ltd (1996) noted that 'Entry by young people into employment and training is still being made on traditional gender lines'. Their figures are reproduced in table 2.17. They indicate that women concentrate heavily in secretarial and clerical occupations while the craft and related occupations are dominated by men. Based on figures from the Equal Opportunities Commission Wales (n.d.) they also found that 'gender stereotyping continues to affect choice at A-level and of vocational qualifications'.

The increase in part-time employment

The growth in part-time employment in RCT is clearly linked to the increasing labour-force participation of women. In the years 1984–91, the most intensive period of pit closures, 12.9 per cent of full-time male employment opportunities were lost, mainly in coal mining (RCTBC, 1996: 5). The relative changes in male and female full-time and part-time employment are shown in figure 2.7. The figure shows that most of the part-time jobs are held by women and that, while women are as likely to work part-time as full-time, only a tiny proportion of men work part-time. Rates of male part-time work in the old mining valleys are lower than in Wales as a whole, whereas women working part-time comprise a share of the workforce that is between 4 and 6 per cent larger than in Wales as a whole (Welsh Assembly, 1998c).

   This chapter has provided an insight into the unique features of the Rhondda Cynon Taff labour market while at the same time indicating how its experience was typical, in some respects, of many industrial areas in recent years. The high levels of male unemployment that resulted from the movement of heavy industry, in this case mining, overseas required a policy response. The nature of the policy response in the study area is the subject of the next chapter.

3

Global Saviours or Local Champions: The History of Inward Investment in Wales

> This town and these communities seem, when one reviews the country's economic history, to have gone through all the economic experiences and related emotions that could be devised by modern industrial man. On the question of self-doubt . . . I should mention that a gentleman who stopped me in the street on my way here, to comment on the wonderful sunny weather, said 'I see from the weather forecast, Mr Rowlands, that we are in between depressions, like the Merthyr economy.'
>
> Ted Rowlands, MP for Merthyr, speaking in the economic
> development debate held there, 13 July 1998

In Wales, from the early 1980s onwards, the most resonating response to high levels of unemployment was a call for more inward investment. Successive Conservative Secretaries of State focused on the attraction of foreign, particularly East Asian, companies, as the most important plank of economic development policy. As outlined below, this policy has had some successes and has provided employment for a significant proportion of the Welsh workforce, although government estimates suggest a continuing need to raise total employment by 135,000 jobs (Welsh Office, 2002a). However, since the faltering and sometimes catastrophic collapse of economies in East Asia, the vulnerability of an employment policy with all its eggs in one basket has been exposed.

The failure of confidence in this strategy towards the end of the last century coincided with institutional change in Wales, particularly the establishment of a Welsh Assembly with a very significant number of Welsh Nationalist members, so that the Assembly does not have an established political direction. This has left the future direction of Welsh economic development policy more open. In this context, employment policy in Wales entered a state of flux, and the simplified debate between 'indigenous business' and 'multinational corporations' was central to the 1999 Assembly elections. In addition, the granting of Objective 1 status to a large area of Wales in 1999 made available large European grants for economic development. The Single Programming Document (Wales European Taskforce, 1999) makes clear how far thinking has changed with respect to job creation and opens up discussion about a range of radical alternative employment policies. This chapter offers a historical evaluation of the twenty years of intense focus on inward investment as the policy option to solve Wales's economic problems as the setting for more radical and creative ideas about an approach to employment policy that Wales might follow, which is outlined in the chapters that follow.

This chapter consists of a statistical and theoretical analysis of the impact of the inward investment strategy on the economy of Wales, focusing on the study area of Rhondda Cynon Taff. The following section attempts to measure inward investment and this is followed by a discussion of its problems. The next section attempts to assess the impact of inward investment on the Welsh economy in terms of its direct, indirect and dynamic effects. The impact of the policy and its consequences for the RCT local economy are then analysed, with a final section suggesting what the future of this policy might be in the Welsh context.

MEASURING JOB CREATION IN WALES

The history of job creation in Wales dates back to the nineteenth century (A. Roberts, 1994: 73), but its recent expansion can be traced to the post-war economic regeneration. Initially foreign investment was mainly by US companies – including Monsanto and Hoover, and later Ford, who arrived in 1965 (Morris, 1993). US companies account for a larger share of foreign employment in Wales than those of any other origin (see table 3.1). However, following the greater integration of the UK economy into the European market more investment in Wales has come from European companies such as Bosch at Bridgend, and Japanese and other Far Eastern companies, such as Toyota in Deeside, who need Europe-based assembly operations to gain access to the European market (A. Roberts, 1994). The first major study of FDI (foreign direct investment) in Wales was carried out in 1976, following a surge in foreign investment beginning in the later 1960s. Its authors concluded that: 'Only during the past decade can it be claimed that overseas factories have begun to make a real impact on the Welsh economy, rather than simply being interesting, but peripheral, "frills"' (Davies and Thomas, 1976: 8).

In the following period, and especially following the election of the first Conservative government in 1979, economic development policy for Wales was focused heavily on the creation of jobs through FDI. Tables 3.1, 3.2 and 3.3 give details of inward investment in Wales for 1991, 1996 and 2001, by origin country of the investing company, by sector and by Welsh county.[1]

Table 3.1: Employment in foreign-owned units by country of ownership, 1991, 1996, and 2001

Country of ownership	Units			Employment (000s)			% share of employment		
	1991	1996	2001	1991	1996	2001	1991	1996	2001
USA	100	139	132	28.1	30.9	30.0	41.6	41.0	44.2
Canada	20	14	10	5.1	3.0	1.2	7.6	4.0	1.77
EU	110	141	117	15.8	20.2	17.9	23.4	26.8	26.4
Germany	40	43	34	4.5	6.3	6.2	6.7	8.4	9.1
France	39	23	17	5.9	4.6	3.1	8.7	6.1	4.6
Others	101	87	71	18.6	21.3	18.7	27.6	28.2	27.5
Japan	29	38	35	11.8	16.9	12.3	17.5	22.4	18.1
TOTAL	331	381	330	67.5	75.4	67.8	100.0	100.0	100.0

Sources: Morris 1993; Welsh Office, 1998b: Table 5.9; Welsh Assembly, 2002b: 7.4

Table 3.2: Employment in foreign-owned units, by industry grouping, 1991, 1996 and 2001

Industry	Units			Employment (000s)			% share		
	1991	1996	2001	1991	1996	2001	1991	1996	2001
Metal manufacturing	18	44	37	4.7	5.7	4.3	7.0	7.5	6.3
Chemical industry	47	55	54	8.2	8.4	7.8	12.1	11.1	11.5
Mechanical engineering	29	32	25	2.4	5.2	3.8	3.6	6.9	5.6
Electronic and instrument engineering	65	69	55	19.1	23.6	19.8	28.3	31.3	29.0
Vehicles and parts	25	40	41	9.5	13.0	13.2	14.1	17.3	19.4
Food and clothing	22	34	29	3.5	5.4	5.6	5.2	7.2	8.2
Paper etc.	23	30	29	4.0	4.7	5.9	5.9	6.2	8.7
Rubber and plastic	29	41	31	3.6	5.0	4.0	5.3	6.6	5.9
Other	83	60	29	12.5	4.2	3.7	18.5	5.4	5.4
Total	341	405	330	67.5	75.4	68.1	100.0	100.0	100.0

Sources: Morris, 1993; Welsh Office 1998b: Table 5.11; Welsh Assembly 2002b: Table 7.6.

Table 3.3: Employment in foreign-owned units, by county, 1991, 1996 and 2001

County	*Units*			*Employment (000s)*			*% share*		
	1991	*1996*	*2001*	*1991*	*1996*	*2001*	*1991*	*1996*	*2001*
Clwyd	70	88	71[a]	12.2	15.0	13.8	18.1	19.8	20.4
Dyfed	26	24	15[a]	4.6	4.4	4.5	6.8	5.8	6.6
Gwent	71	69	17[a]	13.0	11.8	7.4	19.3	15.6	10.9
Gwynedd	14	5[a]	13[a]	2.4	1.9	2.5	3.6	2.5	3.7
Powys[b]	–	9	8	–	2.9	0.8	–	3.8	1.2
Mid Glam	91	98	115	17.9	15.2	17.7	26.5	20.1	26.0
South Glam	30	31	29	8.2	9.4	7.8	12.1	12.4	11.5
West Glam	39	48	41	9.2	15.0	13.5	13.6	19.8	19.9
TOTAL	341	372	330	67.5	75.6	68.0	100.0	100.0	100.0

[a]These totals are not full totals, since some figures have been suppressed to prevent disclosure.
[b]No figures for Powys are available for 1991.
Sources: Morris, 1993; Welsh Office, 1998b: table 2.12; Welsh Office (2002b), table 7.9.

As can be seen from table 3.1, over 40 per cent of the employment provided by FDI in Wales is in US-owned companies, with a further quarter in EU-owned companies, and slightly less than one-fifth in Japanese-owned companies. The EU countries and Japan increased their share of the employment total between 1991 and 1996, but Japan's share has since fallen back. The total number of foreign-funded production units can clearly be seen to have hit a peak around the mid-1990s, having declined since. This suggests that the persistent investors may be those who are well established in Wales and that there was a surge in interest from other companies at this time. This was likely to have been the window of opportunity for Wales before the bursting of the Asian bubble and the availability of access to European markets via the low-labour-cost countries of central Europe. However, all interpretations of inward-investment figures must be made cautiously, since changes in the ownership patterns of the companies, that is, mergers and takeovers, may have undue influence on the data presented.

Table 3.2 shows that the most significant inward-investment sector is electrical equipment manufacture, which provides about one-third of total employment. In 1996 a full 17.4 per cent of this was the manufacture of TVs and radios (Welsh Office, 1998b: table 5.11), although this had fallen back to around 11.5 per cent by 2001. The other significant sectors (providing more than 10 per cent of total employment) are vehicles, which shows a steady rise, and chemicals. Food is also a growing sector (during 2000–2 this sector increased by 13 per cent in Wales: Munday 2003), a fact masked by its inclusion in this table with clothing, which has collapsed in recent years in the face of Asian and eastern European competition.

Table 3.3 shows clearly the uneven geographical distribution of inward investment in Wales, with nearly 60 per cent of the employment provided being in the Glamorgans, the former industrial areas of south Wales. Mid Glamorgan has seen the largest overall number of jobs funded from overseas investment with around a quarter of the total. Rhondda Cynon Taff accounts for 7.6 per cent of this. The most successful boroughs in terms of inward-investment-based job creation are Flintshire, Wrexham, Bridgend and Newport, which all have around 9 per cent of the total. The impact of transport links to the rest of the UK on the success of attracting foreign investment is clear here.

If we divide these percentage employment shares by populations in the various unitary authorities (UAs) we gain a clearer picture of the regional spread of the employment generated by this policy. By calculating a regional investment index for Wales[2] we find that Wrexham and Bridgend have around twice their proportional share, while RCT has an index of slightly less than 1, as does neighbouring Merthyr. The other Valleys UAs of Blaenau Gwent, Torfaen and Neath score more highly on this index. Although RCT has fared reasonably well in absolute terms, because of the large population of this UA, and its high levels of unemployment, it is still relatively worse off in terms of inward investment share than other boroughs that have faced less serious economic problems.

During the years of Conservative administration Wales was the most successful UK region in terms of attracting inward investment: it received 14 per cent of the UK total between 1979 and 1991, and approximately 20 per cent per year from 1988 onwards (Hill and Munday, 1994). However, assessing the extent of inward investment is complex, and is not aided by the caution shown by the development boards in giving precise data about the size of investments made or grants awarded. Begg (1995) presents data for 1994 which indicate that according to his 'Location Quotient' (LQ) Wales was supremely successful: its LQ of 5.26 compares extremely favourably with the next highest scoring region of Northern Ireland with 2.64. The more economically active regions of the UK – the East Midlands, South-East and South-West – all receive LQs of 0.30 or less. However, since these quotients are normalized by dividing the number of manufacturing projects by the size of the GDP of the area, the method itself ensures that economically inactive regions will achieve a higher LQ value and appear to be more successful in the inward investment competition. Indeed, it is because of the low level of GDP that these regions are awarded the assisted status which enables them to offer grants to foreign companies. The quotient is further weakened by being based on the number of projects, rather than their value, thus indicating little of importance about the extent of inward investment in the different regions. Given the unwillingness of the development agencies to divulge the precise size of the investments – and the understandable unwillingness of companies to report such sensitive information – there is little else a researcher is able to do.

I presented more realistic estimates of the LQs of the various UK regions using data for 1996 in an earlier paper (Cato, 2000a), which gave a more balanced picture of the investment situation then, being based on a comparison between the extent of inward investment to the regions (again, unhappily, measured by number of projects alone, data on the extent of investment or number of jobs being unavailable) and the size of workforce of the region. These results showed that even on this better-balanced measure Wales was indeed the most successful UK region in terms of manufacturing investment with an LQ of 2.07. Updated estimates using the same method are presented in table 3.4.[3]

The picture was much less rosy for Wales in terms of non-manufacturing investment in 1996 (LQ 0.3), the inward-investment sector that is most likely to grow in the future, and has not improved much since (the LQ for this sector in 2001 was 0.57). Wales's high level of manufacturing inward investment also compares unfavourably with the levels of non-manufacturing investment seen in London, the West Midlands, the South-East and Scotland. This is of concern, since following the enlargement of the EU manufacturing investment is the most likely to migrate eastwards. However, these data are not very informative, since they conflate data for well-paid sectors, such as financial services, that focus around the South-East, and poorly paid work, such as in call centres.

Suggested explanations for Wales's past success in attracting inward investment include 'rapidly improving infrastructure, low relative wage levels and high levels of regional aid' (Hill and Roberts, 1993: 21; see also Sahara, 1993). Rapid increases in productivity are another attractive feature (Hill and Keegan, 1993). Huggins's (2001) study of Wales's foreign-owned manufacturing plants conducted in 1999 concluded that by far the most important factor influencing companies' decisions about where to invest was the level of grants and subsidies available.

The impact of inward investment on the structure of the Welsh economy is undoubted, with an increase of 47 per cent in the level of employment in the foreign manufacturing employment sector compared with a decline in employment of 5.5 per cent in domestic manufacturing employment in Wales (Munday and Peel, 1997). By 1999 Wales had around 16 per cent of FDI coming into the UK, roughly three times its population share. In the European context Wales attracted around 5 per cent of all investment, compared with its population share of around 0.5 per cent. There were

Table 3.4: Distribution of inward investment by UK region, 2001/2002

Region	Manufacturing projects		Non-manufacturing projects	
	No.	LQ	No.	LQ
North-East	49	2.03	41	1.08
North-West	20	0.30	67	0.63
Yorks/Humbs.	50	1.0	27	0.34
East Midlands	16	0.37	22	0.32
West Midlands	85	1.60	99	1.18
East	19	0.33	78	0.86
London	30	0.39	356	2.93
South-East	42	0.48	247	1.80
South-West	26	0.51	53	0.66
Wales	72	2.67	24	0.57
Scotland	57	1.10	76	0.93
Northern Ireland	19	1.23	17	0.70

Source: *Regional Trends*, 37: tables 3.6 and 13.8, based on information from Invest-UK, Department of Trade and Industry.

Photo 3.1: A view up the Rhondda Fach valley from Ferndale showing typical strip housing and demonstrating the constraints on industrial expansion at ground level

around 380 foreign-owned plants in Wales employing approximately 75,000 people (Huggins, 2001). The foreign manufacturing base in Wales represented around a third of all Welsh manufacturing employment (Munday and Peel, 1997). There is no question that investment on this scale filled an employment gap following major industrial restructuring which, with Wales's history of specialization in heavy industry, hit the economy particularly hard. However, since the start of the policy voices have been raised questioning its expense and its long-term consequences for the Welsh economy. These issues will be discussed in the following sections.

PROBLEMS WITH INWARD-INVESTMENT-BASED JOB CREATION

The government's inward-investment-based employment policy in Wales has attracted sceptical attention since its inception, but it was holed below the waterline by the experience of the disastrous LG investment, which led to a terminal undermining of confidence in the reliance on foreign-based companies to solve Wales's employment problems. As the largest-ever foreign investment in Europe the LG project was always going to attract attention. Aside from the large grants to long-term Japanese companies in the automotive industry, the LG grant accounted for around two-thirds of the value of the other eight offers made to Asian companies (Tewdwr-Jones and Phelps, 1999). In the early days (it was announced in 1996), it was trumpeted by both politicians and the Welsh Development Agency. The project was in two parts and involved the construction of an integrated monitor plant and a microchip wafer manufacturing plant on a greenfield site near Newport. The exact size of the investment was given in evidence to the Welsh Affairs Select Committee (WAC, 1998) as £1,664m for the promised creation of 6,100 jobs. The size of public-sector support was also a record at £248m. A simple calculation makes it apparent that, even according to the official count of the number of jobs to be created, the cost per job of this scheme to the public was slightly in excess of £40,600, a sum which has called into question the cost-effectiveness of this sort of employment scheme (WAC, 1998: para. 6). It is actually not the highest rate per job of any of these schemes, however, that dubious honour belonging to the Ford engine plant at Bridgend at £90,000 per job created (Tewdwr-Jones and Phelps, 1999). This is far more than the average rate per job in England, which the NAO estimates at £4,600 (NAO, 2003).

Worse was to follow, when, as a consequence of a slump in world prices for microchips following a global glut, LG reneged on the deal. Although the TV assembly plant has functioned since 1998, the larger semiconductor operation was cancelled. More than half of the promised jobs never materialized: employee statistics show that 1,600 were employed by the end of 1998, rising to approximately 2,000 employees by the year 2000 (Kelly, 2000). The final blow came in May 2003, when the announcement was made that another 870 jobs were to be cut, leaving a mere 350 employees of the promised 6,000 (BBC Wales website). Following this announcement a spokesman for the WDA expressed his disappointment, admitting that they had 'hoped the jobs would be here for decades'. Kevin Morgan of the City and Regional Planning Department of Cardiff University called the whole experience 'one of the biggest disasters in our history' (BBC *Wales Today*, 22 May 2003).

The experience makes it clear how vulnerable such global agreements are. LG found itself overexposed in its home market as a result of the Asian economic collapse, and its Welsh investment was peripheral and easily sacrificed. To save its own corporate skin, and at the direction of the Korean government, which does not share the UK's laissez-faire approach to economic policy-making, LG's semiconductor division merged with Samsung, which already had spare capacity in semiconductor manufacture. The result is that the new factory, subsidized and built on a greenfield site (opened for development in opposition to local planning rules: see Tewdwr-Jones and Phelps, 1999) as part of the incentive package, has stood empty for five years. It is custom-built for semiconductor manufacture and cannot easily be adapted for another use. Most of the £250 million of development grants has already disappeared into LG's international debts, while the actual size of subsidy per job has now risen to £124,000.

The Welsh Affairs Select Committee concluded that:

> Even when taking into account the potential multiplier effect of such a large enterprise, the value of the public investment in LG must at best be unproven. There has been widespread concern in Wales, outside the Newport area at least, that public sector resources intended to stimulate indigenous industry have been redirected to fund LG. (WAC, 1998: para. 6)

This is, clearly, the most important point: money that could have been invested in locally anchored, community-based businesses has simply been wasted. It has been spent subsidizing an inefficient manufacturer, a policy so decried during the era of nationalized industries, but in this case not even a British one, but one based in East Asia, owing no loyalty to Welsh workers and over whom UK economic planners have no political control or influence.

The LG story epitomizes the negative view of inward investment at the level of narrative. There has also been substantial academic criticism of inward-investment job creation, which has focused on five main issues, outlined in the following paragraphs, to which I add one of my own.

1. *The jobs created are low-skilled.* Part of the enthusiasm for inward investment was the desire to attract world-class companies to Wales. However, the criticism has been voiced since the inception of the policy that companies use their Welsh production units merely for low-grade assembly work. A review of unemployment by Glyn found that jobs generated by the new, high-technology industries are poor in terms of skills levels, as well as rates of pay and conditions of work (Glyn, 1996: 4). It is the case that many of the plants established as a result of inward investment in Wales are only for the assembly of components into goods which are then sold in the EU market, so-called 'screwdriver operations'.

In spite of the prominent example of research and development (R&D) commitment by Sony, which has its European R&D centre in Wales (WAC, 1998: para. 12), rates of investment in R&D by business cast a depressing light on the discussion regarding the low technical standard of much of Welsh TNC-sponsored manufacturing industry. Wales has the lowest value on an index of business R&D spending as a proportion of regional GDP. Its value of 0.4 is lower than those of the UK's other peripheral regions such as Scotland (0.6) and Northern Ireland and Yorkshire and Humberside (both 0.5), and is less than a sixth as much as the UK's most research-orientated region, the East, which achieves a value of 2.8 (ONS, 1998: table 13.8).

A useful case study of the issue of skill levels in foreign-owned companies in Wales is provided by K. Morgan (1987), who focuses on the electronics industry, which was once the heart of inward-investment strategy in south Wales. He identifies the international division of labour operating in the global electronics industry, with production functions being divided between high-level R&D, intermediate high-skilled production, and low-grade assembly in branch plants. Electronics production and assembly facilities in Wales seem to fall mainly into the third group, with only a limited role for product adaptation for the European market. Electronics-based employment in Wales focuses mainly on consumer electronics (that is, the production of TV sets or home computer monitors), with bulk rather than high-skill production. A later review by a different author (B. Morgan, 1993), found that Japanese firms had positively affected productivity in Wales, which suggests that the 'skills' that are spilling over may be of the 'behavioural' variety particularly favoured by Japanese employers (see section 2 below).

The 'international division of labour' thesis is supported by data indicating the location of different corporate activities for the Welsh

Table 3.5: Extent of various corporate research, design and development (R, D&D) activities provided locally or supplied from the parent company for Welsh foreign-owned companies, 1999 (%)

Location of R, D&D	On-site	Parent company	Bought in locally	Bought nationally/ internationally	N
New products	42.2	76.5	3.0	6.0	166
New processes	49.1	68.9	4.3	9.3	161
Design/redesign	60.3	62.2	2.6	3.8	156
Product adaptation	70.1	40.2	1.9	1.9	157
Process adaptation	80.7	42.9	3.7	5.0	161
Product testing	78.3	46.4	2.4	6.0	166
Process testing	78.2	38.5	2.6	6.4	156

Source: Phelps et al., 2003: table 3.

inward-investment projects studied by Phelps et al. in 1999. As shown in table 3.5, most of the higher-level functions of inward investment companies are conducted by the parent company, with very little scope for expertise bought in from, for example, the Welsh higher-education sector. As the skill level required increases from process testing to new product research the proportion conducted on site, as opposed to being supplied by the parent company, falls below 50 per cent. The authors of this study conclude that the plants fall somewhere between branch plants and fully embedded units of the Welsh economy.

TNC commitment to training also appears weak. Although the larger and better-established firms such as Bosch and the Japanese firms invest heavily in training, 40 per cent of firms provide no training at all and consider money spent on training to be a cost rather than an investment (Owen, 1993: 30). This was confirmed by the survey results from the Japanese company included in my sample: at 23 per cent it had the second lowest rate of training, with only five of the twenty-two staff who returned questionnaires having undertaken training in the past year. However, a study carried out in the same year (1999) found that inward-investing companies frequently discovered that the local labour force was not as skilled as they were expecting and so had themselves been forced to spend more on training than similar-sized FDI companies elsewhere in the UK (Huggins, 2001).

The creation of jobs by foreign firms was a policy responding to the desperate situation facing the local labour market after the huge job losses in mining. Its role in taking up some of the slack in the labour market should be acknowledged, and the fact that many of the jobs required only low levels of skills to some extent merely reflected the levels of skills available amongst local workers. However, longer term, this sort of strategy begins to perpetuate some of the problems it is intended to solve. The low level of skill and technological know-how involved in these branch plants limits the possibility for positive spillovers into the local economy and can lead to the degradation of the local labour force. The branch-plant system also reduces the value of grants paid to inward investors because of the absence of a multiplier effect on local suppliers. Estimates of the proportion of components provided by Welsh suppliers centre around the 10 per cent mark (Hill and Roberts, 1993; Sahara, 1993; this issue is discussed more fully below).

2. *The jobs created are poorly paid.* In addition to low levels of skill, criticisms have also focused on pay rates, although the link between low levels of pay and Wales's FDI success is contentious. Wales has the lowest GDP per head (at 80 per cent of UK GDP: Welsh Assembly, 2002b) of any of the UK regions except Northern Ireland, and is one of only two areas to show consistent declines in GDP since 1988 (ONS, 1998: figure 12.2). Evidence is clear that manufacturing inward investment is closely correlated with low levels of disposable income: this relationship is illustrated in figure 3.1 for ONS data on disposable income per head in each region in 2001 (ONS, 2002: table 8.2) and the location quotients calculated in table 3.4.[4] To test the strength of association a correlation was calculated: the resulting Pearson's r of −0.61 ($p < 0.05$) indicates a significant negative correlation between low GDP in a region and the level of investment. Interestingly, in the case of non-manufacturing investment there is a positive correlation of 0.77 ($p < 0.01$), illustrated in figure 3.2. This is an indication of the change in the nature of foreign investment towards financial and service sectors and its corresponding geographical relocation in the more prosperous areas of the country. In spite of these caveats it seems unsurprising that foreign manufacturing companies would seek out lower-wage areas of national economies, especially those that have large numbers of relatively well-skilled and available workers. Munday and Roberts (2001) confirm the low level of wages: in their study Japanese-owned companies paid the lowest average wages, a finding which is replicated in my study, where those who work for the Japanese electronics company have the lowest average earnings.

3. *Insecurity of employment provided by foreign firms.* Since the inception of the policy, questions have been raised about the level of commitment that can

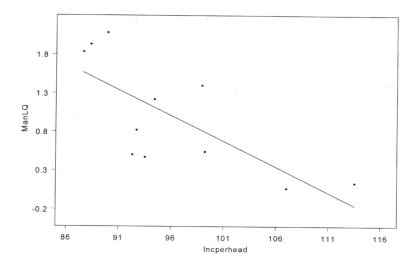

Figure 3.1: Relationship between disposable income per head and manufacturing inward investment

Source: Regional Trends, 37 and author's calculations of LQS

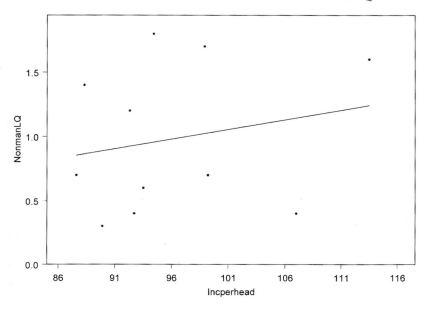

Figure 3.2: Relationship between disposable income per head and non-manufacturing inward investment

Source: Regional Trends, 37 and author's calculations of LQS

be expected from transnational corporations, which have no reason to provide employment in Wales rather than Taiwan or Poland: 'the potential rootlessness and footlooseness involved in multinational branch plant operations' (D. Thomas, 1996: 227). This point has been clearly illustrated in the past few years, following the crisis of the Japanese and South-East Asian economies. In the face of recession in their domestic marketplaces they have withdrawn investment from their Wales-based operations.

This is not just obvious in hindsight. An analysis by Munday and Peel (1997) compared the effects of recession on foreign-owned and domestically owned firms. Data from the Census of Production for the UK showed that from 1981 to 1986 total manufacturing employment fell by 17 per cent, whereas the decline in the foreign manufacturing sector was 28 per cent. The results of their study showed that this finding was not reproduced in the foreign-owned manufacturing sector in Wales over the period 1989–92: during this period of boom to bust for the British economy foreign-owned firms reduced employment levels by only 1.5 employees on average, compared with a reduction of 15.4 employees for domestically owned companies. The authors suggested that this reflects the greater stability of foreign-owned companies. However, it seems more likely that it simply shows the vulnerability of this sector to changes in the international business cycle, and that the business cycles of western Europe and the Far East are not synchronized. Now that the economies of Japan and South Korea have gone into their own recession a similar comparison could be expected to reach the opposite conclusion. This suggests the importance of having a balanced portfolio of employment in foreign and domestically owned firms.

Although data on the performance of foreign-based companies is difficult to come by due to a concern for commercial confidentiality, there is data available on the small and medium-sized enterprise (SME) sector in Wales. Table 3.6 indicates that there is good news in terms of the creation of new businesses in Rhondda Cynon Taff. It presents a comparison of figures for new business start-ups and failures in the twenty-two unitary authorities of Wales. The fourth column is a ratio of VAT registrations to de-registrations in 2001 and shows that the Valleys areas have some of the highest rates, undermining the thesis of low levels of entrepreneurship there.

Research conducted at the Welsh Institute for Research into Cooperatives also stresses the contrast between the longevity of local businesses, especially those that are owned by their workers, and the instability of foreign direct investment. The concept of 'capital anchoring' describes how local businesses are more embedded in the local economy and far less liable to capital flight. The cooperative form is the most embedded business form, since its ownership is diffuse and closely linked to employment, so that individuals have an incentive both to keep the business going and to make it successful through their own endeavour (Arthur et al., forthcoming). This idea is explored further in Chapter 7, which focuses on the Tower Colliery workers' cooperative.

The discussion about the insecurity of foreign-owned firms can work to the firms' advantage. Multinationals' discussion of their employment strategy can also be used to manipulate employees and policy-makers in different countries, or even in different parts of the same country, following the logic of 'regime competition'. According to one commentator:

> Recent studies show how companies use sophisticated management information to 'reward' or 'punish' individual sites by granting or withholding new investment . . . Many companies have used the *threat* of transfer of investment or production as a lever to improve productivity . . . Such 'coercive comparisons' between plants . . . are particularly used in industries where similar or identical plants operate in different countries: a typical case is the motor vehicle industry. (Ferner, 1998: 174)

Even when workers exceed all productivity expectations and perform better than their 'competitors' it is no guarantee of job security, as the workers in Corus's south Wales steelworks recently discovered. The closure of the more efficient British plants to focus business in the Dutch and eastern European plants underlines both the threat to UK jobs from Enlargement and the insecurity of an employment policy when board-level strategic decisions need take no account of worker loyalty or efficiency. As Ferner points out (pp. 178–9) Britain's lax labour legislation means that it is actually cheaper to make workers redundant here than in most EU countries, making British workers more vulnerable in the competition for jobs in spite of the UK winning the race to the bottom in the regime competition.

There was a severe panic amongst policy-makers following a series of damaging closures in 1998 of newly established foreign-based production units in north-east England, particularly based around the electronics industry, as discussed by Pike (1999). In this article the author argues that the devolution of Wales has allowed it an unfair advantage in the competition for inward investment, but this may not protect Wales's inward investment in the long run. The Welsh Affairs Select Committee acknowledged a concern with the insecurity of investment from foreign-based firms, although it found 'as yet little evidence of this in Wales'. However, it has conceded that 'recent closures in Wales and in other parts of the UK are alarming' and left the question of the future of inward investment projects in this era of Asian recession open (WAC, 1998: para. 16). This comment was, of course, made before the steel closures at Corus

Table 3.6: VAT registrations and de-registrations in Welsh unitary authorities, 2001

Area	Registrations	De-registrations	Ratio
Blaenau Gwent	70	70	1
Bridgend	250	205	1.219512
Caerphilly	250	220	1.136364
Cardiff	775	845	0.91716
Carmarthen	390	395	0.987342
Ceredigion	180	145	1.241379
Conwy	230	245	0.938776
Denbighshire	220	220	1
Flintshire	340	290	1.172414
Gwynedd	260	260	1
Isle of Anglesey	125	130	0.961538
Merthyr Tydfil	80	65	1.230769
Monmouthshire	280	285	0.982456
Neath Port Talbot	210	175	1.2
Newport	295	285	1.035088
Pembroke	245	260	0.942308
Powys	350	400	0.875
RCT	355	305	1.163934
Swansea	470	505	0.930693
Torfaen	145	130	1.115385
Vale of Glamorgan	240	265	0.90566
Wrexham	245	225	1.088889
England	154,280	142,630	1.08168
Wales	6,000	5,920	1.013514
Scotland	11,530	10,745	1.073057
UK	175,455	162,725	1.07823

Source: Business Start-ups and Closures: VAT Registrations and De-Registrations in 2001, Small Business Service, *www.sbs.gov.uk*

were announced and before the latest and most serious job losses at LG: in the first case production will continue at plants in eastern Europe; in the second the TV and computer monitors will be manufactured in China.

4. *Promises to provide jobs not kept*. According to a Radio 4 investigation (BBC Manchester, 1998), only two-thirds of the jobs promised by inward investors in the UK are actually created.[5] Establishing a business relationship with an overseas company for the first time inevitably involves a high level of risk. But even well-established foreign companies have no problem in changing investment decisions, with a consequent loss

of jobs in Wales, should circumstances be preferable abroad: 'Since [Ford's] initial, and much lauded, commitment, successive revisions of the company's plans have seen investment transfers to Germany and Spain, with attendant job losses at the south Wales plants' (D. Thomas, 1996: 227). With the proposed expansion of the European labour market into eastern Europe, many more workers will become available to the mobile, branch-plant operation (Hudson, 1994), exposing the vulnerability of the inward-investment strategy. Again, LG provides the most prominent example of the failure of inward-investment companies to create the jobs they promise. The public announcement was of 6,000 jobs. The actual maximum number at any point in time was around 2,000 of which, after five years, some 350 remain. The cynical comment by one of my interviewees that when he hears the official announcements of jobs created he mentally divides the number in half begins to appear optimistic.

5. *Regional imbalance of development within Wales.* The disadvantage of corporate job creation, as contrasted with state regional planning, is that the balancing of local economies within a region is not important: from the perspective of the multinational the only criterion is the availability of a labour force with appropriate skills and wage rates. This has been particularly apparent in Wales, where regional inequalities in employment rates have always been extreme. Thus one result of an employment policy based on inward investment that has been deleterious to Wales as a whole has been the enhancement of regional economic imbalance, particularly focusing around available road links. The result of unplanned develop-ment has been:

> a clustering along the M4 corridor in south Wales and in Alyn and Deeside in north-east Wales, thus creating or amplifying regional growth inequalities within Wales . . . Nearly three-quarters of the employment in foreign-owned plants is located in industrial south Wales (Mid, South and West Glamorgan together with Gwent) with another 20 per cent in Clwyd in the north-east. (D. Thomas, 1996: 227)

The index for regional investment around Wales presented in note 2 indicates that rates range from 2.04 in Wrexham and 1.93 in Bridgend to a mere 0.1 in Conwy and 0.15 in Ceredigion. As will be discussed further in the second part of this chapter, with the institution of the Welsh Assembly the requirement to balance the needs of all parts of Wales, and the need for 'national' economic planning for Wales as a whole, has come to the fore.

6. *The jobs that are created are unpopular*. This final criticism is necessarily more speculative, since reliable data are unavailable. However, the results of my own interviewing (presented in full in Chapter 6) indicate that the kinds of jobs that are provided by inward investment companies are unpopular, particularly with the older male workers who represent the bulk of the unemployed. There are several ways in which factory-based employment, especially in companies run along Japanese-style management lines, contrasts strongly with the heavy industrial employment that formerly dominated south Wales. First, the strict discipline and the visibility of workers to management monitoring typical of factory work is in strong contrast to the 'camaraderie' of the pits, which most miners and ex-miners identified as being the most attractive aspect of mining. Secondly, the jobs are not seen as suitable for men's work in an area with a highly machismo-based culture. This is exacerbated by the need, especially in electronics factories, to wear what might be considered 'effeminate' protective clothing. And, finally, the jobs are considered not to provide 'a living wage': an issue that emerged strongly in the interviews conducted at Tower Colliery. My survey evidence shows that workers at the Japanese company I studied are, indeed, some of the worst paid in the sample. These more anecdotal aspects of the unpopularity of job creation especially in south Wales are addressed Chapter 4, and workers' reactions reported in Chapter 6.

New Labour's national strategy for coping with the long-term unemployed, such as the Welfare to Work policy, which requires job search in exchange for benefits, has been devised to encourage them back to work and has been combined with an ideological attack on the 'dependency culture' and a parallel idealization of work. However, the creation of undesirable employment appears to be leading rather to increasing levels of economic inactivity, particularly amongst men, so that although unemployment rates are declining this does not represent any reduction in the loss of labour activity amongst these mature, male workers (see Dickens, Gregg and Wadsworth, 2000).

This effect seems to be strong in Wales, according to the Welsh Office economic strategy document *Pathway to Prosperity*:

> But now the real problem is that, in Wales, 27 per cent of people of working age are outside the labour market – that is they are neither working nor actively seeking work. For GB, that figure is 22 per cent. It is this higher level of inactivity in Wales which contributes most to our low GDP.

One purpose of the interviewing reported in Chapter 6 is to inform policy-making so as to make the offered employment more attractive to potential workers by assessing what they value about the work that they do. This might prove to be a carrot that is effective, especially in areas such as the Valleys where successive sticks have manifestly failed to have any effect on the donkey.

ASSESSING THE IMPACT OF INWARD INVESTMENT ON THE WELSH ECONOMY

Inward investment is hypothesized as having three distinct effects on the local economy: direct, indirect and dynamic (Williams and Smith, 1998). The direct effects in Wales, in terms of job creation, are substantial, and have been outlined in an earlier section. The issue of the indirect effects, via spillovers and supplier networks, is the subject of ongoing debate, while the dynamic impact of FDI on the host economy in Wales appears to be substantial and lasting.

One of the major reasons for the enthusiasm attached to decisions by East Asian, and particularly Japanese, companies to invest in Wales was the expectation of skill spillovers into the local economic environment. Following Solow's original growth model, New Growth Theory, developed by Romer (1989, 1990) and others, suggests that monopoly power is undermined by spillover effects from R&D and technical knowledge. This model interprets knowledge as a non-rival factor, so that knowledge spillovers can be considered a positive externality. The theory concludes that knowledge and innovation spillovers can permanently increase growth rates. Thus the expectation of such a beneficial effect on the Welsh economy was an important stimulus to the inward-investment policy.

Before the crisis in Japanese capitalism became apparent in the mid-1990s Japan was seen as the apotheosis of a successful capitalist economy:

> Japan has constantly outperformed other free-market economies and, today, in the eighties, she has become an economic superpower controlling nearly 10 per cent of the world's exports by value. So the history of Japan is one from war-torn economy to economic domination. (Munday, 1993)

The hope was that the inward-investment relationship would benefit both sides: the investors would gain a skilled, relatively low-paid workforce and favourable production and trading arrangements, while the Welsh workforce would gain secure employment and acquire new skills.

Evidence for positive indirect effects is rather weak. First, in terms of knock-on effects for components suppliers, according to Hill and Roberts (1993), foreign firms purchased only 12 per cent by value of their components in Wales. A more positive account by a manager from Toyota

Table 3.7: Sourcing of materials and services in the host region and calculations of indirect turnover generated per £1m of direct sales, 1999

Sector	% host sourcing		Indirect turnover (£000s)	
	UK	Foreign	UK	Foreign
Rubber etc.	33.6	28.4	365	301
Metals	30.9	24.5	357	201
Engineering	35.3	27.0	451	360
Electronics	35.1	25.2	435	306
Transport equipment etc.	28.6	33.3	372	339

Source: Brand et al., 2000: tables 6 and 7.

UK based on Deeside claims 60 per cent local content for their product, but this is qualified with the definition of 'local' as meaning 'European'; in fact only 8 per cent of Toyota's components are supplied by Welsh-based firms (Sahara, 1993: 25). Even a firm with such a long history in Wales as Bosch is still only sourcing 20 per cent of its components from within the UK as a whole (J. Salmon, 1993: 28). Later articles confirm that levels of local sourcing remain low, as found by Phelps et al., 2003.

Munday and Roberts (2001) found evidence of low levels of linkages and purchasing, and, interestingly, that the larger companies had fewer local supplier linkages than smaller companies. They also found a discrepancy relating to the origin of the companies, with those with Japanese ownership showing the highest total spend on materials and services (still at only 20 per cent) compared to the lowest level for non-EU European plants (a mere 10 per cent). A study by Brand et al. (2000) attempted to estimate values for local sourcing and indirect turnover that compare levels for UK-owned and foreign-owned firms: some of their figures are presented in table 3.7. The discrepancies of some 5–10 per cent in levels of local sourcing, and up to £150,000 in indirect turnover per £1m of direct sales, raise questions about the value for money offered by a policy that spends public money attracting foreign companies to create jobs in Wales. The National Audit Office (NAO, 2003) assessment of similar schemes in England (where the rates of public investment per job are much lower than in Wales) found that issues of displacement and a relatively low level of additionality (or multiplier effects) limited the value for money offered by these projects.

More negative evidence can be drawn from a study of the indirect regional impact of inward investment by Driffield (1998), who suggests that Wales has lost a significant number of jobs in its car components and its iron and steel-making sectors as a result of employment substitution to other regions where inward investors had located. The Welsh Affairs Select

Photo 3.2: A hopeful appeal in Pontygwaith: the flat landscape gives the clue to the former use of this site for mine workings

Committee concluded that the case for indirect effects was unproven and suggested the need for further research: 'In our view, more needs to be done to monitor and evaluate the effects of inward investment projects on the local economy, and thus the cost-effectiveness of public sector support for such projects' (WAC, 1998: para. 9).

Evidence on the existence of skill spillovers is also mixed. A review provided by Wang (1998) concludes that the extent of technological spillover is limited by the size of the gap between the indigenous industry and the inward investor: where the gap is too large the innovating company can manage to maintain control over its technological advantage. This seems to have been the case in Wales with the national body charged with encouraging small-business development admitting that 'Wales has a poor track record in creating high-tech start-ups' (EAPSG, 1999: 7). Munday and Roberts (2001) confirm that Wales demonstrates particularly low levels of indirect employment creation and technology spillovers.

Discussions about the extent of skill spillovers have tended to be confused because of differing definitions of what constitutes a 'skill'. While Western economists might tend to associate the word with a technical or intellectual ability, foreign, and particularly East Asian, companies tend to use a wider definition:

The foreign firms tend to have a much broader conception of 'skill', which is taken to refer not just to technical qualifications, but is used to include behavioural qualities as well, such as strong identity with the company, low absenteeism, high work rate and quality consciousness and so forth. This behavioural definition of skill is most pronounced among the Japanese firms. (Morgan, 1987: 45)

If we take this wider definition of 'skill' then we have moved on to consider the third type of effect of FDI, namely dynamic effects, the evidence for which is more substantial. B. Morgan finds convincing evidence of increased productivity: during the 1980s Wales achieved the greatest increase in productivity and the largest fall in unit labour costs of any UK region (1993: 16). Debate continues as to how much of the productivity improvement was the result of improved management or workers' behavioural 'skills' and how much was merely the result of the decline in relative wages seen in Wales over the same period (see Hill and Roberts, 1993).

The most important 'skill' that incoming employers required of their workers was 'flexibility', in terms of functional demarcation, as well as hours of work, and, to some extent, pay rates. This point is confirmed in an article written by one of Toyota's managers at its Deeside plant (Sahara, 1993), who wrote the following in connection with positive aspects of the location:

> An excellent skilled labour tradition within the area. We have been very pleased with the quality of the applications we attracted and with the calibre of the workforce recruited. Our selections procedure looked for key personal attributes such as flexibility, dedication and willingness to learn and we have been more than pleased with the results of our recruitment process.

The picture of the behaviourally 'skilful' and 'flexible' worker as sought by Japanese management contrasts strongly with the popular view of the Welsh workforce, which, with its high levels of union militancy and inflexible working practices, represented everything that was hostile to the neo-liberal economic position that dominated policy-making in the UK throughout the 1980s and early 1990s. One of the intentions of introducing Japanese working practices into south Wales was surely the hope that some of the culture of discipline and obedience would rub off on the local workforce.

Munday found evidence that Japanese managers were wary of Welsh workers and aware that they might face difficulties with industrial relations. The first Japanese companies to arrive made clear their requirements in terms of worker organization. Single-union agreements in the UK were pioneered in Wales by Sony and the Amalgamated Union of

Engineering Workers in the early 1970s; a dozen or more followed in the incoming Japanese plants through the 1980s (K. Morgan, 1987; Munday and Wilkinson, 1993). These agreements included the following features: white-collar status for manual workers, pendulum arbitration, the company council, and flexible working arrangements (J. Salmon, 1993: 28).

While union legislation passed in the 1980s limited the scope of action of trade unions, the vast levels of employment fallout resulting from economic restructuring, leading to high levels of structural unemployment in union heartlands such as south Wales, had at least as damaging an effect on union power. Workers were prepared to accept the lack of camaraderie and strict discipline of the Japanese factories as an alternative to unemployment (although their disapproval of this system came out clearly in my interviews; see Chapter 6). In the new factories the role played by unions was largely taken over by managers. As fulfilment of their central corporate value of 'mutual trust and respect between employees and management' (as expressed by a Toyota manager: Sahara, 1993), managers communciated directly with workers and even took over the union's role in the solution of grievances (K. Morgan, 1987).

Research suggests that the spreading of alternative working practices and cultures is a central feature of the corporate manager. As far as the role of the foreign manager is concerned:

> the key skill that TNCs seem to seek in a senior expatriate is their ability to establish, promote and protect the core values of the corporations in other geographies. This incorporates the ability to contribute effectively to the reshaping of economic and cultural relations with others in different geographies. (Sakho, 1998: 125)

Although this research was based on interviews conducted with western TNCs establishing production facilities in developing economies, an interesting parallel can be drawn with the attitude of East Asian managers to the Welsh workforce:

> These have to do with our core values, which are the rules wherever you are. When senior company people are put in charge, they become its face. We are a global company, and it is these people that matter a great deal to us . . . If we accept to work with local rules, there are places where we will never do any business. You have to have the skill to adapt these rules to your values and, *if need be*, to change them, to shape the agenda. (General manager of an oil company – joint venture, China; Sakho, 1998: 121)

So how much impact have the inward-investment companies had on the south Wales economy? The evidence for direct effects is strong, in terms of the number of inward-investment factories established, the number of jobs created, and the extent of foreign investment in the Welsh economy. Although the level of inward investment may wane in the wake of crisis in the East Asian economies, the persisting high levels of inward-investment-based employment indicated in tables 3.1 to 3.3 indicate a strong impact. Despite attempts by the WDA to encourage domestic sourcing of components, evidence of indirect positive effects of inward investment on the supply chain is limited, as is evidence of technology spillovers. Indeed, it may be that negative effects in terms of investment attracted away from indigenous business and weakening of local R&D (Williams and Smith, 1998) could outweigh the positive direct effects.

Specifically in the Welsh case, there does seem to be evidence of dynamic effects of inward investment, especially in terms of work attitudes and the changing of attitudes towards economic development (see Morris, Munday and Wilkinson, 1993), although, as identified by Lovering (1999), there have been few attempts to study these less measurable effects. Morgan, Sayer and Sklair (1988) agree that the restructuring of management–labour relations as a result of the advent of Japanese factories has been lasting, has spread beyond the Japanese-owned factories, and has been beneficial for labour–management relations in Wales.

The most serious lasting question about this strategy is whether it offers value for money in comparison with other possible policies for dealing with unemployment. The huge figures involved immediately make the policy vulnerable to accusations of wastage or even nest-lining. The size of the public subsidy for LG has already been given as £248m, which was the largest single investment. However, Sony has also benefited from what some critics refer to as 'corporate welfare': its Pencoed factory has received £15m in Regional Selective Assistance (RSA) since 1984. Between 1988 and 1998 Tewdwr-Jones and Phelps have calculated that a total of almost £800m in current prices has been offered and accepted in RSA payments in Wales. This compares with £1.4bn spent by all the regional development agencies in England between 1994/5 and 2000/1 (NAO, 2003).

Once Objective 1 was announced the size of these awards was seen as diverting resources from the match-funding that was necessary to draw down the European money. This was the final impulse for a rethink of the whole strategy although, as is discussed in Chapter 8, actual economic development programmes and grants do not seem greatly changed. Since this is public money it is for the public to decide which sorts of job creation we favour. This is a point I develop further in Chapter 5, where I report the results of putting this question directly to workers in Rhondda Cynon Taff. For now it is sufficient to note that the option of spending these huge sums on low-paid, low-skilled jobs with foreign-owned companies, and then to spend additional money in tax credits to subsidize the poor wages, is only one option and one that, in a globalized world where any labour force that is competing on price is facing very stiff competition indeed, no longer appears very attractive.

THE JOB-CREATION STRATEGY IN RHONDDA CYNON TAFF

The history of job creation in RCT dates back to the economic depression of the 1930s. The Treforest Trading Estate, established in 1936, was the first development park in the UK, and was funded under the Special Areas (Development and Improvement) Act, 1934. During the initial period of development some 3,000 people were employed in a variety of light industrial and engineering companies, many of which were set up by refugee industrialists from central Europe (Baber and Thomas, 1980). The real impetus for the expansion of Treforest came with the heavy demand for vehicles and munitions manufacture during the Second World War. This also led to the establishment of the second major industrial park in the study area at Hirwaun at the head of the Cynon Valley. Hirwaun was established in the late 1930s as one of three Royal Ordnance Factories in Wales.

More recently, Mid Glamorgan as a whole has been successful in attracting inward investment in the most recent period for which figures are available, 1996–7, which represented a boom year for inward investment in Wales as a whole. Throughout Mid Glamorgan, Bridgend and Merthyr, more than £150m was invested in twenty projects in the year to April 1997 (Mid Glamorgan tec, 1997: 34). However, the stability of such investment and the jobs it generates is questionable. Much is made in the tec report of the investment by Halla, the forklift manufacturer, at Merthyr in May 1997 ('the first Korean manufacturing investment into Wales'), but this factory has already laid off all staff as a result of the recession in the Korean economy. More positively, in Rhondda Cynon Taff itself inward investments over the period included: an expansion of £6.8m by Rocialle Medical creating 238 jobs in Mountain Ash; 130 jobs created by Dynacast International which built a new plastic components factory at a cost of £4.2m; and a £10.2m investment by Japanese-owned engineering firm Showa, which is to employ 180 people in Aberaman making suspension and steering units.

A survey of twenty-five plants moving into the south Wales industrial belt (including Gwent, West and South Glamorgan, and the Llanelli travel-to-work area in addition to Rhondda Cynon Taff) confirmed that the majority of these firms relocated from within the UK (eleven), with the

USA providing the largest number of foreign-based firms (seven), followed by other EU countries (five) and Japan (two). The predominant sectors were electronics (nine plants) and chemicals (five plants) (Morris and Mansfield, 1988).

An important reason why the attraction of inward investors has made such a small impact on the level of unemployment in the south Wales Valleys is simply the small size of the plants that are established. Based on a sample of twenty-five interviewed in 1986, Morris and Mansfield (1988: 67) found that the average plant size was just over 100 employees, rising to an average of only 116 employees in foreign-owned plants. These are marginal increases in job numbers when compared with the size of losses in the collieries, and also when compared with another sector explored in the same survey, that of expanding existing firms, which had an average workforce size of 247.

A survey carried out to assess the impact of inward investment firms on skills in the Valleys found that a large proportion of the employees of foreign firms are in low-skill categories, and that training budgets in these firms are low (Employment Intelligence Unit, 1991). The survey based on a sample of twenty-five inward investment firms cited above found that skills levels in direct production were 'very low': 'Seventeen plants employed no skilled workers at all, five up to ten per cent of direct workers and only two . . . having large percentages of skilled employees' (Morris and Mansfield, 1988: 66). Another author concluded that the UK industrial policy of freeing labour markets and reducing labour standards has encouraged multinationals to devolve their routine production processes to Britain, while keeping the high-skill R&D and design roles in their home bases, often in newly industrializing countries (Mainwaring, 1995).

Rhondda Cynon Taff local authority has played an enthusiastic part in the attraction into south Wales of foreign-based businesses, and with some success: 9.1 per cent of total overseas-owned plants in Wales are located in the Rhondda Cynon Taff County Borough (Welsh Office, 1998b: table 2.9). The council's campaign to attract foreign businesses, A Vision for Business Success, has won presentational awards, as has the innovatively designed Navigation Park Valleys Innovation Centre, at the southern end of the Cynon Valley. The authority's *Economic Development Statement 1996–1997* (RCTBC, 1996) lists 'To encourage inward investment into the County Borough' as the first economic objective and considers its 'Outstanding record in attracting inward investment' to be its major economic strength.

The study area's employment policy was supported by UK government repeat designation of the whole of industrial south Wales as an Assisted Area in 1993 (D. Thomas, 1996), which enabled it to make sizeable grants to inward investors. In addition the area has received support under the

European Structural Funds Objective 2, assigned to areas suffering deprivation as a result of industrial restructuring, although, as D. Thomas points out (1996: 232), this status seemed vulnerable in the late 1990s, since such restructuring was viewed 'as a finite process rather than an open-ended commitment'.

In March 1999 economic planners in RCT became aware that their area had qualified for Objective 1 status, the highest level of eligibility for European regional aid. The status has been granted to a large area of Wales including the south Wales Valleys, Swansea and Pembrokeshire, rural mid- and west Wales, and north-west Wales. It will have a major impact on economic development in the study area, and the single programming document (SPD; Wales European Taskforce, 1999) suggests that priorities for development may be shifting away from the traditional inward-investment, job-creation strategy. However, the Coalfields Communities Campaign lists the priorities for the funding as: 'expanding and developing small and medium-sized enterprises, developing innovation and the knowledge-based economy, stimulating community economic regeneration, and helping to develop people through training and education'. As they themselves point out

> All these policies are worthwhile – but not so different from the ones that have been tried for many years and have met with only partial success in the most deprived areas. The coalfield communities of North and South Wales need . . . policies that are targeted to meet their specific needs.

The remainder of the book is dedicated to an exploration of what those needs might be and what sorts of policies might address them, rather than the same rather tired list of priorities for Objective 1 funding. (The strategy for Objective 1 is addressed more fully in the final chapter, although it is too early to make a realistic assessment of its consequences.)

WHAT IS THE EFFECT OF JOB CREATION ON THE LOCAL ECONOMY?

The overwhelming bulk of the discussion regarding the consequences of inward investment as an economic regeneration strategy has focused on its consequences in terms of three main factors: the number of jobs created and investment attracted, the possibility of beneficial skills spillovers, and the indirect positive impacts on local components suppliers. A typical example is the study edited by Pain (2000), which focuses on direct productivity improvements and indirect improvements via competition,

R&D and increased trade. It suggests that 'The "ripple through" effects of changes in production and working practices triggered by the presence of new inward investors have been particularly important' (p. 163), but it is a quantitative study and hence has no way of actually measuring these less tangible effects.

Focus and finance

Policy-making involves making strategic choices: if money is spent attracting inward investors it cannot also be spent developing local businesses. This was the choice made in RCT and it is hardly surprising, therefore, that local businesses have failed to thrive. The spending by RCT on economic development is spread between three categories: inward investment projects, indigenous businesses, and community enterprises. RCT itself spent £115,200 on the community enterprise fund in 1997/8, but no money was allocated to this fund for the following year (RCTBC, 1998). As a result of spending in 1996/7 a total of 867 jobs were either created or safeguarded in RCT, which can be put into perspective by comparison with the numbers of jobs lost in coal mining (see table 2.6, above). Grants to inward investors are made by the Welsh Development Agency, as are those to stimulate the expansion of local businesses. Due to the 'sensitivity' of commercial information it is difficult to ascertain the exact spending on inward investment, although the single doomed LG investment of £248m (WAC, 1998) dwarfs the sum RCT spent on community enterprise.

The ideology of neoclassical economics suggests that the choice for policy-makers is between offering grants to incoming corporations or stimulating the indigenous business sector. In fact, as Fevre pointed out in connection with the steel industry (1987), government money was previously spent subsidizing jobs in loss-making industries. It is only because of the way government accounting works, and because the cost of imports kept artificially low by either subsidy or inhumane working conditions is accepted as a given, that it is cheaper to import the goods. In the case of coal, the subsidies paid by our competitors outstripped those in the UK during the period of the pit-closure programme (see Chapter 2, note 5), a cause of considerable resentment in south Wales and a reason for the belief that the closure programme was politically motivated. Moreover, the cost of keeping a person employed in the collieries compared favourably with the cost of keeping a person in unemployment, leaving aside all consideration of the social and psychological costs of widespread unemployment. A simple, back-of-envelope calculation indicates that the cost of subsidizing a job in the Mid Glamorgan coalfield was considerably less than the cost of keeping an unemployed person during the 1980s, before the final large-scale closures.[6]

Fevre compared the costs of keeping 'loss-making' jobs at BSC in Port Talbot with the costs of keeping an unemployed person. Today the more relevant comparison would be between subsidized employment where the British company receives a payment to make it viable and subsidized employment where the inadequate wages offered by the multinational corporations are boosted by one of the Chancellor's tax credits and direct grants to the company. If, as Fevre suggested, we consider all the government's expenditures at once we find that there is still considerable spending on job subsidy. Wage-packet subsidy is no more acceptable within a free-market framework than support grants to nationalized industries. The direct subsidies to employers now come in the form of payments which are kept secret for reasons of 'commercial confidentiality' and become part of the companies' balance sheets rather than that of a nationalized company that belongs to the country and its people.

The grants are also felt to be outside the ambit of the local businesses. The perception amongst local people I interviewed was that grants were only awarded to large-scale businesses: the figure for turnover of £250,000 before businesses were eligible was given by several respondents. There was no shortage of enthusiasm for setting up in business and several of the respondents I spoke to were successful entrepreneurs themselves. However, they perceived that priority was given to 'foreign firms' which were favoured over local businesses. As the proprietor of a successful health shop put it:

> It's crazy! Lots of people will come for five years and then they'll pack up shop and go. A lot of these Japanese companies. I think it would be far more important to give money to . . . I'd expand if I knew I was in a . . . I could manufacture it [a health product] here in Britain instead of bringing it from Europe I would and I'd employ people. But they don't give you grants.

Another respondent ('Sam') had previously established a successful computer shop, which he had later sold. Following another spell of unemployment he was retrained as a fitter of smoke detectors. He had his own personal story about a Japanese company which had set up in Penrhiwbach, employing 175 people for a fortnight with a grant of £30,000, and then closed down. This seems improbable, but that is less important than the fact that this is the perception of inward investors: they are seen as unreliable and soaking up money that could be used to support local investors. But the fact that policy-makers choose to give investment grants to these companies rather than to indigenous businesses is itself a blow to the local entrepreneurs' self-confidence.

When I asked Sam what the priority for spending should be he said, 'I would say encourage local businesses', and in response to my question about whether there was much encouragement given to people setting up their own businesses he replied:

> Hardly any at all . . . I have thought about starting my own fire prevention company up and I was sent on a one-day seminar to talk about it and I said 'Yeah, yeah, let me know, find out about funding and anything else to go with it' and that's the last I've heard.

This respondent clearly demonstrated an entrepreneurial bent and yet could find no support in his local area; he was considering moving to Scotland where he had heard support for new entrepreneurs was better. During a group discussion held at an engineering works the same views emerged, with the employees feeling resentful that there was no support for indigenous entrepreneurs while huge sums were being given to inward investors. They felt that the reason a small local business might not attract financial aid was that 'it doesn't have the 6,100 jobs headline'.

Local reactions and loss of confidence

The local perception of inward employers was negative, both in terms of the conditions of employment and the levels of pay. The sort of work that was created – especially factory work – was compared unfavourably with work in the collieries. For men who had worked in the mines, the constant surveillance and lack of autonomy inherent in factory work was intolerable: 'I couldn't work under that regime. It's repetitive isn't it? It's like you're on a conveyor. You're just like bloody robots working there.' In general, local people were cynical about the motivations of the inward investing companies: they were perceived as interested only in low-waged workers and grants (more details are given in Chapter 6).

Recent economic policy documents in Wales have emphasized the failure of entrepreneurship, particularly the lack of confidence in establishing new businesses demonstrated by people in Wales (Welsh Office, 1998d; EAPSG, 1999). However, they fail to identify the inward investment policy itself as a source of this loss of confidence. As Secretary of State for Wales announcing the LG investment William Hague said, 'It's the biggest vote of confidence the Welsh economy has ever had', but, as I have argued elsewhere (Cato, 2001a), the real consequence of this strategy of reliance on overseas companies has been an undermining of that confidence. The local workers I spoke to suggested that the destruction of the area's main industry, which most local people see as for political rather than economic reasons, followed by the introduction of foreign 'saviours', has served to demoralize and disempower the people of RCT.

One of the careers officers I spoke to during my research, herself from outside Wales, could not imagine that local people could establish success-ful businesses. Discussing the possibility of using European Objective 1 funding to pay grants to attract entrepreneurs from elsewhere in the UK she said: 'I imagine there's going to be some subsidies to attract people to the RCT area – part of the bid is going to include that I'm sure. So the entrepreneurial characters may not be local, but the jobs will be.' Her underlying lack of confidence in local people, which may be a result of the emphasis amongst her colleagues on the need for foreign companies, is unlikely to encourage the young people she advises to follow an entrepreneurial route out of unemployment after leaving school. It also indicates how the inward-investment policy may itself have undermined possibilities for local economic regeneration.

THE FUTURE OF THE INWARD-INVESTMENT STRATEGY

Despite its positive effects on the Welsh economy the employment policy based heavily on foreign-firm job creation which was dominant during the 1980s and 1990s was to some extent a policy of despair resulting from the massive job losses Wales was experiencing. The 'beggars can't be choosers' aphorism that seems to have been the tone of policy-making at this time is rapidly becoming obsolete in the face of a growing self-confidence amongst Welsh politicians. This has led to a more critical evaluation of the inward-investment strategy which suggests that it may attract less attention in future.

The Welsh Affairs Committee was mildly critical of the WDA strategy as concentrating too heavily on inward investment and suggested that the balance should now shift in favour of indigenous industry. Its members drew attention to the fact that most businesses in Wales are indigenous and that only 10 per cent of the workforce are employed by foreign-owned companies (WAC, 1998: para. 22). Most firms in Wales are SMEs, with 52,000 out of 58,000 Welsh firms employing fewer than twenty-five workers (Welsh Office, 1998d). This sector looks set to become the focus of increased attention in future Welsh employment-creation policies with an increase of 18 per cent in support for SMEs and an aim to support 6,000 of them per year (Feld, 1999).

Competition is fierce from other regions within the UK that 'can offer similar, if not better, attractions to Wales with respect to market oppor-tunities, transport, training facilities, professional and technical staff, business support and aftercare together with close buyer–seller relations' (D. Thomas, 1996: 236). This competition is likely to increase, with regional development agencies arguing for equal status with those in the devolved regions, and with the move to establish regional parliaments. The inward-investment strategy is also threatened by the availability of low-wage workers in eastern Europe and the developing Asian economies who are rapidly acquiring relevant employment skills (Young, Hood and Peters, 1994).

The future expansion of the European Union eastwards will allow east European workers to compete with Welsh workers on equal terms. And this movement eastwards is already well under way:

> Estimates published by the European Bank for Reconstruction and Development . . . show that inward investment into the former Soviet bloc countries rose by a factor of ten between 1990 and 1993, with the lion's share going to the Visegrad countries, especially Hungary and the Czech Republic. (Begg, 1995: 104)

Wales also seems handicapped by the fact that future inward investment is likely to be concentrated in its weaker economic sectors. Already by 1992, 20 per cent of UK FDI was in the finance and business service sectors (B. Morgan, 1998: 26); figures presented in table 3.4 above indicate that only a tiny fraction of investment in this sector comes to Wales. Given the weakness of Wales's services sector this type of investment is unlikely to find its way to the country. Indeed, a recent study indicates that the overwhelming majority of Japanese financial FDI – 176 out of 181 establishments – was concentrated in London and the home counties (Roy, 1998: table II). Welsh MPs have recently urged the encouragement of non-manufacturing inward investment and suggested that priority sectors should be 'software development, design, and international telephone call centres' (WAC, 1998: para. 13). However, it is clear that these are exactly the sectors that other regions of the UK and Europe are competing for. India, in particular, is attracting large amounts of call-centre business, the Prudential being the latest large company to move its operations there, due to an 80 per cent saving on wages (Scott, 2002). The more positive side of the growth in global communications, however, is the fact that Wales's position on the periphery of Europe and its poor transport networks are becoming less of a problem, and in the personal-service sector the use of the English language will always offer an advantage over the eastern European economies, although not India.

As mentioned previously, the debate on the issue of economic develop-ment during the 1999 Welsh Assembly elections focused around the choice of supporting indigenous business or sponsoring investors from overseas, a clearly nationalistic argument that favoured Plaid Cymru. The large number of Plaid members in the Welsh Assembly has certainly changed the terms of debate. The chair of the Economic Development Committee, Christine Gwyther, is now required to provide a breakdown of Regional Selective Assistance grants according to whether the companies receiving them are Welsh, based elsewhere in the UK, or based overseas. It is clear from offers made in 2001–2 that although the rhetorical emphasis may have changed, the weight of funding still goes to foreign companies: 54 per cent of grant aid in this period has gone to overseas-owned businesses, with 19 per cent going to companies based elsewhere in the UK and barely more than one-quarter (26 per cent) going to Wales-based companies.[7] The latest Welsh Development Agency Corporate Plan for the period 2003–6 suggests that the economic development strategy has seen little change.

It is too early yet to assess the outcomes of the spending of Objective 1 European funds, but early signs suggest that much of it will be awarded to the usual round of public-sector initiatives. Objective 1 projects are not considered in this book, partly because it is too early to make a considered assessment, and partly because news of the award of the status was made during the course of the research project with the period of grant-making to run from the year following the conclusion of the research until 2006. So attitudes expressed by respondents in most cases reflect the situation pre-Objective 1, although those policy-makers I spoke to were already considering its possible consequences.

This account of inward investment as the miracle solution to Wales's employment problems has the feeling of a historical assessment. Perhaps it has been excessively negative in tone; but such a tone is hard to avoid a mere month after the near-collapse of the LG project, the jewel in the crown of the whole policy. It is also important to acknowledge that there are a number of foreign-owned firms that are a lasting source of employment in Wales, making up around a third of Wales's manufacturing sector. But this is not to accept the view of employment policy that relies on such companies as foreign saviours for people who are too inadequate to resolve their own economic problems. That attitude, which infused many policy-making documents towards the end of the last century, has been replaced by a renewed confidence and by a realization of the need for us, the people of Wales, to revitalize our own economy. The remaining chapters in this book focus on how this may be achieved, by offering hints about the sorts of employment we might favour and examples of firms and individuals who are already offering us the vision we need to build a new working Wales.

4

The Story of the Waxwork Miners: Cultural Aspects of Employment Policy in Rhondda Cynon Taff

The cruel logic of market economics with its arid terminology seems indifferent to the social consequences of the policies it advocates. Those directly affected are not merely units of labour any more than a pit is a site of production. They are ordinary men and women who ask no more than the right to work and the economic self-sufficiency and social respect which accompanies it. This is perhaps the greatest single social impact of pit closure. Because the pit is the basis of the local culture as well as economy, its removal attacks the very basis on which pit communities have traditionally depended: their capacity to help themselves.

Waddington, Dicks, and Critcher, 1992

In Chapter 1 I introduced the image of the railway to communicate the importance of the work of the Valleys. Since then we have enjoyed a rather breathless ride through a couple of chapters of potted history packed with statistical detail. I would now like to invite you to step off the train and enjoy the scenery. One of the fortunate insights of the postmodernist movement is the realization that evidence presents itself in many forms. So far in this book, the conventional academic forms have predominated, but in this chapter literary references will break the confines of the epigraph and be presented as data central to the analysis.

In her book *Science and Poetry*, Mary Midgley addresses the public revulsion against science that has occurred in recent years, which she sees as a reaction to its 'strange, imperialistic, isolating ideology'. Anti-science feeling is, she claims,

> a protest against this imperialism – a revulsion against the way of thinking which deliberately extends the impersonal, reductive, atomistic methods that are appropriate to physical science into social and psychological enquiries where they work badly. That they do work badly there has often been pointed out. Yet these methods are still often promoted as being the only rational way to understand such topics. (Midgley, 2001: 1)

In relation to this book I take the lesson of this passage to be that we cannot understand the situation of employment in Rhondda Cynon Taff merely in terms of statistics. In order to engage effectively in policy-making a first step must be to have a deep understanding of the situation we are intruding into, and this should include the poetry as well as the science that together make up the everyday life of that community. This chapter offers a more poetical look at work in the context of the south Wales Valleys particularly in terms of the role it plays in people's sense of identity, and the impact this has on the kinds of work they feel prepared to undertake.

As discussed in Chapter 3, the response to unemployment that has been followed in Wales over the past twenty years prioritizes the creation of jobs. Economists have focused on explanations and solutions originating from the supply side of the labour market. Workers are required to 'price themselves into jobs' and threats to worker flexibility ranging from overgenerous welfare benefits to trade unions are undermined at the policy level. The nature of those jobs, their psychological consequences and cultural resonances, or lack of them, have been barely considered. Discussion of job creation is situated firmly within the discipline of economics, yet its consequences are clearly social as well as economic. It is important that the sociological insights concerning the identity con-sequences of the jobs that are created are brought to bear in a critical discussion of job creation. This chapter addresses these issues in the setting of Rhondda Cynon Taff and concludes by proposing a way of reorientating the local economy along a path defined by its own cultural preferences.

I begin the chapter by establishing the crucial importance of employ-ment to the identity of individuals in an industrialized society. I move on to consider how the globalization of the economy, with employment now being under the control of multinational corporations with bases in several different countries, has affected the building up of identity through work. To demonstrate the contrast between work in a pre-industrial setting and work in the modern, globalized economy I use the example of George Eliot's character Adam Bede. This general consideration is then applied to the workers of the south Wales Valleys, whose confused and polarized identity is examined with reference to Baudrillard's concept of the simulacrum. Finally I explore alternative sources of work-based identity in Wales, culminating in the suggestion that relocalizing the economy might provide the most positive way forward.

THE CENTRALITY OF WORK TO IDENTITY

Traditionally, identities within society have been determined largely by the work that people do. We all know the first question asked in many situations of primary social encounter: 'What do you do?' by which we really mean 'What is your job?' The German sociologist Ulrich Beck has a passage describing this in his *Risk Society* (1992: 139–40):

> Nowhere, perhaps, is the meaning of wage labor for people's lives in the industrial world so clear as in the situation where two strangers meet and ask each other 'what are you?' They do not answer with their hobby, 'pigeon fancier', or with their religious identity, 'Catholic', or with reference to ideals of beauty, 'well, you can see I'm a redhead with a full bosom', but with all the certainty in the world with their occupation: 'skilled worker for Siemens'. If we know our interlocutor's occupation then we think we know him or her. The occupation serves as a mutual identification pattern, with the help of which we can assess personal needs and abilities as well as economic and social position.

In this context job creation is a far deeper social and psychological process than the guaranteeing of an income. The central place that work occupies in our conception of ourselves, our status, and our relationship to others in our community implies far deeper consequences from the loss of employment than the mere loss of income.

In a ground-breaking piece of research, based on ethnographic study in a town in deep and lasting recession in the 1930s, Marie Jahoda (1982; see also Jahoda, Lazarsfeld and Zeizel, 1933) discussed the consequences of unemployment from a social-psychological perspective. She identified that, aside from financial considerations, work played a number of vital functions in maintaining psychological well-being: it gave a clear time structure to the day; it provided social contact with people outside the household; it involved participation in activities with a wider collective purpose; and it offered social status and identity. Her findings were confirmed by a regression analysis carried out to test the theory in 1996 (Gershuny, 1998). It was found that, even after controlling for income effects, the loss of all the factors she identified had a significant negative effect on psychological health. Dennis Marsden, in a small-scale ethnographic study conducted in the early 1970s, similarly found that 'loss of a sense of meaning and identity' was one of the more distressing consequences of unemployment (Marsden, 1975).

So there is clear evidence that unemployment brings identity stress and psychological harm, but researchers have also discovered that those in insecure and temporary employment, exactly that sort of employment that we have seen the strategies for inward investment described in Chapter 3 have brought, can suffer equally damaging effects. Burchell (1994) found that those in insecure employment with a history of unemployment are as distressed as the unemployed. Moving into secure employment was found to increase their psychological well-being, and both these findings remained after controlling for income levels, indicating that financial pressure was not the explanation. In drawing conclusions from their similar research study Gallie and Vogler (1998) stated that unemployment could merely be considered 'a more extreme case of the general phenomenon of labour-market insecurity'.

In their conclusion, the editors of a collection of research studies exploring how employment had changed in the later decades of the twentieth century (Gallie et al., 1998) identified a polarization of the workforce along class lines with a reduction in autonomy for those in the unskilled, manual-work categories. The security of the job was the most important factor in determining its negative psychological impact: 'Employees who felt that their jobs were under threat felt much lower levels of involvement in their work, they experienced higher levels of strain and, most crucially, they were more likely to display the more severe symptoms of psychological distress' (p. 305). It is important to note here that these conclusions relate to workers who 'felt' that their jobs were under threat, in other words the perception of insecurity is what does the damage. In a context of flexible labour markets, where lean management can mean the constant threat of 'downsizing' as a productivity motivator, the consequences for the psychological health of the workforce can be predicted to be negative. In addition, the nature of the jobs that are created, in terms of their security, are seen to be important, in contrast to the focus on quantity that drives employment-creation policies. It is in this context of proven harm from such employment that we turn to a discussion of the impact of developments in the international economy on the identity of workers who find their place in it.

THE IMPACT OF GLOBALIZATION ON WORK-BASED IDENTITIES

The concept of 'globalization' has engendered a vast amount of academic research, including several analyses of its impact on employment prospects (e.g. Rifkin, 1995; Hines, 1993). Yet little research has explored the consequences of a global market for production and consumption on personal identity. It is taken for granted that, as creatures who evolved in a local world and grew up in a world of nation-states, we can effortlessly move into a world where factors on the other side of the planet have an enormous impact on our lives. Before I come to addressing the consequences of this global economy for the work-based identities of people in Rhondda Cynon Taff I would like to address this issue in a more homely, human-focused way, and develop a theoretical understanding based on an archetypical example of a worker.

The analysis begins by contrasting the identity consequences of a modern, globalized job with those of a craftsman worker in the eighteenth century. This comparison is based on a literary data-source, which provides useful qualitative material that is missing from numerical economic accounts. The source is George Eliot's novel *Adam Bede*. The eponymous hero of the novel is a carpenter who lives in a village in rural England almost exactly 200 years ago. Like all George Eliot's novels the book has many themes running through it: several disastrous love affairs and a great deal of social comment and beautiful description. But the underlying moral position of the book is about work, with a view of work heavily influenced by the 'Methodies', several of whom feature as characters, especially Adam's eventual wife. So work is central to the novel, which actually opens with a description of Jonathan Burge's 'roomy workshop' where Adam works.

> The afternoon sun was warm on the five workmen there, busy upon doors and window-frames and wainscoting. A scent of pine-wood from a tent-like pile of planks outside the open door mingled itself with the scent of the elder-bushes which were spreading their summer snow close to the open window opposite; the slanting sunbeams shone through the transparent shavings that flew before the steady plane, and lit up the fine grain of the oak panelling which stood propped against the wall.

This is, of course, a romanticized view of work even at this time. I am certainly not supporting Eliot's picture of work as joy and salvation (E. P. Thompson's (1963) critical review of the development of Methodist ideology as a support for capitalist work forms lends a necessary critical edge). The reason the focus is on Adam Bede is that his reality can illustrate the complex network of social relations that bound people together through their work in the days when work was locally based. This point is best illustrated by another, longer, quotation from later on in the novel. Adam is dreaming of Hetty, the girl he has set his heart on, and planning how he can make fancy furniture to generate enough money to afford to set up on his own and take a wife.

> No sooner had this little plan shaped itself in his mind than he began to be busy with exact calculations about the wood to be bought and the particular article of furniture that should be undertaken first – a kitchen cupboard of his own contrivance, with such an ingenious arrangement of sliding-doors and bolts, such convenient nooks for stowing household provender, and such a symmetrical result to the eye, that every good housewife would be in raptures with it, and fall through all gradations of melancholy longing till her husband promised to buy it for her. Adam pictured to himself Mrs Poyser examining it with her keen eye, and trying in vain to find out a deficiency; and, of course, close to Mrs Poyser stood Hetty, and Adam was again beguiled from calculations and contrivances into dreams and hopes. (Eliot, 1901: 318)

Hetty works in Mrs Poyser's dairy, so Adam's aim in manufacturing the cupboard is twofold: he hopes to win the money and the girl. But the point I want to draw from this is a general one: that in a locally based economy people know who made the articles that they use every day in their homes. And the people who manufacture those items have an idea where they will be sold and to whom. So the actual work of making and selling and using items provides identity to everybody involved in the exchanges.

What is the nature of the workshop where my MFI sofa was made? Of course, the answer is that I do not know and I probably cannot find out.[1] Various uncomfortable images come to mind: Manila sweatshops, rainforest destruction, children sewing footballs. My trip to a furniture warehouse to buy a 'fitted kitchen' only serves to undermine my identity, as the identity of the person who worked in the factory making the kitchen units, whether in Huddersfield or Havana, is similarly undermined. There are no connections and the result is a feeling of alienation, confusion and loss of identity.

This loss of identity in economic and social structures has been observed and commented on by numerous sociologists, particularly those of the Frankfurt School. A prominent example is the work of Habermas, who developed a critical response to modern social life, which grew out of his initial Marxist position. In *The Theory of Communicative Action* (1987), Habermas appraises the social philosophy of G. E. Mead, and extends it to provide an explanation of the process of identity development in modern society:

> Corresponding to the ideal communication community is an ego identity that makes possible self-realisation on the basis of autonomous action. This identity proves itself in the ability to lend continuity to one's own life history. In the course of the process of individuation, the individual has to draw his identity between the lines of the concrete lifeworld and of his character as attached to this background. The identity of the ego can then be stabilised only by the abstract ability to satisfy the requirements of consistency, and thereby the conditions of recognition, in the face of incompatible role expectations and in passing through a succession of contradictory role systems. The ego-identity of the adult proves its worth in the ability to build up new identities from shattered or superseded identities, and to integrate them with old identities in such a way that the fabric of one's interactions is organised into the unity of a life history that is both unmistakable and accountable. (p. 98)

Habermas emphasizes the importance of continuity, consistency and autonomy in the creation of personal identity. He acknowledges the need to change through life, and indeed he stresses this as the key to successful identity-building. But the reintegration of former identities, and their combination with present roles in an overall personal identity, is to be carried out against a 'background', which is the 'concrete lifeworld'. It is clear that this process is complicated by changes in that background. Change is a pervasive and one might argue the dominant feature of the globalized economic system, with its emphasis on flexible work patterns and employment provided by a network of international companies, whose base in any given country is always contingent. If Habermas's view of the building of identity is correct then a global economy inevitably undermines this process, and hence undermines our ability to build secure personal identities.

It might again be helpful to draw a distinction between the lifeworld of Adam Bede and that of an employee in a multinationally owned furniture factory to illustrate this point. Early on in the novel Adam's drunken father is drowned in a flood. This represents, in Habermas's words, 'incompatible role expectations' and part of 'a succession of contradictory role systems', since Adam will now become head of the household. Adam's role is to take control of the funeral arrangements and bury his father, as well as supporting his mother and brother. Adam's work as a carpenter plays a central part in this process, since he will make the coffin himself, staying up all night in what becomes a testament of love for his father, expressed through work. So the central role of Adam's joinery in linking his two identities becomes clear.[2]

In contrast we may think of an employee in a furniture factory, whose work has no meaning outside the money economy. Such an employee will not even feel an identity as a skilled worker, since he is likely only to play one small part in the process of manufacture. He will have no idea who will purchase the furniture he produces, or where it will be transported to. He has no human connection with his product or its purchaser. His is an entirely market relationship with his work: it is narrow and money-based. What is more his employment is insecure, as a change in the relative prices of wages in his country and another country may well result in the movement of the productive unit overseas, possibly to the other side of the globe. In such a situation it is much more of a challenge for him to create a meaningful identity.

Let us consider a twenty-first-century contrast to Jonathan Burge's 'roomy workshop': the Bertrand Faure automobile upholstery factory in Tredegar. The company announced its investment of £12m in a new factory in Tredegar in December 1996, part of the 'record year for inward investment' lauded in *Contemporary Wales* (Drinkwater, 1997). The factory's existence was used to support the Conservative government's economic development policies in Wales in a speech to the House by then Welsh Secretary William Hague on 10 February 1997 (along with a glowing reference to the ill-fated LG investment). With a promise of 290 jobs, the factory opened in November 1998. So what do we know of Bertrand Faure? According to its website it produces car furniture, as well as other components for multinational car producers such as VW and General Motors, and has operations in France, Germany, Belgium, Spain, Portugal, the UK, Luxemburg, Italy, Turkey, Canada, the USA and Argentina. Its registered address is in Boulogne. Between the announcement of its investment and the opening of the factory the identity of the company had already changed, due to its takeover by a rival firm. Since June 1999 Bertrand Faure has been part of the international Faurecia group, with a workforce of 30,000 and 100 production sites located in twenty-five countries.

So how would the identity of a worker finding herself in such a factory compare with that of a craft worker, or even a worker in a locally owned factory as Bertrand Faure was in Boulogne fifty years ago? It seems inevitable that the sense of being part of a worldwide network of related factories selling to an equally widespread list of customers cannot provide the same rooted identity as a local business. What is more, the repeated changes of ownership of one's employer, whether by takeover or merger, is bound to increase the feeling of job insecurity.

The academic studies cited in the first part of this chapter identified 'job insecurity' as the aspect of employment change with the most damaging psychological consequences. They also established that these consequences relate not to income, but to the loss of identity such insecurity brings. We might therefore suggest that employment in the factory of a foreign firm, which has arrived recently on a local industrial estate and is expected to leave equally suddenly (see the attitudes towards the footlooseness of such multinational companies in the interview results reported in Chapter 6), may have similar negative psychological consequences. We will now turn to consider the consequences of this sort of employment change in the study area, in terms of both job insecurity and identity conflict.

GLOBAL PRODUCTION AND IDENTITY IN THE SOUTH WALES VALLEYS

'We want people who thrive on change and are not the victims of it.' This statement is drawn from a Labour government economic consultation paper, *Pathway to Prosperity* (Welsh Office, 1998d). In the previous section I outlined how personal identity, based on Habermas's definition, is undermined by constant change. Such an understanding of personal identity suggests that a workforce that thrives on change may be an unattainable goal. The south Wales Valleys is one area of Wales which has experienced rapid social and economic change. The previous chapter discussed the economic problems confronting such an economic development strategy based so firmly on the one policy of inward investment. But such a strategy has other, perhaps more serious, human consequences. There I discussed how the efforts to attract outside 'saviours' to solve the Valleys' economic problems may have undermined the confidence of local people in their ability to regenerate their own economy (see also Cato, 2001a). Here I would like to consider other psychological consequences of such a policy, this time in terms of the impact it may have on the identity of the people for whom such jobs are created.

To begin with it is helpful to have the view of the national government of the role of change in our economic future. A publication from the Department for Education and Employment (the linking of these two under the rubric of 'lifelong learning' is itself an indication of the direction of government thinking) describes the relationship between economic and social change and the workforce as follows:

> We are in a new age – the age of information and global competition. Familiar certainties and ways of doing things are disappearing. The types of jobs we do have changed as have the industries in which we work and the skills they need. At the same time new opportunities are opening up as we see the potential of new technologies to change our lives for the better. We have no choice but to prepare for this new age in which the key to success will be the continuous education and development of the human mind and imagination. (DfEE, 1998: 9)

This message has been received loud and clear in Wales. According to the 'Statistical Profile' of Wales published in *Contemporary Wales*, 1996 was:

> a record year for inward investment, with more than 15,000 jobs being created. The new investments included 300 jobs by Halla forklift trucks in Merthyr, 300 at Matsushita electronics in Cardiff, a further 1,000 by the Sony corporation at Bridgend and 300 by the Bertrand Faure Group who manufacture car seats in Tredegar. (Drinkwater, 1997)

It is surely worth noting that the range of production and national origin of the companies listed in the quotation is bewildering even to academic observers, never mind to local people. Companies we have never heard of, frequently from countries we would have difficulty pinpointing with confidence on a world map, are to be the underwriters of our financial future. This future for work requires considerable mental flexibility.

What is more, there seems to have been no strategic planning, no Wales-based decisions about priority sectors for development, no attempt to attract jobs which have cultural affinities or match the skills of the people who live in Wales. Rather than a coherent economy with compatible manufacturers participating in positive linkages within a unified economic structure we see a mishmash of multinationals whose sole common aim is to make a profit out of their investment in Wales.

The south Wales Valleys are regularly highlighted for special attention within Welsh economic planning. This is a dubious honour awarded on the basis of the area's continually high scores on such measures as rates of unemployment and levels of chronic sickness (as described in Chapter 2). The strategy for the Valleys, under the rubric 'Industrial Villages' (*Pathway to Prosperity*), is based on attracting component manufacturers supplying larger corporations outside Wales and marketing the area as one of scenic beauty and loyal workers: the 'green valleys, green workers' approach. The campaign headquarters, at the Valleys Innovation Centre, Navigation Park, presents an image of a skilled and modern workforce. This is obviously designed to appeal to inward investors, but it is interesting to explore its impact on the unemployed people who live within this authority's area. Many of those seeking employment are ex-miners: their identities are undermined by comparison with a clean-cut, skilled worker in a sharp suit or a white coat. This is one side of the insecurity of the identity of the Valleys worker.

There is another, diametrically opposed, identity available to Valleys workers: the image of the worker in a heavy-industry setting, typified by the miner (see photo 4.3). This is an identity now being repackaged and sold through the Rhondda Heritage Park. As part of what has been referred to as the 'museumization of life', in the Rhondda, as in many former industrial areas, the historical work patterns and images of workers are being used to publicize the area, to attract both tourists and inward investors: 'the creation of new or reinvigorated cultural identities is now central to the standard response to deindustrialisation' (S. Watson, 1991).

The genuine historical work experience of the Valleys, with its social consequences for community life, is a fundamental part of the lifeworld of a worker in the Valleys. It was for this reason that many people in the Rhondda supported the idea of a heritage park to celebrate and safeguard their identity in what had been. According to a researcher who studied the progress of what was to become the Rhondda Heritage Park:

> many local people supported the RHP as a space through which to remember the past. The requirements of a discourse of memorialism are for authenticity, safe-keeping and commemoration of prized objects – which are shared with

traditional museum discourse. These were the desires of local residents when they handed over their domestic artefacts to the RHP. (Dicks, 1996: 71)

The idea for a heritage park came from the people themselves, as a way of safeguarding the past, but they felt betrayed by the way this idea was repackaged and turned into an exercise in image-selling to tourists. Dicks (2000: 24) identifies the 'defensiveness' shown by the Welsh Tourist Board resulting from 'the political sensitivity of the "character" of the Valleys – their cultural and economic identity', in connection with a debate over the re-greening of the area's environment.

The different motivations towards establishing the Heritage Park are illustrated by the following quotations, which may be contrasted with the wishes of the local people as expressed in the quotation above. First, the view of the Steering Group which was set up to carry through the project:

> The purpose of the scheme . . . is to assist in the rebuilding of the valleys communities and their economy, on the basis of new and potentially prosperous businesses, be they manufacturing or service industries. To do this requires a change in the character and image, as well as the actual jobs, within the valleys. (Dicks, 1996: 59)

The second quotation is from a speech made by Peter Walker, then Welsh Secretary, on 14 June 1988:

> I consider this to be an extremely exciting project which epitomizes many of my aspirations for the valleys. Based on the industrial heritage of the valley communites it involves transforming a derelict site with its symbols of former glories into an attractive heritage park with much needed alternative employment. It will strengthen the local economy through the attraction of substantial numbers of visitors and help to change many of the unwarranted perceptions that still exist about valley life.

These two quotations make clear that the work history of the Valleys is treated differently by the two groups: for the local people it is a real and cherished part of their community's identity; for the planners and politicians it is an image that can be used to attract money for investment and from tourists. Indeed, for the latter group, the genuine identity of the local worker is dismissed as being based on 'unwarranted perceptions'. The distinction between reality and virtualism that distinguishes these two attitudes can be linked to the critical position on modern culture adopted by postmodernist critics.

In his essay 'Simulacra and Simulations' Jean Baudrillard discusses the distinction between image and reality in the modern social and economic world, focusing on his concept of the 'hyperreal'. He outlines four successive phases of the image:

1. It is the reflection of a basic reality.
2. It masks and perverts a basic reality.
3. It masks the absence of a basic reality.
4. It bears no relation to any reality whatever: it is its own pure simulacrum.

In the first case, the image is a good appearance: the representation is of the order of sacrament. In the second, it is an evil appearance: of the order of male-fice. In the third, it plays at being an appearance: it is of the order of sorcery. In the fourth it is no longer in the order of appearance at all, but of simulation. (Baudrillard, 1988: 170)

The apotheosis of the simulacrum is taken to be Disneyland, that original and prototype of all theme parks. While the Rhondda Heritage Park may only aspire to such status, the image it presents does attempt to relate to what was once reality, and so, in terms of its reflection of the history of work in the Valleys, we might take the Rhondda Heritage Park as representing stage three of Baudrillard's scale: it provides a false picture of work to conceal the fact that there is no longer any real work in the area. This is illustrated by a visit to the Park or the nearby Big Pit mining museum in Blaenavon, where tourists are shown round by one ex-miner, dressed in what were once work clothes but what is now costume. Where once thousands were true workers these few who have found work are now mere cast members.

John Evans, who has produced a short postmodernist critique of the Valleys communities in his *How Real is my Valley* (1994), goes even further and suggests that the Heritage Park actually represents Baudrillard's final-stage simulacrum, the copy for which no original ever existed. He describes the creation of the myth of the Valleys through novels such as *How Green was my Valley* by Richard Llewellyn, translated into celluloid in the Californian dream factory, and sold back to the unemployed workers of the Valleys as a false image of their lost past, a process Dicks (2000) refers to as 'romancing the coal'. Evans quotes at length from the novel *Shifts* by Christopher Meredith (1988), which exposes this myth-making:

'Up comes Donald Crisp and Dai Bando on a tandem', Jack said. He slipped his arm around Keith's shoulder again and held Jude under his other arm. 'Look you boy bach', says blind Dai. 'There's been an explosion up at the pit. Hurry you along now begorrah' . . . They pedal and reach the scene. Young women in shawls wring their hands. Old women in shawls wail and gnash their gums. Robert Donat bandages Paul Robeson's arm. 'Ianto Full Pelt it is',

Photo 4.1: Waxwork miners at the Rhondda Heritage Park
Photograph © Neil Turner

cries lovely Blodwen wringing her shawl. 'Stuck he is in the big hole he is look you. Too small is the passage mark you for the big guys.'

So the Valleys worker is torn between a once-genuine but now fantastical and commodified image as a physical worker, and an equally unreliable image of the information worker in the new economy that does not have any point of contact with her or his everyday reality.

This confused identity is illustrated perfectly by the RCT borough crest (see photo 4.2). We might note at the outset the unusual choice of men as supporters of the shield, where we might expect to see real or fantastical beasts. This expresses the centrality of the worker – the male worker – to the borough's identity. It may also allude to the perception of local workers as caryatids of local political hopes and, perhaps, as beasts of burden. But the central point is the conflict between the miner and the scientist. The historical archetype who is now an endangered species of the miner, contrasted with the white-coated scientist of the local economic planner's aspiration. Somewhere between lies the reality – a confused factory worker, possibly with white wellingtons or a paper hat, wondering why he is neither brawny nor brainy but just a human robot. This is another classic example of Baudrillard's simulacrum.

The overall conclusion for a worker in south Wales might well be that the choice of the devil you know would be preferable. An interesting light

Photo 4.2: The modern image of Valleys workers
Reproduced by permission of Rhondda Cynon Taff County Borough Council.

can be cast on this discussion by the response amongst local workers to the Tower Colliery 'narrative'. The story of the buy-out has itself become a local myth, directed by the charismatic leadership of Tyrone O'Sullivan (see e.g. Llewellyn Jones, 1998).[3] The Tower Colliery project is based on the belief that locally based work is vital to sustaining the life and culture of the Valleys; this commitment stands in direct contrast to the profit-maximization policies of multinational corporations. It also offers a much stronger identity to the workers employed there. This emerged clearly from interviews conducted at the mine and reported in Chapter 7.

BUILDING A WELSH WORK IDENTITY

In spite of the manipulation of the image of the worker in Wales and elsewhere, the stereotype of the muscular male industrial worker persists. When the Valleys worked the image of the worker was of a well-built, physical male, possibly bare-chested, almost certainly covered with coal dust. Women were nowhere in the picture (and in fact were prevented by local custom from working outside the home: see Beddoe, 1995; John, 1995), and other forms of employment that made a significant contribution to the local economy were also marginalized in the public imagination, particularly the public-sector workers who have always played such a major role. The image of the male industrial worker is as prevalent

**Photo 4.3: Prototypical worker as
chosen by Oxford University Press.**
The cover from *The Oxford Book of Work*,
edited by Keith Thomas (1999).
Reproduced by permission of Oxford
University Press.

amongst academics as amongst local people in former industrial areas. The image chosen for the cover of the *Oxford Book of Work* (reproduced as photo 4.3) is exactly this one: a miner. This book was published in 1999 – the same year I conducted my research in the Valleys – by which time 90 per cent of Britain's coal industry was dead. Yet the image of the miner lives on in the imagination of researchers and working people alike.

It is a powerful marker against which other jobs in areas once dominated by mining are judged. This was acknowledged with some irritation by one of my respondents. I will resist the temptation to refer to him as an 'ex-miner' for reasons that will become clear; he is now in his fifties and works as a tour guide at the Rhondda Heritage Park. This is how he expressed the attitude towards mining in the Valleys:

> Yes, well, people always go on about miner, miner, miner. This person is an ex-miner. I'm an ex-army person as well, and an ex-finance consultant. I'm an ex- . . . I've had over thirty jobs, so I'm an ex-many things. But people tend to categorize you as ex-miner and there's no such animal really. Unless you're

talking about somebody who left school, went in the mines, worked in the mines for forty years. That's a true ex-miner. But many miners worked in the pits after doing other jobs as well. So to categorize someone as that is wrong, really. I mean most of the people of my generation were industrial workers and I think that's an important way of describing people as 'an industrial worker'. There isn't any more industrial work to be had.

The sort of attitude he found frustrating is typified by a passage in the account of the Tower Colliery buy-out by its leader, Tyrone O'Sullivan. He describes reports he read in *Coal News* about redundant miners who had found 'rewarding careers' elsewhere.

I did not feel encouraged, however, by stories of miners picking up a hamburger franchise or setting up a small business installing electrical fittings. I found a lot of the reports to be very sad. I am sure the man who spends his days 'driving a Ford Transit along the leafy lanes of Nottinghamshire with his own same-day delivery service' is completely fulfilled, but as a former underground mechanical engineer he must find life very different if not difficult. Similarly, the gentleman who ended up as a noise consultant may enjoy his new job, but I wonder if he misses the camaraderie of mining work after spending 28 years in the industry. (O'Sullivan, Eve and Edworthy, 2001: 143–4)

My respondent had his own view of this kind of romanticized view of heavy, dangerous industrial work:

Well, if they said where would you like to go back to I'd like to go back to the army. It's all very well to go on about the camaraderie in the mines, which is the main aspect people like about the mines. But there are other places that have equally good camaraderie, like the forces. Any job which involves danger has a certain amount of camaraderie, just like the oil-rigs. I mean it's like a macho thing, you know, men against the elements, things like that that perhaps attracted them. Perhaps they felt, like, to be more of a man working in that type of environment. These places where people say `I wish I was there again' are places where one works to the exclusion of women. So I wonder how much that has to do with it. Do these people see women as a threat?

Whatever the source of admiration for the dangerous physical labour of which mining work is the prototype, this sort of work is highly esteemed in Rhondda Cynon Taff, and other jobs that are created will inevitably be compared with it – and frequently found wanting.

So where are local workers to find their identities since the demise of the pits? One answer may be in a resurgent nationalism. There is some evidence that in the Valleys a nationalist identity is replacing the traditional work-based identity. B. Roberts (1994) explored how the Valleys' identity has changed in response to rapid social and economic changes. Previous research had shown the strength of mining and radical traditions in the Valleys' identity, but this seemed to be being replaced by a 'feeling of Welshness'. Respondents sought to establish a Welsh pedigree or 'roots' by mentioning Welsh and especially Welsh-speaking antecedents. The Welsh identity, and particularly the Welsh-language identity, is more ambiguous in south Wales, where so many people are the descendants of workers who immigrated from England in the last century:

> The issues surrounding language and nationality raise deep sensitivities and confusions: Welsh nationalism is often equated locally with political extremism (bombing and other violence) and Welsh language use with exclusivity and ostracism . . . there seems to be an emergent, stronger sense of cultural nationalism rather than a discernible trend towards national self-determination as a political demand.' (B. Roberts, 1994: 89)

The success of Plaid Cymru, the Welsh nationalist party, in the Welsh Assembly elections of May 1999 suggested that the nationalist identity has a strong appeal. The party did particularly well in the area where this research was carried out, where Labour has always relied on massive majorities. The Plaid candidate won in the Rhondda seat and the party was within 700 votes of Labour in Cynon Valley and 1,500 votes in Pontypridd (B. Morgan, 1999). Some of these results were reversed in 2003, but Plaid has certainly established an enclave in the Valleys and still runs the RCT local authority. However, the nationalist response may not be healthy for society as a whole. Gellner (1983) sees nationalism as a specific response to the modern form of economic organization, and one that he considers can be problematic for the effective functioning of human society. One particular concern is that the yearning for a national identity, in the absence of an identity with any other foundation, can be exploited by unscrupulous politicians to facilitate their own rise to power: we can think of examples as diverse as Indian religious nationalism and the ethnic conflicts of former Yugoslavia and Chechnya.

Although it is difficult to develop a real sense of how the dark side of nationalism is distributed in time or space, there is some evidence that exclusive nationalistic attitudes may be encouraging the spread of racism in the Valleys. Research carried out by Jonathan Scourfield of Cardiff University (2002) suggested a worrying growth of such attitudes. As part of this study Mairja Kempenaar of the charity Barnado's in Wales said: 'My gut feeling is that it's not comfortable in the Valleys or in other areas of Wales like it, as compared to areas of Cardiff like Grangetown or Butetown where there is a higher concentration of minority groups.' As a children's worker in the Valleys area she is particularly concerned about racism there and its consequences for the 'invisible' ethnic minorities who dare not appear in public.

Their fears may be well founded. Two stories from the Welsh papers from March 2002 give an idea of the practical results of nationalist ideologies. The first tells of an English man living in the Valleys who committed suicide after being subject to racist taunts by Welsh people (Pearson, 2002); the second is a more typical example of an Asian shop-keeper who was threatened and abused (*South Wales Echo*, 2002). In connection with the findings of his research study Dr Scourfield said: 'I thought that sort of abuse [calling people "Paki" and telling them to "Go to their own country"] went out in the seventies, but it's alive and well in the Valleys.' And members of ethnic groups have more than abuse to deal with. A group called Valleys Anti-Racist Initiative has been set up in response to concerns about bullying as well as abuse and is campaigning for political action (Trainor, 2002). The response from the Welsh Assembly in holding a plenary session on 'social injustice and racism' in June 2002 suggests that the concern is treated seriously at the highest levels and several senior Labour politicians are happy to make the link with the growth in support for Plaid Cymru.[4]

This is the unpleasant face of the human need for a sense of identity through place and community. The strength of this need can be judged from its political consequences when exploited for political gain. But taking on board the desire for a locally based identity that is one response to economic globalization, we may consider that a more constructive route for the Welsh economy would be one based on Welsh values and cultural preferences. Since the devolution of the power over economic development from London to Cardiff in 1999 there has been a need for the development of a specifically Welsh model of economic development. As I have already discussed in Chapter 1, this process may be considered analogous to the route taken by nations that have been subject to colonialism. They need to undergo a 'decolonization of the mind' (Marglin and Marglin, 1996), challenging the assumptions of the colonizers and replacing them with their own perspectives and priorities. It is the role of the academic community in Wales to put flesh on the bones of politicians' aspirations to achieve an authentic national model of economic development. A useful contribution was made by a team investigating the failure of entrepreneurship in Welsh-speaking communities. They identified the vital requirement that this issue

> must be addressed in the context of a strategy of empowerment, not the imposition of ideas and values from outside. Effective cultural and economic

change must therefore be seen as coming from within the culture, through a process of reinvention and reassertion of its core values in its economic life. (Casson et al., 1994: 19)

It should be made clear that this research was conducted amongst the Welsh-speaking culture of north Wales. This automatically suggests the question: which culture is Welsh culture, or even whether there is an underlying Welsh culture at all or merely a kaleidoscope of cultures made up out of the mixture of immigrant and indigenous peoples who now live here. This question is a highly sensitive and political one, tied up as it is with the deeply resonant issues of language, land and identity. For the purposes of my argument in the rest of this chapter I do assume that the culture I found in the Valleys area can, to some extent, be generalized elsewhere in Wales, and that some findings relating to north Wales can be applied to the Valleys. However, it should also be borne in mind that a similar culture can be identified in other working-class areas (compare Lamont, 2000). Aside from this necessary caveat, it also seems reasonable to suggest that economic sociologists and cultural anthropologists would be most welcome to expand on our understanding of the local cultures of depressed regional economies.

Casson et al. proceeded to identify aspects of Welsh culture that would need to be included in the building of an authentic, culturally grounded model of entrepreneurship. First, they identified that the people they had studied placed a high value on the concept of *service to others*.

> Rather than seeing both private and public employment as equally legitimate domains there has been a popular tendency to equate esteem and worth with service to the community . . . This may be described as the result of the predominance of an 'other-regarding' rather than a 'self-regarding' value system (Casson et al., 1994: 15; see also Trosset, 1993)

Further evidence that this attitude is alive and well in Rhondda Cynon Taff is provided by the results of a survey of the social valuation of occupations presented in Chapter 5.

In the context of mining communities it is easy to explain how such a culture of mutual support would have developed. In the interviews reported later many miners took it for granted that, underground, your lives quite simply depended on each other. A. Morgan describes this feeling in his history of the early years of mining in the Rhondda:

> The danger and darkness underground were perhaps the main reasons why coal miners developed a unique sense of togetherness and comradeship. This

sense of identity was to spread to many other aspects of life in the mining areas of South Wales. (A. Morgan, 1983: 8)

This is what is meant by the word 'camaraderie', which miners so often use when describing what they particularly valued about underground work. Morgan also concludes that the mutual dependence of the work situation spilled over into the communities where the miners lived: 'The dangerous nature of underground work created a unique comradeship which enriched the mining communities in innumerable ways' (Morgan, 1983: 8).

In the era of economic success in south Wales this sense of community explains the strength of the social institutions that were developed. In the era of depression, these bonds still held and offered support to those who were out of work. During the 1984/5 miners' strike, the level of solidarity shown by Welsh miners (admittedly bought at the expense of episodes of shocking violence) again illustrates the sense of mutual dependence (O'Sullivan, Eve and Edworthy, 2001). Even today, evidence from the interviews I conducted at Tower Colliery suggests that the desire to support community life is a more important motivation in keeping the pit open than economic or financial rewards. Without dramatizing or romanticizing the point, it does seem fair to say that economic life in the Valleys has always been based on mutual support, and that this may be used as a cultural support for certain types of employment development, while it may well undermine the success of other types.

Dicks (2000: 105–6) analyses this 'discourse of community' which she sees as three separate discourses: first, that based on shared values founded on working lifestyles; second, that relating to the commitment to the power of collective action; and third, that of the 'community of deprivation', which is now taken to typify the 'backward Valleys hinterland'. She concludes that there are two related imaginary communities: that of the 'archetypical mining community' as 'a world apart' and the broader one of the industrial working class which is portrayed as 'experiencing a special and other way of life in particular bounded places'.

In a geographically limited study such as this it is hard to pin down how much of this culture is specific to the Valleys and how much is typical of all working-class communities. An interesting comparison can be made with the blue-collar workers from New York and Paris who form the subjects of an ethnographic study by Lamont (2000). She also found that her interviewees valued camaraderie and the morally organized community. Interestingly, the 'caring self', which she identified as a nexus of admired attributes and which has parallels in the responses I found in the Valleys, was found only amongst the Black Americans she studied. This may help to explain the mutual attraction between the US singer, actor and activist Paul Robeson and the Valleys communities.[5]

Secondly, Casson et al. (1994) identify the *sense of enterprise as alien*, resulting from the almost exclusive role played in entrepreneurial activity in Wales by English industrialists. Val Feld, the late chair of the Assembly's Economic Development Committee, made a similar point in a presentation on the future of media entrepreneurship in Wales (Feld, 1999). Again the point is perhaps more about perception than reality, but her experience in building plans to encourage the development of enterprise had taught her that Welsh people had learned from a history where most of the industries had been based on exploitation of both the land and other people. They were perceived as 'extractive' and 'exploitative' and these were words that had been extended to describe the process of business in general, which was thus considered to be unattractive and almost immoral.

In her study conducted in a rural community in mid-Wales the US anthropologist Carol Trosset found a similar attitude that 'personal power over other people and society itself is often dubbed an English attribute' (Trosset, 1993: 58). In the context of south Wales it is perceived that most of the mine-owners were English (we can think of examples such as the Crawshays and the marquess of Bute). There is a parallel refusal to include the Welsh entrepreneurs in the myth of King Coal, although the notable example of David Alfred Thomas, later Viscount Rhondda, indicates that there is no incapacity on the part of the Welsh to succeed in business. However, there does seem to be an attitude that business enterprise is not a naturally Welsh attribute, which may help to explain the mythological focus on English entrepreneurs. In the case of the notable Welsh business-man David Davies of Llandinam (who made his own money out of the Barry docks: Pride, 1975: 31), this is expressed by reference to the Welsh language: 'I am a great admirer of the old Welsh language', he said in a speech to the Eisteddfod crowd, 'but I know that the best medium to make money by is the English language.' If entrepreneurialism itself is identified with 'the English' then it is unlikely to prove a popular economic strategy at a time when Welsh nationalism is stronger than ever, and when, as identified above, it may be seen as a response to the loss of identity that the New Economy brings in its wake.

The so-called *radical tradition* in Wales, which is particularly strong in the south Wales Valleys, also acts as an impediment to the establishment of an entrepreneurial culture since, as Casson et al. identify (1994: 11), 'a socialist counter culture which emphasized values based on human solidarity rather than competition had probably more purchase in Wales than anywhere else in Britain'. This tradition, remembered with nostalgia now by older members of Valleys communities, is portrayed in Chris Williams's

(1996) book *Democratic Rhondda*. This explains the hostility shown by some respondents to the hierarchical working patterns of Japanese factories.

Linked to this radical, egalitarian tradition is a related problem with the concept of the 'entrepreneur' that is expressed in a reluctance in Welsh culture to seem to acquire, or to wish to acquire, a superior status to others. In her ethnographic exploration Trosset (1993) identified the importance of 'acting to support the ideal of an egalitarian society'. The wish to 'deny having power, and to seek to avoid at least the appearance of being in a position of authority' is likely to work against the need for strong leadership that is taken to be one of the key characteristics of the entrepreneur (Casson, 1991).

The results of the interviews presented in Chapter 6 indicate that the workers of RCT do indeed have an ambivalent attitude towards self-employment and towards money in general, so the idea of following the example of Richard Branson or Terry Matthews has little appeal. *Competition* also tends to be perceived negatively: several respondents stated that the competitive ethos had been, and still was, a handicap to economic development: as the human resources manager I spoke to put it, 'I definitely think the cooperative ethos works better'. However, a sense of solidarity can also work to encourage individuals to be successful to reduce the burden they place on others: an economic development officer told me that 'the dependency culture is changing to "Well if I feel better in myself I'm not going to be such a drain on everyone around me and we will drag ourselves up by our bootstraps"'.

Judging a culture as superior or inferior is not a useful exercise when the objective is successful policy-making. Instead, as Casson et al. (1994: 13) put it, 'The key to success, rather, is realising a culture's innate potential, developing and enhancing the relationship between people's "mental programming" . . . and their economic environment.' If, as identified by the Tower managers I spoke to, the motivation for them to make a success of the buy-out was to 'provide decent terms and conditions for as long as possible, and increase employment opportunities for young people', a policy to stimulate entrepreneurship should be introduced that focuses on this, rather than maximizing profit, when, according to the same manager 'It's an extra. It's not the most important.'

The Menter a Busnes report (Casson et al., 1994) identifies Welsh culture as fundamentally associationist, rather than competitive, using Casson's (1991) terminology which is based on his analysis of different cultures in terms of such factors as mutual trust, atomistic versus organic social commitment, the quality of scientific or technical judgement, and the drive to succeed as an individual. The report concludes that, in spite of the dominance of the US-style competitive model of economic development, a more cooperative business form, one we might term 'associative entre-preneurship', might take firmer root in Welsh economic soil. One of its authors co-authored a later book entitled *The Associational Economy*, which develops these ideas further. They see successful innovation as

> dependent on the *associational* capacity of the firm – that is its capacity for forging co-operation between managers and workers within the firm, for securing co-operation between firms in the supply chain, and for crafting co-operative interfaces between firms and the wider institutional milieu. (Cooke and Morgan, 1998: 1)

The cooperative business form is a specific example of this sort of firm, and it is in the context of such a view of Welsh economic culture that Tower provides such an interesting example, as discussed in Chapter 7.

The Menter a Busnes report that has provided a basis for much of the discussion in this section was targeted towards Welsh-speaking entrepreneurs, but the following paragraph provides a positive conclusion to this section in terms of the whole Welsh economy:

> Much has been said, of course, about the more negative aspects of Welsh-speaking business culture that act as a brake on business and economic development. Perhaps it is now time to focus on the more positive aspects as possible elements in a distinctively Welsh model of business practice, a far more robust and better-networked business culture that may begin to express, in economic terms, the values and aspirations of Welsh-speaking society.

RELOCALIZING THE WELSH ECONOMY

An alternative approach to building a Welsh work identity could be made through reducing the gap that the globalized economy has created between production and consumption. For many postmodern critics of the existing economic order the response to the loss of identity in work that globalization has caused is to seek identities in consumption rather than production. In his essay 'The System of Objects' Baudrillard identifies consumption as the new basis of the social order, replacing the productive order of an earlier phase of capitalism:

> we can conceive of consumption as a characteristic mode of industrial civilization on the condition that we separate it fundamentally from its current meaning as a process of satisfaction of needs. Consumption is not a passive mode of assimilation and appropriation which we can oppose to an active

mode of production, in order to bring to bear naive concepts of action (and alienation). From the outset, we must clearly state that consumption is an active mode of relations (not only to objects, but to the collectivity and to the world), a systematic mode of activity and a global response on which our whole cultural system is founded. (1988: 21)

With high levels of unemployment, increasing numbers of people being outside the workforce due to other factors (long-term sickness or retirement), and with the homogenization of work (revolving around the computer and the telephone), identity must now be sought outside the work environment, in the shopping arcade. This appears to be the response to the removal of identity from work roles which has accompanied the globalization of the economy. From one perspective this could be viewed as a negative development: since incomes in the Valleys amongst employed and unemployed alike are very low (see Chapter 2), a universe in which identity is achieved through purchasing decisions is unlikely to be a fulfilling one in this and other economically depressed regions. However, from another perspective, the consumer identity could link with efforts to create a Welsh economic model to build strong identities for people in south Wales. Steps have already been taken in this direction, by attempting to revitalize the local economies of Wales by creating a 'Welsh brand'; the WDA is now using the slogan 'Cymru y Gwir Flas' or 'Wales the True Taste' to market Welsh food and drink.

Green economists have been proposing the strengthening of local economies both to enhance security of supply and to reduce the damaging environmental impacts of what is referred to as 'the great food swap' (Lucas, 2001; see also Hines, 1993, 2000; Goldsmith and Mander, 1996; Douthwaite, 1996; Desai and Riddlestone, 2002). Desai and Riddlestone explicitly quote the example of recent factory closures in south Wales to illustrate the insecurity of globalized economic planning:

Economic risk increases with specialisation, when we put all our eggs in one large basket. A country or region dependent heavily on one product or service is of course very vulnerable. For example, the valleys in South Wales were badly hit in 2000 by the closure of five clothing factories when Marks and Spencer decided to source their products from less expensive manufacturers in North Africa and Eastern Europe. (Desai and Riddlestone, 2002: 77)

Economic planners in this region should really take heed of such warnings, supported as they are by the historical experience of the specialization of the mining past, and the increased threats posed by European Enlargement in the future.

Some have also identified the reinforcement of community and personal identity as an additional benefit that such a relocalized economy would bring (see, for example, Norberg-Hodge, Merrifield and Gorelick, 2002). Desai and Riddlestone describe how 'creating stable regional economies can help create a sense of community and security . . . A sense of community can be supported by fostering a sense of place, through locally distinct neigh-bourhoods and industries linked to the ecology and heritage of an area' (2002: 75). The use of the word 'heritage' is interesting in the context of south Wales, where it is considered the basis of a whole 'industry'. But these bioregionalists are keen to point out that true heritage requires respect for the traditions of the people and community of an area – they discuss in particular their revitalization of the lavender industry of south London – rather than the packaging and reselling of people's memories that is criticized in examples such as the Rhondda Heritage Park. Applying similar lessons to Wales, a project at Bangor University is exploring the possibility of reintroducing into Wales two of our traditional textile crops, flax and hemp, as part of an effort to revitalize the Welsh agricultural sector.

The argument has been developed most fully in the case of the production and distribution of local food. Systems such as organic box schemes and, particularly in the USA, community-supported agriculture, offer a sense of enhanced local identity in addition to their economic and environmental benefits. The first system involves the ordering and delivery of boxes of seasonal organic vegetables from a local supplier via a wholefood shop or direct to homes. In the second (CSA) a more complex relationship is built up, with the eventual consumers of farm produce paying for their year's supply at the beginning of the growing season, thus offering a high level of commitment to the farmer and providing her or him with the capital to produce the year's crop. Another link between local producers and consumers is offered by the network of farmers' markets that are springing up all over Britain, from the first in Bath in 1997 to more than 270 by the turn of the century (Norberg-Hodge et al., 2002: 21).

Rural economists in Wales focus on the concept of 'provenance' as the link between localization of the economy and quality enabling the capture of a niche market and increased added value to the producer. Murdoch et al. (2000: 117) argue that

> any assertion of quality, especially as it is linked to nature, must be brought into some kind of alignment with the industrial and commerical criteria that ensure economic survival and economic success . . . the discovery of embeddedness – especially as it relates to issues of spatial proximity – can lead to a 'festishizing' of localness and a downplaying of the more universal factors that are necessary for the acquisition of competitive advantage.

However, this argument may suffer from taking economics too seriously on its own terms. After all market advantage is always dependent on political as well as economic factors, and in no sector so much as agriculture. It seems that there is a developing constellation of the interests of the consumers, regional developers, and farmers which is causing agriculture to move inevitably towards localization.

The argument in favour of local production and distribution appears to have been made successfully in the case of food, with even a judgement from the European Court of Justice going in favour of local supply against free competition,[6] and support for such ideas from the government's proposals for the future of agriculture (see the Curry Report: Policy Commission 2002; in the Welsh context see Morgan and Morley, 2002; Williamson, 2003). The movement in spending on agricultural subsidy away from production and towards environmental production, known in the jargon as 'modulation', can only encourage trends in this direction (K. Morgan, 2002).

We began this discussion not with a farmer but with a craftsman. The argument for local production and distribution can be most easily made in the case of food, which is subject to rapid deterioration and does not travel well. It is far harder to make a similar argument in the case of the furniture that was once made in Adam Bede's workshop but is now made in Manila. But the arguments about the importance of identity in work, and the consequences of the alienation caused by the global production and distribution system should not be sidelined by policy-makers in favour of a unique focus on economic considerations, primarily that of competition. Organizations concerned to establish Welsh national and sub-national brands suggest that in some parts of Wales there are positive steps in this direction. The Welsh Development Agency has adjusted its priorities slightly in response to the changed focus of economic development following the establishment of the Welsh Assembly in 1999. There is now an enhanced emphasis on Welsh branding. An example is Coedbren Ceredigion, produced by an alliance of local authority and timber industry groups to publicize the availability of Ceredigion-based timber suppliers and woodworking craftspeople. Bangor's Flax and Hemp project may result in similar development in the future in the textile industry. Rethinking our economic planning along these lines offers us the hope of a sustainable and socially reinforcing future to replace the fractured and insecure global economy we participate in today.

This chapter has concerned itself closely with the psychological and sociological impacts of the structure and organization of work. In spite of the decision by policy-makers to downgrade these aspects of the activity people spend most of their lives carrying out, their importance has been established. This gives us a basis on which to consider the views of local people about the work that is being created for them, and also establishes their right to have those views taken seriously. The next two chapters present the views of local workers in Rhondda Cynon Taff.

5

Handbags and Glad Rags: What is Work for in the Valleys?

No, I don't like work. I had rather laze about and think of all the fine things that can be done. I don't like work – no man does – but I like what is in the work, – the chance to find yourself. Your own reality – for yourself, not for others – what no other man can ever know. They can only see the mere show, and never can tell what it really means.

Joseph Conrad, *Heart of Darkness*

In Chapters 2 and 3 we looked at the recent history of employment and employment policy in Rhondda Cynon Taff. Chapter 4 then explored how these real-world events, combined with changes in the global economy, have affected the behaviour and outlook of local workers. In this chapter we arrive at the heart of the matter: how local workers perceive the work that they do, or do not do, within this framework. This chapter and the following one report the results of a research study carried out to explore directly local people's reactions and attitudes to their employment situation. I attempt to arrive at answers to two related questions: what do local people in Rhondda Cynon Taff think of the work they and others do, and what is it about their work that they value?

It is an interesting fact that these questions are rarely asked, especially rarely by economists. Sociologists have paid more attention to this field and have labelled it 'the subjective valuation of occupations'. Yet to economists these issues seem of little interest. This is curious, since, in a number of different ideological frameworks, considerable amounts of public money are spent manipulating our labour markets. In spite of the dominance of the rhetoric of the market, there are very few governments that do not intervene in their labour markets. During the 1970s in the UK large amounts of public money were invested in nationalized industries, which provided both consumption goods and well-paid highly skilled employment. Looking even further back, the agricultural sector has been in receipt of considerable levels of public subsidy to ensure food production and the management of our land since the Second World War. And, in this era of rhetorical commitment to free labour markets, governments are still subsidizing jobs, although this is now labelled as 'the attraction of inward investment' or the Working Families Tax Credit. Whatever the label, these policies result in the spending of public money on the creation or maintenance of jobs. In the Scandinavian context unemployment has traditionally been soaked up by creating more public-sector jobs in the health service or education – a strategy which might have been at least discussed in an economy as dependent on public-sector employment as Wales is.

It is bizarre that the form this public spending should take has received so little scrutiny by either the public, academics or policy-makers. There is no public debate about whether we would prefer to spend our taxes revitalizing the south Wales coal or steel industries rather than as subsidies for Japanese or Korean electronics companies. Instead of paying subsidies per tonne of coal, poor wages in factories are supplemented by public money in the form of tax credits, with few questions asked. But since this is our money we have a right to choose how it is spent. And the first people who deserve to answer this question are those who will undertake the jobs that are subsidized. For this reason, in this chapter an attempt is made to measure people's assessments of the value of various occupations, as well as how much they would like to have those occupations and how much they think people who do have them are paid. These numerical results are supplemented in Chapter 6 with the results from a series of in-depth interviews asking local people about the work that they do, and for their opinions of the employment policies of which they have been the object.

THEORIES OF WAGE-SETTING AND JOB SATISFACTION

Although few questions are asked within the discipline of economics about the quality of jobs, there is an extensive literature on the issues of wage-setting and job satisfaction that is relevant to the discussion that follows. From the perspective of neoclassical economics, 'man' is a rational agent, and tends to view the employment contract as an exchange of time for money, with very little attention paid to the nature of the work that is undertaken. In an unpublished paper I have explained the different theoretical frameworks within which neoclassical economics discusses the rewards from employment (Cato, 1998; see also Bosworth, Dawkins and Stromback, 1996.); a brief summary follows. The basic proposition of labour-market theory is that individuals choose to supply their labour according to a formula that will maximize their personal utility. They perform a mental trade-off between goods they would like to be able to buy with the proceeds of the work and the leisure they sacrifice by doing it (see Bosworth et al., 1996: 20–32). Although it has been acknowledged since

Adam Smith that the subjective preferences of individuals affect their labour-supply decisions, economists have 'been rather slow to recognize the influence of the psychological or motivational aspects of these decisions' (ibid.). Economics presents two basic models for how personal characteristics and characteristics of the job itself influence wages. Personal characteristics' influence is explained by 'human-capital wage theory', while the characteristics of the job itself are covered by the 'theory of compensating differentials'.

According to the human-capital theory of wage determination, education and training are the main determinants of earnings. Workers who have undergone more training have sacrificed potential earnings by staying out of the labour market in order to gain greater compensation in the form of higher earnings once they enter the labour market. From the employer's perspective a trained worker will have the capacity for a higher marginal product and so is worth a higher wage. Details of empirical tests of this model especially by Mincer (1974; 1991) and Gary S. Becker (1975) have shown that the level of skill of the individual worker is indeed a good indicator of her/his level of wages. However, analysis of Welsh data, at least at the aggregate level, suggests that the theory does not work well in the Welsh context. A correlation analysis between skill levels (as measured by GCSE passes) and levels of GDP per head at the level of Welsh local authority areas fails to yield significant results. Nor is there a relationship between skill levels and level of employment.[1]

The alternative explanation of wage-setting – the theory of compensating differentials – proposes that workers are compensated for the unpleasantness of their working conditions. The empirical evidence for this theory is mixed, with convincing differentials only being shown in cases where the worker faces a significant risk of dying at work (Marin and Psacharopoulos, 1982). An alternative exploration of the same differentials by Krueger and Summers (1988) suggests that the nature of the employer's business is critical in deciding the wage levels of employees rather than the actual unpleasantness of the work undertaken by employees. The literature on the theory of compensating differentials is inconclusive with authors finding conflicting results. This may be because, while the conditions of the work itself are important, the subjective perception of these is different for different workers. In other words, a discussion of compensating differentials is incomplete without a consideration of the individual differences between the workers who are to be compensated.

Two rather less conventional considerations of wage-setting introduce the idea that workers may substitute psychological returns in the form of status or social approbation for some part of their wages (the concept of 'psychic wages' as an important part of the 'utility' that employees derive from work was first introduced by Robert Lucas (1977)). In his 1985 book R. H. Frank suggested that status might be one of the commodities contributing to workers' utility gained from employment, and that in exchange for an increase in status workers might be prepared to accept lower levels of wages. More recently, using insights gleaned from the psychology literature in an economic context Bruno Frey (1997) has explored the motivations of human agents in various economic situations. His conclusion is that employees are motivated by more than just the financial rewards of their employment and that they have 'intrinsic motivations' relating to the nature of the work they do as well as 'extrinsic motivations' represented by financial rewards.

The workers interviewed during the research study (details are given in the following section) are divided between three sectors for some of the analysis according to whether their workplace is in the private, public or cooperative sectors. This is because research has shown that workers in these three sectors are differently motivated. In their analysis of wage discrepancies between the public and private sectors, Disney et al. (1999: 34) conclude that 'some thought must be given as to why the discrepancy occurs . . . why, for example, people with certain characteristics "select" themselves (or are selected) into particular occupations'. This suggests that insights from the sociological literature might be able to strengthen the economic analysis of the wage consequences of occupational choice. Rather than allocating people to sectors on the basis of the task they perform or function they fill, some sociologists have suggested that the concept of a 'situs' may be more useful in considering work motivations. Situs describes 'a cluster of economic functions' (Wilson and Musick, 1997: 257). Bell (1973), who developed this structure for considering employment locations, distinguished economic, government, academe, non-profit, and military as the five relevants 'situses' in a modern, developed economy. According to Wilson and Musick,

> The situs concept recognizes that the same occupation can be located in very different economic environments. In other words, occupations can be ordered not only on a vertical dimension . . . but also on a horizontal dimension. For example, the job of a physician working for the army is different from the job of a physician working for a mining company.

Research into the empirical significance of the concept of 'situs' has found that people working in different situses tend to share specific orientations towards their work. In an early analysis of the impact of situs on work motivations, Samuel and Lewin-Epstein (1979) found that people working in situses where the purpose of the occupation was socially orientated (such as education or social work) had more strongly collectivist values, that is, values that take the wider community into account rather than merely one's personal interests, than people working in production-orientated occupations (such as manufacturing and maintenance). Later empirical research has shown that, unsurprisingly, workers in the public sector are motivated by objectives such as providing a service or product that is helpful to others, while people working in private-sector companies were more strongly motivated by monetary rewards (Cacioppe and Monk, 1984). A study of work attitudes in the USA (Reinarman, 1987) found that private-sector workers tend to have more individualistic attitudes and tend to divide their lives rigidly between work and social life; by contrast public-sector workers, whose work is more likely to be the result of a personal vocation, have lives where work and social life are more integrated.

As part of an exploration of the employment policies followed in Rhondda Cynon Taff it was important to undertake a study of subjective work motivations there. The results reported in the rest of this chapter come from a questionnaire study that I undertook in a number of workplaces in Rhondda Cynon Taff in 1999. The questionnaire explored issues such as the different levels of work satisfaction in different work-places, workers' perceptions about different kinds of employment in terms of skill levels, rates of pay, and the worth of the work itself, and their perceptions of the inward-investment employment strategy. I was also interested in whether a different employment 'situs' influenced opinions and, as a rough method of approximating this, I divided the workplaces into three sectors: private, public and cooperative.

The following section discusses the method followed in conducting this research including technical details of the survey, information about the response to the survey, and a brief outline of the ANOVA technique to be used in the analysis of the survey responses. The results are then presented and provide a foundation for exploring differences by workplace and sector in the social valuation of occupations in Rhondda Cynon Taff. Once we have gathered this empirical data we are able to draw conclusions about the sorts of jobs that are popular in Rhondda Cynon Taff and offer this as part of an ongoing discussion of how employment policies are developed there.

THE SURVEY QUESTIONNAIRE

The questionnaire which was administered in the study area consisted of twenty-two questions and took some 15 to 20 minutes to complete. The first twelve questions were concerned with demographic variables that might require control during the data analysis.[2] These included information on such variables as age, sex, qualifications, caring responsibilities for children or elderly people, health, marital status, employment status, number of working hours, and training during the past year. Data on income were ascertained from a question asking respondents to locate themselves in one of five income brackets. Only the data which are useful to the analysis have been reported below.

Four of the questions required respondents to assess, for example, their level of job satisfaction or social approval of an occupation on a 1–7 scale. In the case of the three such questions that explored workers' perceptions of the worth of eleven jobs, the amount their incumbents are paid, and their preference for undertaking these jobs themselves, the jobs to be compared were selected roughly according to the ISCO–88 classification schema. This is a rather narrowly based measure favoured by economists, taking into account only skill level and skill specialization, based on the International Standard Classification of Education. The negative consequences of basing a categorization so narrowly on 'skills' (for this purpose defined as 'the ability to carry out the tasks and duties of a given job': ILO, 1990: 2) results in anomalies such as a faith healer being placed alongside a robot operator and nurses being identified as part of the 'craft and related trades' category. Although the ISCO categorization was used for guidance in the selection of jobs to include in the questionnaire, it was not followed slavishly. The category related to agricultural and fisheries work was excluded, on the basis that this is such a small sector in the area under study that respondents are unlikely to be able to assess the nature of this type of work.[3] The armed forces category was also excluded, on the basis that it is anomalous to distinguish it as a separate category on the basis of 'skill'. Instead extra jobs were included in the 'professional', 'service workers', and 'craft and related trades' categories, particularly because employment in these categories is highly sex-segregated, and so one job predominantly occupied by members of each sex was included in each.

The decision to include 'nurse' as one of the jobs in the comparison may have introduced bias, since a large number of the respondents are themselves nurses. However, nursing is the central occupation in the sector that forms the focus of much of this research and is a highly significant form of employment in an area where so much employment is in the public sector; it therefore seemed necessary to include it. It is also a rare example of a female-dominated occupation in ISCO category 7, which is mainly composed of 'male' trade-based occupations such as bricklaying and plumbing. The average approval values for occupations by sector, presented in table 5.7 below, indicate that there is a higher level of approval amongst public-sector workers, possibly indicating bias. However, the differential is not as great as for 'midwife', an occupation which is not represented in the sample.

The respondents were asked to rank the eleven selected jobs on a 1–7 scale according to the following questions:

- How worthwhile do you think the following jobs are to society as a whole?
- How much would you like to do the following jobs, if you had the right qualifications?
- How much do you think people earn for these jobs?

In some of the tables of results below, means for the variables, particularly those derived from the 1–7 scales, are presented. Such means should be interpreted with caution, since there is no objective justification for assuming that respondents perceive the intervals as being evenly spaced, so that a job awarded a value of '3' is really three times more valuable than a job awarded a '1'. While these limitations should be borne in mind when using such scales, they do allow subjective data to be converted into a pseudo-numerical form so that quantitative analyses and comparisons can be made.

Two questions required respondents to select three reasons for wanting work or priorities for job creation and to rank these from most to least important. The results from the reasons-for-working question were not analysed due to space limitations, while the second question was a central issue in the research. The possible considerations suggested were:

- The usefulness of the work itself;
- Attracting competitive international companies;
- A job that pays a living wage;
- Creating jobs that require high levels of skill;
- Creating jobs that offer long-term security;
- Work that strengthens the community.

A number of respondents had difficulty in understanding how to respond to this question: for twenty-three cases there were missing values, and some respondents had simply ticked three boxes without expressing their 1 to 3 ordering. For these cases I inserted their answers at the mean value, i.e. 2, rather than lose more cases. Responses to two final questions asking respondents whether they thought their job was useful to society and whether they felt a pride in their work were not analysed, since only a very few respondents answered negatively.

The survey questionnaire respondents were drawn from a sample of employers in the study area. Because of the nature of the research interest, relating attitudes to the relative importance of pay and the social value of the work, and the relationship of both these to job satisfaction, it was important that the respondents were derived from the two main sectors of the economy, that is, public and private, and from employers typical of the two sectors in the study area. Although the choice of companies to approach was to some extent theoretically guided, it was inevitable that the final sample would be largely selected pragmatically, since some employers were unwilling to participate. The final sample was drawn from three private-sector and four public-sector employers, together with a workers' cooperative colliery. In order to protect the anonymity of respondents, the names of the companies reported in this chapter are fictitious.

As displayed in table 5.1, the employer sample consists of four large employers (the exact number of employees varies around the 200 mark in each case), combined with two small providers of health care, each with between twenty-five and fifty employees. The employees of the local sorting office and the school secretaries who responded to the question-naire have been combined into a single 'Publicadmin' category because the response rate from both groups was so poor. The combined group would fit in the ISCO category number 4 (clerks). The intention was to obtain responses from teachers, but no teaching staff at the school that agreed to participate returned questionnaires, and the numerous other schools in the area that were approached declined to participate in the research.[4]

The level of support shown by company administrators varied widely between the different employers. The greatest support was shown by the administrator of a large local hospital, who sent a memo to heads of departments asking them to request their staff to fill in the questionnaire, and sent me late returns by post. This contrasted sharply with the attitude of the factory of a multinational company where, having received per-mission from the branch-plant manager to distribute questionnaires, I was then turned away at the door, and only after two phone calls was per-mission granted again by the local head office.[5] The response rates mirror the level of support given by the employer, and this may bias the results reported below.

The fine-grained nature of the data analysed here is balanced by the small size of the sample. The small number of cases means that the statistical power of the results is reduced, although this is allowed for with-in the methods of statistical significance testing that form part of the ANOVA technique (see Bryman and Cramer, 1997: 113). So results that are reported as significant below are important findings and may be treated

Table 5.1: Details of companies selected for survey sample and response rates

Company	Nature of work	No. of employees	Responses N	%
Engineerco.	Skilled engineering maintenance	*c.* 250	41	16
Minitaki	Electronic goods assembly	*c.* 200	22	11
Sunnyside	Private nursing home for the elderly	49	25	51
Cynon Hospital	Large general hospital	*c.* 200	56	28
Hillside Hospital	Small cottage hospital	24	12	50
Publicadmin	Sorting office workers	*c.* 100	9	9
Publicadmin	School secretaries	*c.* 12	6	50
Tower[a]	Workers' cooperative coal mine	239	36	15
Total			207	

[a]Although the other names reported here and in the text are fictitious, it seemed futile to attempt to conceal the identity of Tower Colliery since it is the only worker-owned colliery in the world.

Note: The percentage of responses does not represent a 'response rate' as such, since questionnaires were not distributed but made available, with a box to return them to. Thus it merely represents the approximate proportion of employees in each company who returned a questionnaire.

seriously in spite of the small sample size. As a corollary it may be that results which are significant cannot be treated as such because the small sample size means that they fail to achieve statistical power.

For some of the analyses presented in this chapter I have used the ANOVA (analysis of variance) method of statistical analysis. This method (based on the statistical F-test) compares variability within and between groups of data to explore whether differences observed between subjects in two or more groups subject to different influences are significantly different or merely the result of random fluctuations. In most of the tests conducted below, the groups are distinguished on the basis of employment sector, on the suggestion that the culture or economic conditions of his or her sector of employment might influence an individual's attitudes towards various aspects of employment. These tests follow the classic one-way ANOVA model. In addition, it is also possible to consider the respondents in the different groups as subject to two or more influential factors simultaneously. In this situation the appropriate technique is the two-way ANOVA model. When this technique is used an interaction effect can occur in addition to the effects of each of the factors individually. The F-tests conducted (using SPSS) distinguish between the effects of the factors and the interaction effects (for further details of the method see Tacq, 1997).

DESCRIPTIVE STATISTICS FOR THE RESPONDENTS

The total number of completed questionnaires was, as shown in table 5.1, 207: 96 in the public sector, 75 in the private sector, and 36 from Tower Colliery. The following tables present basic information about the dataset. Table 5.2 indicates that there are wide divergences between the employers in terms of pay and the levels of training their employees possess. The highest rate of pay is found at the workers' cooperative, where the mean value is 9.52 (i.e. £9.52 per hour on average), while Engineerco has only slightly lower pay rates with a mean of 9.38. The lowest rate of pay is found at the private nursing home (4.67), closely followed by Minitaki (4.71) and the administrative public-sector jobs (5.55).

The sex variable indicates a high degree of sex segregation in the sample. In the case of the cottage hospital all the employees are female, and from the larger general hospital only one man returned a questionnaire. By contrast, all employees at Tower are men, apart from the women working in the on-site canteen. Minitaki and the Publicadmin employees are more evenly spread between men and women, but in the case of the latter group the two workplaces making up this group are themselves divided between female secretaries in a local school and (mainly) male postal workers. The data derived from the question on health are not reported, since they vary little between employers and are difficult to interpret due to their basis in self-assessment.[6]

The gender segregation between the sectors is also apparent when the workers are aggregated into public, private and cooperative sectors, with all workers at Tower being men, a 60:40 split between men and women amongst the private-sector employees, and an overwhelming majority of 86 per cent women in the public sector. Rates of pay also show considerable differences by sector with the highest pay rates at the colliery (mean = 9.52), and a considerable differential between the cooperative workers and those in the other sectors. The public-sector workers receive the second highest level of remuneration (mean = 7.67), with the private-sector workers paid least (6.79). The public-sector value also has a higher standard deviation (3.30), indicating a larger spread of salaries in the hospitals studied, between the doctors, on the one hand, and the unqualified care workers on the other.

The level of qualification of employees also shows large differences between the employers (for full details see Cato, 2000b). In terms of technical qualifications, unsurprisingly the HNDs and HNCs are concentrated in the engineering company where 28 have such a qualification, with a smaller number amongst the workers at Tower (6). Equally expected is the concentration of nursing qualifications amongst the hospital workers (19 at Cynon, 7 at Hillside, and 6 at Sunnyside). The academic qualifications are

Table 5.2: Summary statistics for demographic variables by employer: means (standard deviations in parentheses)

Employer	Pay per hour[a]	Sex	Training
Engineerco	9.38 (1.94)	0.95 (0.22)	0.73 (0.45)
Minitaki	4.71 (1.37)	0.41 (0.50)	0.23 (0.43)
Sunnyside	4.67 (2.09)	0.16 (0.37)	0.46 (0.51)
Hillside	8.85 (2.91)	0.00 (0.00)	0.83 (0.39)
Cynon Hosp	8.01 (3.48)	0.05 (0.23)	0.75 (0.44)
Publicadmin	5.55 (1.66)	0.60 (0.51)	0.13 (0.35)
Tower	9.52 (3.13)	1.00 (0.00)	0.51 (0.51)

[a]The process used to derive this variable from the response data is outlined in n. 2.
Note: Because the sex and training variables are dichotomous, the values in the table translate easily into percentages.

quite evenly spread, with a high level of qualification at Engineeringco, with proportionally even more degrees than the hospital workers (8 compared with 9 in the two hospitals combined), where all doctors, physiotherapists etc. fall into this category.

Table 5.3 presents mean values for the job-satisfaction variables, measured in terms of overall satisfaction and satisfaction with pay, security and the actual work carried out. Again there are large differences between the different employers. The highest levels of overall job satisfaction are found at Hillside, Sunnyside, Tower, and Cynon Hospital, in that order, with mean values ranging from 5.75 to 5.36 on the 7-point scale. The lowest overall levels of satisfaction are found for the publicadmin workers (4.21), followed by Engineeringco (4.46) and Minitaki (4.77).

In terms of satisfaction with the rate of pay they receive, the workers at Tower are the most satisfied, perhaps because, as members of a cooperative, they have a greater role in deciding their pay. Their satisfaction level of 4.56 is in strong contrast to that of the publicadmin workers' level of 2.86. Workers at Engineeringco, Minitaki, and Sunnyside, the three private-sector companies, are in a middle position in terms of pay-based job satisfaction, while those working in the two public-sector hospitals are slightly more satisfied. Apart from the low level for the publicadmin workers these results do hint that levels of pay satisfaction tend to cluster by sectoral type, a finding which is explored further below.

Findings about workers' satisfaction with the security of their employment should be assessed against the background of the history of high levels of unemployment outlined in Chapter 2. Given the strong emphasis on job creation based on inward investment by multinationals it is

Table 5.3: Summary statistics for job-satisfaction variables by employer: means (standard deviations in parentheses)

Employer	Satisfaction with			
	Job overall	Pay	Security	Work itself
Engineerco	4.46 (1.42)	3.34 (1.53)	2.54 (1.23)	5.07 (1.40)
Minitaki	4.77 (1.85)	3.23 (1.57)	5.23 (1.60)	4.59 (1.85)
Sunnyside	5.64 (1.50)	3.36 (2.06)	4.96 (1.84)	5.52 (1.56)
Hillside	5.75 (0.97)	3.92 (1.31)	5.67 (0.89)	6.08 (0.79)
Cynon Hosp	5.36 (1.47)	4.13 (1.73)	4.74 (1.67)	5.46 (1.56)
Publicadmin	4.21 (1.63)	2.86 (1.61)	3.93 (2.02)	4.79 (1.72)
Tower	5.44 (1.34)	4.56 (1.58)	5.09 (1.63)	5.69 (1.20)

interesting that the second highest level of satisfaction with security (mean = 5.23) is found for the Minitaki workers, who in the other respects show some of the lowest levels of satisfaction. This may suggest that the emphasis on foreign investment as the focus of local employment policy has persuaded these workers that their jobs will be protected. At any rate, they appear to have confidence in the future of this Japanese company. The highest level of satisfaction with job security is found for the workers in the cottage hospital, with workers at Tower also feeling very satisfied with their job security, a finding which must again be influenced by the fact that they in some sense 'control' the company they work for.[7] The other health-care workers also feel secure, whether in public or private sector, with the Publicadmin workers slightly less happy with the security of the work. The lowest score by far on this measure, the mean of 2.54 representing less than half the mean for the highest-scoring company, are the employees at Engineeringco, who clearly feel that their jobs are not secure. The fact that engineering is a sector that is shrinking in the UK as well as in the study area may explain this finding.

The final job-satisfaction measure indicates employees' satisfaction with the actual work that they do. Here, the workers in the cottage hospital scored very highly, with a mean of 6.08 on a 7-point scale. They were followed by the workers at Tower and then the other health-sector workers. In general, the means for this measure were fairly tightly clustered, with a smaller range than for the other job-satisfaction measures.

Once the public- and private-sector workers of different employing companies are combined (results not reported here), the values on the job-satisfaction measures for the Tower workers begin to stand out. Tower demonstrates the largest mean value on all four of the measures, with particularly large differences on the job-security measure (mean = 5.09). In the case of pay satisfaction the public sector workers are as happy as the

Tower workers (both means = 4.56), which is surprising given their lower mean wages and higher levels of qualifications. This may fit the compensating-differentials theory summarized at the outset of the chapter, in the sense that miners are rewarded for their unpleasant working conditions, whereas public-sector workers are expected to enjoy some of their rewards in terms of a high level of social esteem. The private-sector workers (mean = 3.32) are the least happy and, as we saw above, do in fact receive the lowest levels of hourly pay.

In terms of qualifications by sector, the proportions of workers with degrees is quite similar across the sectors, although the Tower workers have notably lower levels of school qualifications (a full 55.6 per cent have no academic qualifications at all). In terms of technical qualifications, as expected the nursing qualifications are concentrated in the public sector (31.3 per cent of employees have them), in spite of the presence of Sunnyside nursing home in the private-sector group, with HND/HNC qualifications correspondingly concentrated in the private (33.0 per cent) and cooperative (16.7 per cent) sectors. Given that the public-sector workers are better qualified than the workers at Tower, their equivalent level of pay satisfaction is worth noting.

COMPARING JOB SATISFACTION AND PAY ACROSS SECTORS

This section explores how the nature of the work carried out affects employees' levels of job satisfaction. As a proxy for the nature of the work carried out, for the initial analysis workers are put into three groups according to their employment sector: public sector, private sector and cooperative. ANOVA tests were then run on the mean values of the job-satisfaction measures between the three groups. The results of this basic ANOVA test are presented in table 5.4. There is a significant difference between the three sectors in terms of satisfaction with levels of pay and amount of job security. However, there is no significant difference between the groups on the third individual measure of job satisfaction – that measuring satisfaction with the work itself – or on the overall job-satisfaction measure. This is an interesting finding given that the rates of pay do vary significantly between the different sectors. It begins to suggest that pay rates may not be the most important determinant of job satisfaction.

Earlier studies have shown (e.g. Clark, 1997), that women are much more satisfied with their work than men and this proves problematic in the case of these tests, given the heavy degree of sex segregation between the different employment sectors noted earlier. To attempt to control for this, a two-way ANOVA test was conducted. As explained in the methods section,

Table 5.4: Results of ANOVA tests by employment sector for various variables

Dependent variable	F-value	Sig. F
Job satisfaction measures		
Pay	7.29	0.001***
Job security	7.08	0.001***
The work itself	2.32	0.101
Overall	1.99	0.140
Other variables		
Pay per hour	8.34	0.000
Training	1.62	0.201

Levels of significance: *** p < 0.01; ** p < 0.05; * p < 0.1.

Table 5.5: Results of ANOVA tests by employment sector and sex for various variables

Dependent variable	Sector		Sex		Main effects	
	F	sig. F	F	sig. F	F	sig. F
Job satisfaction measures						
Pay	9.59	0.000***	5.82	0.017**	6.92	0.000***
Job security	12.2	0.000***	26.57	0.000***	14.19	0.000***
The work itself	2.63	0.074*	1.42	0.235	2.02	0.112
Overall	4.13	0.018**	10.56	0.001***	4.91	0.003***
Other variables						
Pay per hour	7.96	0.000***	12.70	0.000***	10.13	0.000***
Training	2.06	0.131	0.957	0.329	1.40	0.245

Levels of significance: *** p < 0.01; ** p < 0.05; * p < 0.1.

the two-way ANOVA allows for the testing of significant difference between groups, while simultaneously controlling for the effect of a third variable. In this case the difference between groups in terms of earnings, training and job-satisfaction measures is tested for significance, while the ANOVA procedure also indicates the independent impact on that significant difference of sex, as well as the impact of the combination of sex and sector combined. This procedure can also produce an interaction effect – so-called 'two-way interactions'. In the case of this first two-way ANOVA test the procedure detected no interaction effect, although this does emerge in the second such test reported below.

The results of the two-way ANOVA are reported in table 5.5. For the variable indicating satisfaction with pay, the variation is greater in terms of sector, indicated by a higher F-value. However, in terms of job security and overall job satisfaction the sex variable has higher significance, reflecting women's generally higher degree of job satisfaction. No significant difference at the 5-per-cent level was found between sectors in terms of satisfaction with the work itself. In terms of the actual variables, there are significant differences in terms of pay per hour, again explained mainly by the sex variable, where the two variables are significant individually and jointly. There are no significant differences in training by sex or sector. Despite the observed concentration of women in the public sector and men in the cooperative sector, no two-way interaction terms were significant.

So the data analysis suggests that levels of job satisfaction do indeed vary depending on the kind of work undertaken, although it appears that it is the variables that relate to concrete aspects of the job – the rate of pay or security – that vary, whereas the measure concerned with the nature of the work itself does not.

THE SOCIAL VALUATION OF OCCUPATIONS

At the heart of this analysis of employees in Rhondda Cynon Taff is an interest in their subjective valuation of forms of employment. As well as exploring their levels of job satisfaction, an analysis of respondents' appraisal of the social value of various occupations, and the correlations between these responses and their views of the amount people in these jobs are paid and their subjective desire to have such a job themselves, casts light on the evaluation of occupations by workers in the area. The question guiding this section of the research concerns whether the subjective rating of occupations differs significantly by sector of employment.

The suggestion is that the subjective evaluation of the different types of occupation will differ by employment sector, with public-sector workers valuing broadly caring occupations more highly than those in the private sector, who may be expected to value individualistic occupations relatively more. To illuminate these questions workers were asked to assign a mark from 1 to 7 to a selection of eleven jobs depending on their social worth, the financial return they thought people in that occupation received, and how much they would like to be in that occupation themselves. By comparing the strength of the relationship between, first, the popularity of the job and its earnings and, second, the popularity of the job and its social worth, some conclusion can be drawn about whether financial remuneration or social approbation has a greater influence on the popularity of the

Table 5.6: Mean values of variables measuring perceived earnings, by sector, and results of F-tests for significant variation

Occupation	Public	Private	Coop.	F	Sig. F
Bus driver	3.11	2.96	2.79	1.03	0.360
Dustman	2.99	3.03	3.21	0.403	0.679
Executive	6.77	6.82	6.48	2.06	0.131
Factory worker	3.47	2.97	2.97	3.74	0.026**
Fast-food server	2.39	1.92	2.00	3.65	0.028**
Midwife	4.83	4.12	4.24	7.18	0.001***
Nurse	4.27	3.76	3.64	4.02	0.019**
Plumber	4.55	4.69	4.79	0.37	0.695
Professor	6.49	6.05	6.27	4.83	0.009***
Secretary	3.83	3.49	4.00	2.71	0.069
Surveyor	6.16	5.79	5.70	3.99	0.020**

occupations. These relationships are compared across the three sectoral groups established earlier – private, public and cooperative – to assess whether there are systematic differences between the groups in terms of what influences their members' perceptions about what makes a job attractive.

The first stage of the analysis is to present the mean values assigned to the jobs in terms of the three issues being considered by the three groups. Table 5.6 presents the mean values for the subjective evaluation of earnings; table 5.7 presents the mean values for the social worth of the occupations; and table 5.8 presents the mean values for the subjective preference for each occupation by the respondents in each of the groups. To test whether the apparent differences between the groups are significant an ANOVA procedure is again followed, in this case an F-test for the three groups. The results of these F-tests are presented in the appropriate tables, together with indications of their significance.

In terms of the perceived earnings received by people working in the different occupations (reported in table 5.6) the largest measure of disagreement arises in the case of midwives, who are thought to earn more by those with experience of their work, that is, those in the public sector, than by private-sector or cooperative workers. Public-sector workers similarly estimated the earnings of nurses higher than did those working in other sectors. In the case of all the other occupations where there was significant disagreement – factory worker, fast-food server, professor and surveyor – in each case the public-sector workers estimated their earnings higher than did those working in other sectors. This might result from their lack of knowledge of private-sector work; or perhaps it just indicates a

Table 5.7: Mean values of variables measuring perceived social worth, by sector, and results of F-tests for significant variation

Occupation	Public	Private	Coop.	F	Sig. F
Bus driver	5.23	4.74	4.61	4.07	0.019**
Dustman	5.88	5.43	5.54	2.71	0.069
Executive	3.92	3.96	4.31	0.84	0.431
Factory worker	5.31	4.82	5.18	2.84	0.061
Fast-food server	4.40	3.34	3.42	9.97	0.000***
Midwife	6.60	6.19	6.37	3.46	0.033**
Nurse	6.68	6.39	6.51	2.13	0.122
Plumber	5.76	4.90	4.82	13.20	0.000***
Professor	5.47	4.86	4.94	4.31	0.015**
Secretary	5.01	3.89	4.24	16.56	0.000***
Surveyor	4.67	4.44	4.97	1.84	0.162

Table 5.8: Mean values of variables measuring extent of preference for occupations, by sector, and results of F-tests for significant variation

Occupation	Public	Private	Coop.	F	Sig. F
Bus driver	2.15	2.10	2.19	0.051	0.951
Dustman	1.60	1.78	2.22	2.91	0.057*
Executive	2.76	3.31	3.85	3.45	0.034**
Factory worker	1.72	2.73	1.70	10.79	0.000***
Fast-food server	1.64	1.64	1.41	0.52	0.593
Midwife	4.04	2.76	2.55	9.71	0.000***
Nurse	4.95	3.74	3.24	9.05	0.000***
Plumber	2.13	2.93	3.84	12.37	0.000***
Professor	2.94	3.65	3.64	2.73	0.068*
Secretary	3.21	2.27	2.06	7.42	0.001***
Surveyor	2.38	3.11	4.70	17.44	0.000***

generally more optimistic expectation about wages, resulting from the nature of wage settlement in the public sector.

The results for subjective evaluation of social worth, presented in table 5.7, indicate that there are some major disagreements about the social worth of some of the occupations between the different sectors, especially in the cases of secretarial work, plumbing and fast-food serving. In each case, public-sector workers value all these jobs more highly than do workers in the other sectors. Overall, the public-sector workers rate all the jobs as more socially worthwhile than do employees in the other sectors, except for the case of the chief executive. This suggests a general attitude amongst public-sector workers that all employment is socially useful, and indeed, one respondent refused to rank occupations, writing in the 'comments' section at the end of the questionnaire that all work is useful and that such distinctions between the value of different types of work are invidious. The other occupations which were rated differentially to a significant degree between the different sectors are: bus driver, midwife and professor.

Table 5.8 presents the mean values for the different groups' preferences for undertaking the various jobs themselves. The largest differences in means in terms of the preference for actually undertaking the considered occupation were found in the cases of surveying, factory work and plumbing. The workers at the cooperative colliery were particularly keen to work as surveyors, perhaps because it is one of the few professional types of employment found in the mining sector; many of the miners also appear to be plumbers *manqués*. Factory work is rated a whole point lower by those in the public sector and the cooperative workers than those in the private sector, a minority of whom themselves work in the Minitaki factory. The three female-dominated occupations in the list – secretary, nurse and midwife – all receive a much better approval rating from the public-sector workers who are, of course, predominantly women. Finally, and intriguingly, the chief executive was rated significantly higher amongst workers at the cooperative colliery, and lowest amongst public-sector workers – perhaps the experience of 'being your own boss' does affect your attitude to managers?

In general, the most striking differences between the sectors are found in the case of highly sex-segregated occupations, where the fact that the proportions of workers of each sex in the three sectors tested is so unbalanced clearly undermines the strength of the findings. The large amount of variation in the subjective preference for the jobs as nurses and midwives is unsurprising once we recall that all the workers in the cooperative group and nearly 65 per cent of those in the private sector are men, who are unlikely, especially in the traditional culture of RCT, to aspire to nursing work. The same applies in reverse to the high F-value found for the attractiveness of the job of plumber.

The correlation of the results found on the perceived earnings and social-worth scales with the workers' preference for undertaking the particular occupation provides an interesting test. To explore whether workers in the different sectors are more influenced by earnings or by the social worth of a job when considering which job they would like to have themselves, correlations were carried out, separately for the three groups, between the earnings variable and the preference variable, and between the social-worth variable and the preference variable. The correlations are tested using

Table 5.9: Ranking of various occupations by social worth, perceived earnings, and subjective preference, by sector

Factor	Earnings			Preference			Social worth		
Sector	Pub.	Priv.	Coop.	Pub.	Priv.	Coop.	Pub.	Priv.	Coop.
Occupation									
Bus driver	9	9	10	7	9	8	7	7	8
Dustman	10	8	8	11	10	7	3	3	3
Executive	1	1	1	5	3	2	11	9	9
Factory worker	7	10	9	9	6	10	6	6	4
Fast-food server	11	11	11	10	11	11	10	11	11
Midwife	4	5	5	2	5	6	2	2	2
Nurse	6	6	7	1	2	5	1	1	1
Plumber	5	4	4	6	7	3	4	4	7
Professor	2	2	2	4	1	4	5	5	6
Secretary	7	7	6	3	8	9	8	10	10
Surveyor	3	3	3	6	4	1	9	8	5

Table 5.10: Correlation and rank correlation of earnings and preference and social worth and preference, by type of employer

	Pubearn	Pubsoc	Privearn	Privsoc	Coopearn	Coopsoc
Pearson's r						
Publike	.336	.546				
	(.312)	(.082)				
Privlike			.751	.384		
			(.008)***	(.244)		
Cooplike					.854	.188
					(.001)***	(.581)
Spearman's ρ						
Publike	.591	.272				
	(.056)	(.417)				
Privlike			.809	.382		
			(.003)***	(.247)		
Cooplike					.864	.227
					(.001)***	(.502)

Note: The suffix 'earn' indicates earnings; 'soc' indicates social worth; and 'like' indicates the preference variable.

Pearson's r and also using Spearman's r for rank correlation.[8] The rankings assigned to the different occupations by the different groups are presented in table 5.9; the results of the correlation tests are shown in table 5.10.

There is a remarkable degree of consistency in the rankings shown in table 5.9. All three sectors rank the same three jobs, in the same order, as highest in terms of earnings: namely, chief executive, professor, followed by surveyor. Fast-food server is certainly the Cinderella occupation, only escaping the lowest ranking by public-sector workers because they would like to be dustmen less (presumably because these mainly female workers see it as a mainly male occupation), and only avoiding a uniform last place in terms of social worth because those in the public sector have such a low opinion of chief executives. The first three places in terms of adjudged social worth are also consistent across the sectors, with nurses in first place, followed by midwives and then dustmen in third position. Amongst these workers practical, craft-based occupations are considered of more social value than professional occupations such as surveying and the academic life.

The Pearson's correlations in table 5.10 indicate that for private-sector workers there is a close relationship between the amount they perceive a member of an occupation earns and their preference for this occupation, and this link is even stronger in the case of the cooperative workers. This correlation does not exist in the case of public-sector workers, for whom there is no relationship between the level of pay they think a job will bring them and their wish to do that job. In this analysis the Spearman correlation shows a similar pattern. Overall, there is no hard-and-fast indication in these results that workers would favour working in occupations that have high social worth, since the coefficient for all these correlations is non-significant. It almost reaches significance, however, in the case of the public-sector workers, who, as hypothesized at the outset, might be expected to have made their occupational choice on the basis of intangible, social rewards rather than money alone. The failure of the r value to reach significance may well be due merely to the small number of cases. So it seems that the hypothesis that the social valuation of occupations varies by sector is supported by these data, although perhaps the most striking conclusion from the results is the strong favouring of practical 'working-class' jobs, rather than elite occupations, amongst all the workers studied.

WORKERS' PREFERENCES FOR JOB CREATION

In the final section workers were asked directly about their attitudes towards the inward-investment policy. Respondents were asked a direct

Table 5.11: Mean values and ranking of job creation rationales, by sector

Sector	Private	(Rank)	Public	(Rank)	Coop.	(Rank)	All	(Rank)
Compint	1.91	3	1.60	5	2.00	3=	1.84	3
Commwork	1.67	5	1.47	6	1.53	6	1.58	6
Livewage	2.17	2	2.53	1	2.19	2	2.31	1
Secure	2.28	1	2.03	2	2.25	1	2.19	2
Skill	1.62	6	2.00	3	1.83	5	1.76	5
Useful	1.83	4	1.72	4	2.00	3=	1.80	4

Note: Job rationale abbreviations as follows: Compint – Attracting competitive international companies; Commwork – Work that strengthens the community; Livewage – A job that pays a living wage; Secure – Creating jobs that offer long-term security; Skill – Creating jobs that require high levels of skill; Useful – The usefulness of the work itself.

Table 5.12: Number of respondents selecting each rationale from six, by employer sector

Sector	Private		Public		Coop.		All	
	N	%	N	%	N	%	N	%[a]
Commwork	51	61.4	34	51.5	19	63.3	104	57.1
Compint	22	26.5	10	15.2	5	16.6	37	20.3
Livewage	65	78.3	57	86.4	26	86.7	148	81.3
Secure	74	89.1	58	87.9	24	80.0	156	85.7
Skill	17	20.5	7	10.6	6	20.0	30	16.5
Useful	30	36.1	32	48.5	9	30.0	71	39.0
Total	83	312[b]	66	299.6	30	296.6	546	299.9

[a]The percentages are calculated as the number of those who chose the rationale in any of the first three positions as a proportion of all those who answered the question correctly.
[b]This number is slightly high (the column percentages should sum to 300), because a few respondents chose four rather than three responses.

question about the issues that are important when jobs are created. As outlined in Chapter 3, the emphasis of job-creation policies in the study area has been on attracting competitive international companies, on the assumption that the jobs they create will be secure. Considerations such as the rate of pay, the skill level of the jobs, and the contribution the employer may make to the local economy have carried less weight with policy-makers. The survey provided an opportunity to ask the workers who have

**Table 5.13: Number of respondents selecting each rationale as first preference,
by employer sector**

Sector	Private		Public		Coop		All	
	N	%	N	%	N	%	N	%[a]
Commwork	8	9.6	4	6.7	3	10.7	15	8.8
Compint	7	8.4	2	3.3	2	7.1	11	6.4
Livewage	27	32.5	33	55.0	10	35.7	70	40.1
Secure	33	39.8	13	21.7	9	32.1	55	32.2
Skill	1	1.2	2	3.3	1	3.2	4	2.3
Useful	7	8.4	6	10.0	3	10.7	16	9.4
Total	83	99.9	60	100.0	28	99.5	171	99.2

Note: [a]The numbers here relate to slightly fewer cases than in the previous table, because of the absence of first preferences in the cases of respondents who only ticked three boxes but were still kept in the sample (as explained in n. 2).

to undertake the jobs that are created whether their priorities are reflected in recent employment-creation policies implemented in the area.

Data for this part of the analysis are drawn from one question in the survey that asked respondents to choose their three most important job-creation rationales (from a list of six) and to rank these. The means of the responses, with three points given for a first preference, two for a second preference, and one for a third preference, are presented in table 5.11. It is clear from the table that the most important factors in job creation for workers in RCT are that the work pays a living wage and that the jobs are secure: the means for these responses are clearly larger than for other factors, although the public-sector workers place more importance on wages rather than security. These preferences are not reflected in policy-making, which has been primarily based on attracting foreign companies which often remain for a very short time and whose rationale for choosing Wales always includes the lower wage levels there than in others parts of the UK. For the private-sector and cooperative workers the next highest mean is for attracting competitive international companies, whereas public-sector workers are more concerned with the skill levels of the jobs.

Table 5.12 indicates the number and percentage of respondents in each sector and overall who chose each rationale for employment creation. This offers a slightly different perspective. Again, the need for security and a living wage are the rationales selected most often by all groups. However, the third most commonly chosen rationale for all groups is the role of the employment in strengthening the community. This is an aspect of job creation that is rarely considered by policy-makers, and yet is clearly of significance to Valleys workers. It is also interesting that the emphasis placed on attracting competitive international companies by policy-makers is not reflected in workers' priorities. Only 20.3 per cent of workers overall chose this as one of their three most important guiding factors in job creation. For all groups 'the usefulness of the work itself' is chosen by more workers, particularly in the case of public-sector workers, 48.5 per cent of whom chose this rationale.

Finally, table 5.13 indicates the first-choice rationale for employment creation chosen by the workers in the various sectors. The general pattern is similar, with the overwhelming preference being given to a living wage and job security, but the extra preference placed on a reasonable income by those in the public sector is apparent: 55 per cent of the respondents in that sector chose 'a living wage' as their most important rationale in job creation. Correspondingly more emphasis was placed on job security by workers in the other sectors. This may simply reflect workers' favouring that feature of employment that is less strong in the sector in which they currently find themselves. This finding was confirmed during the interviewing stage of the research project. The general attitude towards companies investing from overseas was summed up by a surface worker at Tower who said: 'If they're here for a long time and they give us a good living wage then all well and good', confirming the importance of job security and a living wage in local people's priorities for job-creation policies.

The other interesting conclusion from the table is the confirmation of the relatively low level of importance accorded to the attraction of competitive international companies. For all groups more people chose the role of work in strengthening the community as a first preference, and the usefulness of the work also attracted the same or more first preferences than this rationale that is such a driving force of existing job-creation policy-making. A final point worth noting is the tiny proportion who consider the skill level of the work the most important factor in job creation.

JOB CREATION IN A DEMOCRATIC SYSTEM

An important first point that should not be overlooked is the confirmation provided by the results of the high degree of sex segregation of occupations in Rhondda Cynon Taff. This is a fundamental factor that needs to be borne in mind not only in interpreting the results of this survey, but also when devising job-creation policies for the area. The survey also revealed the expected pattern of disparity in earnings, with the highest levels of pay received by miners at the colliery. This is another important piece of information for policy-makers. Since the closure of the pits occurred relatively recently, many in the area are used to the sorts of levels of pay currently enjoyed by miners at Tower (in the range of £20,000). This explains their reluctance to accept the sorts of jobs that are being created in the enterprise parks, where the wages might be half that amount. In the case of this survey even the skilled workers at the engineering company – a firm attracted to the area by the lower costs of operation and so also technically an inward investment company – earn less than the manual workers at Tower.

In terms of job satisfaction the highest levels were found amongst the workers in hospitals, and amongst women: clearly these two sources of satisfaction cannot be isolated when gender segregation is so strong. However, a significant difference emerged in terms of satisfaction with pay and with job security that was not entirely dependent on gender: in all cases private-sector workers were least satisfied, followed by public-sector workers, with workers at the cooperative showing the highest levels of satisfaction. That this type of workplace structure generates a high level of employment satisfaction is also related to the culture of the area (as discussed in Chapter 4) and its political history. These issues are explored further in the case study of Tower presented in Chapter 7, and might also influence the decisions of policy-makers about what sorts of jobs to subsidize in the future in the area.

In terms of their assessment of the social worth of different occupations, workers in RCT are in agreement in favouring caring and practical forms of employment over the role of an 'executive'. This universal and unexpected finding should ring alarm bells amongst policy-makers who enter the area with an entirely different concept of who is most valuable to society. The sorts of jobs most frequently created – in factories – are considered of average social worth, but do not rank high in local workers' preferences, perhaps because they are not considered to pay well – accurately, as is shown by the actual figures for pay reported above – as well as because of the routine nature of the work and the high levels of monitoring, a point that was made repeatedly in the interview transcripts reported in the next chapter. The most popular jobs, both in terms of personal preferences and subjective evaluation, are those in caring roles in the public sector, which might suggest that investing money in such forms of employment might be a more popular policy, as well as tackling RCT's poor levels of health, which in themselves operate to undermine other employment-creation programmes.

In terms of the findings relating directly to priorities for job creation, we have evidence that employment-creation policies are not responding to the priorities of local people. Given the history of RCT it can hardly come as a surprise that local workers are most concerned with pay rates and job security. However, these issues are not of paramount concern to job creators. As Chapter 3 demonstrated, few of the incoming companies offer either living wages or job security. Once these are guaranteed, local people would rather have useful work that strengthens the community, although this does not feature in the policy-makers' priority list at all, and their interest in competitive international companies is limited. These attitudes are explored in more depth in the following chapter, where the constriction of the questionnaire is abandoned, leaving respondents to discuss employment policy in their own words.

It is clear from these results that the valuation of work in RCT is based as much in the past as in the present. The industrial jobs that have gone were valued not only because they paid well, but because they engendered pride, especially pride for the male, physical worker. In an exploration of low-paid work in modern Britain, Polly Toynbee describes these 'old "heroic" jobs of the old days' where pay was:

> Well above the national average for occupations and professions and that pay gave them the status of worker-kings. It made the jobs desirable despite the hard conditions that showed on every melting-shop man's face, pitted with black marks from the spitting metal branded deep into their skin . . . it was money and industrial power that conferred pride: money and power are what counts, as every rich man knows. (Toynbee, 2003: 224)

If she is right, then the workers of RCT have lost any hope of pride in these days of poor pay and Japanese factory work practices. Tax credits are no substitute for acceptable wages; rather they draw attention to a person's inadequacy in not being able to earn a living wage by their own efforts. Toynbee also points out that 'without WFTC employers would have to put up wages until they made it worth people's while to go back to work'. This is the layman's statement of the obvious fact that an economist might refer to as a failure of incentives. Workers' loss of power is the other side of this coin. The following two chapters explore local workers' political perspective on the changes in the local employment situation over the past twenty years. Their political weakness is manifested not only in their poor rates of pay and standard of living but also in their marginalization from debate about the future of their labour market.

The data presented here offer some pointers towards the kinds of work that are valued by the workforce in RCT. The most striking conclusion to be drawn is that this research is, by itself, wholly inadequate and needs to be supplemented by thorough and wide-ranging research into what are the preferences and attitudes of local workers in RCT and in other areas. To refuse to conduct such research is a tacit admission on the part of policy-makers that they have no interest in the job satisfaction of people in economically depressed areas, whom they perceive as troublesome blips in labour-market statistics that need to be smoothed away by a combination of statistical manipulation and shunting from one unpopular and demoralizing employment situation to another. Or perhaps that they would rather not open a debate about the way that public money is used to distort the labour market.

Taking a longer-term approach to employment policy, and one that was committed to addressing genuine local needs, would require as a first step a thorough exploration of the preferences and attitudes of local people, along the lines of the very preliminary work presented here. But, more importantly, we should establish our right to find answers to these questions, and to have our employment preferences as workers taken seriously by policy-makers. It is our money that is spent on creating jobs, good or bad, and it is therefore our right, and the right of the people of RCT, to have jobs that we choose, not those that are chosen to suit the profit-drive of global corporations.

6

Instrument of Virtue or Secret Happiness? Local Views of the Economy

> Much writing about work is deficient because it expresses the external view of a comfortably placed observer, with an eye for the picturesque and a taste for the sight of the human body under strain.
>
> Keith Thomas in *The Oxford Book of Work*

Chapter 5 presented a statistical analysis of responses to a structured questionnaire seeking pre-defined information. Such questionnaires are always subject to the prejudices of those who draw them up, so to supplement this data with the perspectives of local people themselves I also carried out a series of unstructured interviews. In most cases the respondents were happy to talk about their experiences of work around a series of themes that I suggested. The amount of structuring that took place depended on their willingness to direct the discussion themselves, but it is fair to say that this chapter presents genuine views of local workers.

ECONOMIC SOCIOLOGY AND WORK

It is a cliché amongst critics of economists that they are not terribly interested in people. As a discipline economics deals rather in abstract concepts, in tidy diagrams where straight lines cross each other at the expected point. Data that may have at one stage been contaminated by the complexity of real human lives have been cleaned and ordered long before they are entered into econometrics packages. There is some truth in these accusations. A combination of a desire to arrive at unassailable scientific conclusions and a recognition of the mismatch between statistical analysis and everyday life has led to economics becoming one of the most ivory-tower-bound of all the disciplines. This is a status which is particularly inappropriate for a science which, given that its subject matter is the resource exchanges between people, is pre-eminently a social science, however its central actors might like to portray themselves. However, it would be unfair to suggest that economists do not care about people and the economic problems they face. The acres of pages in academic journals addressing the problems of unemployment and employment policies referenced at the end of this book testify to economists' concern for the central issues I am addressing.

Perhaps the Post-Autistic Economics Society, recently established by disillusioned young economists in Paris, is closer to the mark. Economists are not indifferent to the major economic problems of our world; rather, perhaps they are not well equipped to make connections and to communicate their findings. In the case of the subject of employment policy, the most important connection that needs to be made is between economics and the related social science disciplines of sociology and anthropology. The field of economic sociology has made great headway in bridging this divide, both by prioritizing people and their behaviour in its study of economic issues, and in using the methods and approaches of sociology (see Swedberg's *Economic Sociology*, 1996). Since to the lay reader it is blindingly obvious that one cannot consider employment without understanding the people who are working, their relationships with each other and the social structures they have experienced and developed, we may conclude that the rigid structure of academic disciplines within universities is the culprit here. In developing employment policies we need to overcome these divisions and deal with the people and the situations as we find them.

The recent increased interest in economic sociology suggests there is movement in this direction within academia (Trigilia, 2002; Woolsey Biggart, 2002). However, the dicussion surrounding the issue of 'embedding' foreign-owned companies into the Welsh economy demonstrates the inability of economists to take the social context properly into account. All the theorists base their thinking on Granovetter's (1985) paper, which has become a classic of economic sociology. Huggins (2001) echoes Granovetter's identification of the fact that 'economic action cannot be isolated from the social relationships, conventions, rules, habits and norms within which the individuals involved in such action are positioned', which is an understanding central to this book. However, Huggins himself, and the authors he cites in support of his position (Amin and Thrift, 1994; Pavlinek and Smith, 1998), immediately remove everything sociological from their study by 'narrowing this definition to the particular case of the economic action of inward investment' and then claiming that 'embeddedness can be said to revolve around the integration of such investment into local and regional economies'.

A similar study by Phelps et al. (2003) again begins by discussing the importance of 'embedding', which the authors define as relating to 'the social conventions and norms that serve to frame economic action'. But the features that they actually study only include corporate status and functions, R&D, the supply chain, skill levels, and the possibility of repeat investment. Thus an interesting departure in the field of economic sociology, which might suggest a focus on issues such as the relationships between investors and employees, the clash of cultures, or the reaction of Valleys people to the jobs created, has been cut down to a dry study of institutions, primarily the training institutions with which academics feel most comfortable.

There are also notable examples of researchers who have followed a similar path and generated useful results. Truman Bewley of Yale University interviewed local workers when trying to understand the reasons for the failure of the labour market of Connecticut to clear during a time of economic recession. Bewley (1995) states the questions that drove his decision to undertake ethnographic research into a local labour market as follows:

> Unemployment is extremely difficult to reconcile with the main body of economic theory. Why is the labor market so different from other markets in that the price of labour does not adjust to clear it? Why do not workers and companies avoid layoffs by having workers continue to work at reduced wages until adverse conditions disappear . . . If labor markets do clear, then why during recessions does one meet or hear of so many very unhappy unemployed people? (Bewley, 1995: 250)

He admits that 'In doing the survey, I violated many of the implicit rules of economic research', but justifies his decision to do so on the grounds that 'it is possible to learn the answers to the questions posed only by violating those rules'. Qualitative interview-based research has also been used to increase the depth of analysis of a research project into the intra-household distribution of income (see Pahl, 1989).

I share Bewley's interest in the motivations of workers, and, while his long research record in the field of econometric analysis indicates his commitment to that methodology, he felt that some questions, particularly those concerning human behaviour, could only be answered by a more direct approach to those who were exhibiting the behaviour, that is, the participants in the labour market. Bewley made discoveries which were unexpected, and which provided useful information about the real functioning of labour markets. He identified that it was the employers, rather than the employees, who were unwilling to cut wages, and that the reason they were inflexible in this regard was to do with how wage-cutting and laying off workers might be perceived by current and future em-ployees. Employers wanted to foster a positive public image and a positive spirit amongst workers; pay cuts would undermine this and reduce worker morale.

The use of such an ethnographic, human-scale method in a field where it has been used only rarely may yield particularly valuable insights, as James (1998) discusses in terms of her decision to base her (1996) thesis on interview research in another field where it has rarely been used: that of international relations. In terms of a research study that aims to contribute to developing employment policy in a specific area such a novel method may be especially valuable. According to an economic development officer I spoke to during my research,

> The only way that we are going to make anything work in the long term and give it sustainability is by getting ownership by local people. Again they have even more of a vital role to play in making it work and making it happen than the council or the WDA, or the tec, or the Assembly or all of us thrown in together.

If this is true then a necessary first step in policy-making must be to ascertain the views of the 'local people' referred to.

While the insights gained from in-depth interviewing are of great interest they face severe methodological limitations in terms of the extent to which they can be generalized because their internal and external representativeness are both limited. In terms of this research, internal representativeness is limited by the very small size of the sample, and the fact that it includes a large number of workers from the mining sector. However, although this sector only employs a small number of local workers today, the attitudes and culture of miners and ex-miners are important for policy-makers, since these people represent the bulk of the unemployed and economically inactive (see details in Chapter 2).

The demographic details of the whole sample of interviewees are presented in table 6.1, which indicates the age, sex and sector of each person I spoke to (most of the ages are estimates). The 'No.' column indicates how many respondents were present at the interview, since in one case I spoke to two safety workers together and thirty of the respondents were members of three, hour-long focus groups. The average length of the other interviews was twenty minutes. The interviews were mostly conducted in person at the respondent's workplace, although some were conducted by telephone. All interviews were tape-recorded and later transcribed; the transcriptions are available as an appendix to Cato (2000b). Respondents are drawn from across genders, age groups, sectors, income levels and occupations, but it is obvious that many perspectives are not represented. It is therefore not possible to conclude with certainty that the views expressed represent the general view of the RCT community.

In terms of external representativeness the applicability of the insights gleaned in connection with employment policy-making are also limited.

Table 6.1: Demographic details of the interview sample

Occupation	Sex	Age	Sector	No.
Human resources manager	F	c.40	Private	1
Contract electrician	M	c.55	Private	1
Careers officer	F	c.40	Non-profit	1
Careers officer	M	c.25	Non-profit	1
Shopkeeper	F	58	Private	1
Auxiliary nurse	F	c.50	Public	1
Charity shop manager	F	c.30	Non-profit	1
Tourist guide	M	53	Private	1
Mines Rescue Service	M	c.45	Non-profit	2
Miner	M	c.30	Cooperative	1
Colliery environmental officer	M	c.50	Cooperative	1
Colliery fitter	M	55	Cooperative	1
Marketing manager	M	c.50	Cooperative	1
Manager	M	c.55	Cooperative	1
Matron-manager	F	c.60	Private	1
Economic development officer	F	c.30	Public	1
Technicians, administrators and engineers	Both	25–55	Private	30
Total				47

Rhondda Cynon Taff is a highly specific local labour market with a unique employment history, as outlined in Chapter 2. For this reason the tentative conclusions drawn throughout this chapter cannot be freely generalized to other employment situations.

The following sections present the views of local people in Rhondda Cynon Taff on a range of issues relevant to policy-making: their general views of the local economy; an appraisal of the inward-investment strategy that has been the focus of recent employment policy-making; an insight into the perception of supply-side labour-market policies; in view of the discussion of the failure of entrepreneurship in Wales, the following section presents the views of the interviewees about this important subject; while the next two sections explore the issue of work motivations; and, finally, local people's views about the various leakages from the RCT economy, particularly into the informal economy.

GENERAL VIEWS OF THE LOCAL ECONOMY

The lack of confidence in the future of the Valleys economy was clear in nearly every interview: most of the people I spoke to were severely demoralized and several made the same joke when I asked them about the future of work in the area: 'There isn't one.' The repeated blows to the local economy over the past half-century have had a powerful impact on local levels of self-confidence, and have created a 'helplessness' that was identified as the central problem facing the local economy by many respondents. One cynical respondent expressed his demoralization in the following terms:

> What's the word you use for these kinds of areas? – The word I use is Third World economy areas, but I think what you'd say is 'deprivation areas', where employment has gone from previously industrial bases and is taken over by either service industries or electronics or other types of product who want to sell into Europe but don't want the commitment of joining the Common Market.

Many identified this demoralization directly with the policies of the Thatcher years and this respondent's identification of the area as 'Third World' was not unique. Another respondent, one of the Tower management team who had worked as a miner himself during the years preceding the miners' strike, judged that 'the Conservatives believed that to compete with the Third World you've got to have Third World wages here'. Another member of the Tower board gave a depressing assessment of the legacy of the Thatcherite period in south Wales:

> the damage they done wasn't closing coal mines, the damage they done was ruining communities . . . In that period they destroyed the moral fibre of people working here. It was getting to the stage where there was no hope, because everything you'd done was ending up in failure. And because of the political situation in south Wales I suppose we were bound to be a target. They weren't going to lose many seats whatever they done to us in south Wales. So I suppose it does have a bearing on their decisions.

Regardless of the accuracy or otherwise of this political assessment, this quotation sums up the perception of some Valleys workers that they are the target of economic policies. In this context, any government initiative, even from a Labour government, is going to be met with hostility and resistance. Overcoming this sense of alienation must play a fundamental part in the development of a new employment policy in the Valleys.

The economic ideology of competition that characterized this period was also considered to have had a negative impact, causing a retrenchment that made introducing any change difficult. According to a Tower respondent:

> We have had a major influence in the valley. I think one of the major things what Tower done at that period of time, I don't know if it's still out there, I

don't know. But I think a lot of working-class people in Wales had dug in the trenches. They were in the trenches after eighteen, nineteen years of Conservatism. The desolation. And I think what we done was we made them put their heads up over the trenches. There was a feeling there. And I'm hoping that we did achieve that, and I think we did, and I'm hoping it's going to go on from there. Not just us. I've heard tons of bloody stories about how confident the boys are compared to how they were under British Coal when they had no knowledge of how the colliery was run: there was them and there was us.

The economic development officer I spoke to considered that the competitive ideology of the economic policy of that time had caused divisions within the bodies responsible for economic planning and made it difficult for them to work in partnership:

There's also a huge task in breaking down cultures and breaking down barriers and getting people to work together in a far more coordinated way. There has been moves over the last five years, but we still have territory, blinkered approaches, blockages. We still haven't yet recovered from the competition element that we were thrust down in the Thatcher years. That is still rife. Everyone is in competition with everyone else. It's going to take a long time to overcome that as well . . . Instead of win–lose, which is the competition state, we need win–win. And there's got to be a middle ground somewhere.

One central feature of the modern economy met with general disapproval amongst respondents: globalization. Most respondents accepted that the globalization of the economy could not be reversed, but they were very pessimistic about the opportunities for them in such an economy, a view summed up by one respondent who said: 'Going global has ruined it all.' Another offered a more critical analysis:

It's a strange old world, though, isn't it? They've got these mines abroad where they're digging into these sensitive minerals and things, radioactive stuff. I've seen photographs of the mines where they work, in their bare feet with loin cloths, digging this stuff out. And yet they're paying them some ridiculous amount of money. I can understand a capitalist taking it on board and saying 'Yeah, that's great, why not? Why should I dig coal in a coal mine where I've got to pay a man all that money when I can get somebody for a bowl of rice and a bar of soap and a tube of toothpaste?'

One respondent, the head of the union at Tower Colliery, proposed the renationalization of the 'basic resources' (water, gas, oil and coal) since these 'should be owned by the nation', although he acknowledged that this was now an 'old-fashioned view'. He expanded this point by saying that 'The making of cars and the making of bloody toy factories and balloon factories, I suppose that's all well and good in private hands. But once you've got the main resources of the country in private hands you could have serious difficulties.'

The importance of local commitment to economic strategies was identified by the economic development officer I spoke to who said: 'It's easy to bring in a consultant or an expert to say you could do this, that, that, or that, but they're not going to make it work.' However, gaining popular support is going to be difficult, particularly given the cynicism about any employment policy as expressed by respondents earlier. Several respondents, though, expressed support for the Welsh Assembly, which was in the process of being established. At that time this body had a relatively high level of regard that could have been used to gain support for its employment policies, particularly if these are seen to be authentic Welsh economic models, as discussed in Chapter 8. One of the Tower managers I spoke to said: 'There's a lot of people like myself who believe that the Assembly gives us hope. And we believe, a bit like Tower, that we'll have control of our own destiny a bit more than we've had in the last twenty years or so.' This same respondent developed his point further:

> I want people to end up in it with the belief that they are working for the people of Wales and for the benefit of Wales. I'd be a very disappointed person if a Labour-controlled Assembly in Wales stopped doing some of the things that the people in Wales wanted to do, which could be afforded, because Mr Blair or somebody says 'We don't like you doing that.' I don't think there should be a complete cut-off but the Assembly should be close enough to us folks to know what the people want. I would hope that every single member, no matter what area of Wales they're from, they feel what their community needs.[1]

A survey conducted by RCT as a basis for the drawing up of a five-year strategic plan had yielded interesting results about the priorities of local citizens. The first priority was employment, but the second was the environment, including visual enhancement and improvement of the housing stock: employment policies would fail, they reasoned, if the local area was not pleasant to live in and adequately equipped. This was a surprise to the local councillors, who would have put social services and education higher up their priority lists, according to the economic development officer I spoke to. She agreed with a manager from Tower Colliery who viewed the environment of the Valleys as an important economic asset and suggested that tourism might play an important role in the local economy in the future.

ASSESSMENT OF THE INWARD-INVESTMENT STRATEGY

As identified in the survey results presented in the previous chapter, local workers' foremost concern was that the jobs created by inward investors pay 'a living wage' and that they are secure. The role of work in strengthening the community was considered more important than the attraction of competitive international companies, which has been the priority with economic planners in the area. The results of the interviews confirm these views. Most of the respondents were ambivalent about the benefits of the inward-investment strategy for job creation pursued in recent years, an ambivalence summed up in the view of the nurse I spoke with who said: 'I'd just rather keep Britain British and the only good thing about it of course is putting people into employment.' I interviewed two members of the Mines Rescue Service together and they neatly summarized the debate. When asked whether he thought inward investment was a good way of taking the economy forward one said: 'Yeah, I do, because it's a skilled employer employing British people in them', while they other said: 'Any work is good, like, but they would rather invest in foreign people than our own people I think.'

The first response to inward investment is positive, in that at least some jobs are being created in an area where such vast numbers of jobs have been lost. In the words of a human resources manager of one company attracted to the area from elsewhere in the UK:

> I think it has to be good for the area because there's such a big hole left from the old coal and manufacturing base that's gone. So it has to be good. I think it's good that they've concentrated on it because they have to have something to replace it.

However, the economic development officer I spoke to was more realistic about the inward-investment policy, and critical of what was promised that could not be fulfilled:

> It's the quick fix isn't it? It's this short-termism all the time that we've been brought up with through the eighties and nineties. 'This is a new initiative. We're going to go for this, we're going to go for that, and that will solve the problems overnight.' But it's not. We must take a longer-term view of it.

Other respondents were sceptical about the commitment to the long-term future of the south Wales economy of foreign-based companies, several mentioning examples of companies coming to the area, receiving grants and then reducing staff numbers or closing down altogether. This had further reduced morale and undermined local workers' faith in inward investment as a solution to their employment problems. An extreme statement of this view was expressed by one miner: 'The multinational companies will milk the system. If the system is there to be milked, they'll milk it for the benefit of their shareholders of course, that being the way of the world today.'

The lack of control over such 'foreign' companies was also identified as a problem:

> I think the danger is with those multinationals that are outside the European Community, where we could never really have had any control over their movements. It was quite obvious to me that they could come in very quickly, with massive subsidies, but they could just as easily leave very quickly . . . I think possibly at the time it originated: in the eighties or seventies – when these things first started – and we had Panasonic and some others at that time. And of course LG was mooted three or four years ago, and the enthusiasm was still there at the time. But I think people are starting to realize now that those companies (with the experience of LG) that they can go as quickly as they came. (Careers manager)

She was also aware of the threat posed by competition from cheaper but equally skilled labour in eastern Europe and Asia, as identified in Chapter 3.

Another criticism of inward investors' contribution to the local economy, their low level of local sourcing, was also identified:

> The very big projects – like the Bosch and the LGs of this world, and the Sonys – do take a very long time to be integrated into the local economy and to have all their sourcing and supplying locally. They take a long time to embed. It's only now, twenty-five years later, that an awful lot of companies supply Sony locally. Bosch still, when they first moved into Junction 34 [of the M4], were importing 98 per cent of their materials for production and they're still importing about 80 per cent. And they've been there quite a few years now. The main purpose of attracting inward investment into this area is not just to mop up the unemployment and to give people jobs, but it's also to revive the other supply industries in the area. That takes a lot longer to achieve than overnight.

However, this local authority employee, who is closely involved in implementing the inward-investment strategy, suggested that part of the reason was the poor quality of components supplied locally.

There was scepticism about the number of jobs created by these policies. One senior technician at Engineeringco. described his disbelief for the jobs totals claimed by the development agencies: 'Whenever you see those figures for the number of jobs you cut them straight in half.' The quality of jobs in the foreign-based companies was also criticized, with most respondents feeling that wages were too low, and in fact that that was the reason the area was attractive to such companies: 'There's one reason they come here: cheap wages', said an engineer at Engineeringco. The following comment represented the most negative view of inward investment, one which was held by a significant minority of the interviewees:

> Whenever you dangle a carrot you can have somebody trying to bite it. But whether they are genuine people and whether they are in it for their own personal reasons, to grab a chunk of the carrot and then disappear after a couple of years, or whether it's a long-term thing. It's all about how honourable these people are.

Most respondents agreed that there was too much emphasis on attracting inward investors relative to the effort invested in local businesses. A Tower worker agreed with this view and felt it unfair that the colliery had been unable to obtain grants while Japanese companies could:

> It's all well and good, but they should also make sure that they protect local-based companies and locally owned companies like ourselves – indigenous. They seem to forget about people like us. I mean they'll pay Sony or LG or Hitachi or any of them people vast amounts of money to attract them here and make sure they'll stay here. They've just paid BMW now God knows what amount to make sure those jobs remain. If this company was under severe financial difficulties they wouldn't do the same for us.

A member of the Tower board agreed with this comment and expressed his hope that these economic priorities would change under the economic direction of the Welsh Assembly.

The local perception of inward investment as a job-creation policy tallies with that provided by academic commentators and outlined in Chapter 3. It includes three main aspects. First there is a widespread scepticism about the number of jobs created and the commitment of the employers. Secondly, local people are concerned about the poor quality of the jobs that are on offer, and the low rates of pay that are offered in return for them. Finally, there is a general conviction that local entrepreneurs are not given the support they need.

ACTIVE LABOUR-MARKET POLICIES

Alongside the demand-side policy of attracting inward investors to create employment opportunities, policies have been implemented with the aim of strengthening the supply side of the labour market by using 'active labour-market policies' and improving the level of local human capital via training schemes. For a local economy where jobs with a single employer and for life had been the pattern for generations (whether in a colliery or the public sector) adjusting to the rapidly changing nature of the modern labour market has proved one of the most important challenges facing policy-makers:

> that is another area where the lifelong learning agenda is going to have a big impact. That needs to concentrate on not just learning as in school, or doing your training course, but that you are continually learning and training so that you can cope, then, with sudden changes in your career pattern. Instead of working for a local authority all your life we're very much moving to the American model where every ten years there may be a drastic change, a completely different direction, and people need to be continually trained and developed ready to cope with those things. (Economic development officer)

This is an ideal view, but the careers officers were aware that training opportunities were limited: one identified the Modern Apprenticeships as improving the likelihood of employment but admitted that 'there hasn't been a lot of training around here. I'd say it's declined over the last six or seven years.' This is on top of the decline in skill levels that followed the closure of the collieries, which were acknowledged to train workers to a high level of skills, for example as electricians. The careers officer went on to say that 'the training market's been cut back so much. Last summer we had practically no training to offer.' His colleague described the situation as follows:

> One of the problems we've got in RCT, specifically in Pontypridd, actually, Rhondda's slightly better placed, is lack of training provision, the traditional route for education leavers to go into . . . In Pontypridd the training provision is little or zero. We're in a very bad position. So the word among young people gets out on the street: if they haven't got the training why go in?

Given that the careers officer quoted earlier is actually based in the Rhondda, their two contributions provide a gloomy view of the training situation in RCT.

The role of the New Deal was also questionable. A careers officer said about one local engineering employer who had recently reduced staff numbers: 'I've met someone who works there, and he said perhaps the people they took on were from schemes like the New Deal and they might not have the skills to cope with the work.' If such active labour-market policies are to have credibility with the unemployed and with employers it is clearly essential that the skills provided are of a sufficiently high standard.

Other respondents were more sceptical about the New Deal and other government training schemes. One respondent, who had herself worked as a trainer on government schemes, said: 'All these training tecs are a con; they're a great big government con.' Another, an ex-miner, had participated on a nineteen-week New Deal training course of which only three days actually consisted of training. For the other eighteen weeks the course administrators were unsuccessfully trying to find him a job. The respondent's reaction was that it was 'Excellent training, but the back-up to find jobs after was absolute rubbish'. This account also raises the suspicion amongst local people that the New Deal may be as much about massaging unemployment figures as providing the unemployed with skills.

The level of skills required in the new electronics factories was generally considered to be low, which, contrary to one of the important aims of the inward-investment policy, may have actually reduced skill levels in the local economy. According to a human resources manager, whose job involves recruiting new staff from the electronics factories, including the one sampled in Chapter 5:

> If you're in Minitaki and you work on the assembly line they'll give you a City and Guilds in electronics, for example, but you don't actually need that to do the job. You could actually do the job quite happily without that. It's just 'take this component and put it there', and they show you what to do. So they give you skills training but they then give you something on top of that. But you don't actually need that to do the job, whereas in our place you actually need it to do the job. It's a higher-skilled job so you couldn't actually do it without that qualification. And the X industry won't let you do it without the qualification.

In spite of their possession of City and Guilds qualifications, applicants to Engineeringco from Minitaki would still enter at the lowest level, as if they had no qualifications.

> Well I would say that it does mean that the people who get trained at Minitaki but who do their qualifications, they would stand a chance of getting a job with us. Because we would take somebody with a year's experience at the lowest level of intake. We also do apprenticeship schemes and obviously we'll train people from scratch ourselves. So we'll take people with no qualifications but a year's experience, or with the basic City and Guilds. And we'll provide the career ladder. But, if you like, they're providing the experience below, for the intake to us. And there are a lot more companies coming into the area because of that skills base that's there.

So the role of the new electronics companies seems to be mixed. They do give their employees basic skills which make them more attractive to other employers who require higher-skilled employees. However, without the commitment to training of these other employees (both of those mentioned by this respondent were British-based), skill levels would decline further. This appears to confirm the suggestion in the literature about the 'international division of labour in electronics' (K. Morgan, 1987), contrasted with the need on the part of British companies to have employees at all levels of skill. The same respondent described how these companies also work with local colleges to ensure that young people are given the skills they, as employers, need.

As a conclusion to this section, three suggestions may be made about the effect of active labour-market policies in RCT. Firstly, the provision of training is inadequate, so that young people leaving school feel pessimistic about training opportunities and, linked to this problem, there is not sufficient commitment to training on the part of employers, which also contributes to the problem of low skills. Secondly, the inward-investment strategy may itself have undermined skill levels, since these employers do not require high levels of skills from their employees. Thirdly, the New Deal does not appear to have the confidence of the unemployed or employers.

OPPORTUNITIES FOR ENTREPRENEURSHIP

The evidence that there is a lack of confidence in the ability of Valleys people specifically to become entrepreneurs came clearly through the interviews. A careers officer pointed out that starting out in business was generally perceived as one person, say a plumber, working as an individual on single contracts. The only possibility for job creation was if he employed a mate, although most self-employed craftsmen would keep that position open for their sons: 'It is often meant to be a family thing.' The overall view of the prospects for creating sufficient jobs through this type of business was bleak. A careers officer told me:

> It isn't an answer for society totally because you can't have an area that is everybody dependent on self-employment. You've got to build the infrastructure, the medium-sized companies have got to be there. Britain's decline in that area has been so bad that we'll only meet the same problem again later if we don't do it now.

Her colleague in a related career centre made a similar point: 'It's not going to cure the numbers of unemployed. You're not going to get everyone doing it.' He felt that the answer lay instead with encouraging successful large employers into the area: 'Ideally you need big employers coming in . . . It's not a bad thing because at the end of the day people just want money. Enterprise has got to come later really.'

It is perhaps to be expected that those whose business is in findings jobs for people are not inclined to see self-employment as an effective job-creation strategy, but it may be discouraging for young people who approach them with this in mind. It may be that in some places official attitudes are working against the entrepreneurial strategy. These quotations also seem to suggest that the emphasis on the importance of large and especially foreign employers in job creation has undermined local people's self-confidence in their ability to generate enterprise themselves.

The cultural dimension

The point emerged repeatedly in the interviews, as in much anecdotal literature on entrepreneurship in Wales, that the Welsh national culture is simply unsuitable for creating successful entrepreneurs. The baldest statement of this folk wisdom came from a technician at Engineeringco. who said that 'The culture is not for our people to start their own business'. According to a human resources manager at the same company:

> I think it's to do with the Welsh psyche for the area. Because you've got people there who are third-generation unemployed, and there's never been an ethic of entrepreneurial skill there. Second, those people who are third-generation unemployed, their parents, the people who were employed, were promised a job for life in coal or government industries, coal or rail or steel or whatever. There's still the psyche there that the government owes them a living. That's taking a while to break down.

However, the same person pointed out that the success of Tower Colliery demonstrates that there is entrepreneurial energy in the area, although she qualified this by suggesting that part of the reason for its success there was the desire to prove they could do better than the former managers, and that 'a lot of it is talk'. One of the Tower managers I spoke to felt that the success of the cooperative had increased the self-confidence amongst local people in their own ability to succeed. As one manager expressed it:

> I don't know whether the coal is there, or whether the market's there, but Tower's not gonna close because we failed to work a head. It may fail because somebody says: 'We're not gonna have coal any more: we'll have nuclear energy and we'll have this and we'll have that': I've got no control over that. But the determination to have that control over your own destiny and to say it

won't fail because I've failed, I think that has fed into people's attitudes and where they're coming from.

The lack of confidence in the ability of native workers to be entrepreneurs was so great that one respondent, herself a careers officer from outside Wales, suggested that the only solution would be to bring enterprising people from outside into the area, attracting them with development grants:

> That's where you do need your entrepreneurial character to come along and say: 'There's a niche in the market: I'll go there.' But where do you attract them to? I imagine there's going to be some subsidies to attract people to the RCT area – part of the bid [for Objective 1 funding] is going to include that I'm sure. So the entrepreneurial characters may not be local, but the jobs will be.

By contrast, a local economic development officer found opportunities in the nature of the local culture, particularly in terms of the developing sector of e-commerce. She felt that this might overcome the innate 'fear and trepidation' of exporting and that the close-knit nature of local economic networks might suit the network-building that was the basis of internet commerce. However, she herself conceded that 'the competition model just won't work in those areas'.

Although not stated explicitly by many respondents, a sense emerged that the culture of south Wales is ambivalent about the role of money. One respondent said of her husband, a self-employed businessman: 'He wants to have money, he wants to make money, but at the same time there's an inner conflict if he makes money off the back of other people: it's wrong, as it were.' She admitted that she was similarly lacking in motivation to earn money, and that when she tried to run her own business she did not feel inclined to expand the business beyond the point of being able to draw as much in personal income as she had had when in employment.

The prime motivation for the self-employed appeared to be to guarantee jobs for themselves and to support their families, not to create expanding companies that could generate vast profits. This was true of the manager at Tower Colliery I spoke to, who stated that the priority was secure jobs rather than high pay rates (the full quotation is given in Chapter 7). The commitment to family and community is the motivating factor, not the opportunity to generate wealth. This was confirmed when I asked to which valley he was referring when he used the phrase 'my valley': 'It's the Cynon Valley. It isn't really my valley, but . . . I own part of it!'

A second Tower manager made a similar point in connection with the payment of dividends to the stakeholders at the end of the first year of cooperative ownership:

And in the first couple of years when dividends were paid people saw that as a boost. It's an extra. It's not the most important. Our commitment from the Tebo days was to form a company that would provide decent terms and conditions for as long as possible, and increase employment opportunities for young people.

A priority area for one (female) economic development officer was the encouragement of women to become entrepreneurs. She spoke enthusiastically about a network of Women into Business and the specialized training courses they run for potential female entrepreneurs. She considered that women could be more effective than men:

Interestingly the women who set up in business are far more viable in a long-term perspective than the men setting up in business. Because the women are more imaginative and then they listen and when they put their business plan together they stick to the business plan and follow it and evaluate it and rethink their strategies. Whereas men tend to say: 'I've done my business plan and I'm going to get on with running the business now', and they never look at it again. Whereas the women tend to use that as a valuable management tool.

One of the most successful female entrepreneurs in the sample was the manager of a health-food shop which had been 'a cracking small family business', but had been undermined by the growth in out-of-town shopping and the loss of trade in the high street of the small Valleys town where it was located:

Three years ago it changed overnight. They closed the electricity, they closed the gas [showrooms/shops], they opened Pioneer [Co-operative supermarket] and my turnover dropped one-third within a month. These shops brought people into town to spend their money in town. I'm not the only person . . . but a lot of traders find the same things.

One respondent, now employed as an auxiliary nurse having spent several years working in a factory, discussed her own decision not to start a business. She recalled that she had thought of opening a café at an out-of-town shopping centre. Although she felt the idea was a good one and that there was a market for her service she had not seen it as an opportunity to make money and was put off by the risk involved. She concluded that: 'I wouldn't really [want to start a business]. I don't think I'd like the headaches that go with it, and the stress you know? As it is now I can do my job, my pay's there at the end of the month, and that's it, and I'm quite happy.'

Supporting new businesses

Encouraging new business set-ups was considered of primary importance by the economic development officer I spoke to:

> the culture of expecting to work for somebody else and being told what to do needs to be changed. We need to encourage more self-employment, more companies to be born. The business birth rate is incredibly low in Wales compared to other parts of the UK, and compared to other parts of the world.

However, she admitted that support to small business, in terms of grants and training, had been inadequate in the past. She also felt that it was important to encourage those in employment to become self-employed, rather than targeting only the unemployed, who might have fewer skills to make a business successful. The limited provision currently available to small, new businesses in the area were small set-up grants, grants for training, and reduced rents on premises in units such as the Tonypandy and Treorchy Development Areas.

One respondent had previously had success in running a computer retail outlet which he set up by investing his redundancy money and had later sold to another retailer for a large profit. He was interested in setting up again but could find no support. In fact, rather than supporting small businesses, he felt that local authorities presented them with problems, since they employed contractors to carry out services such as house repairs but were slow payers and put pressure on the small businesses who had limited cash flow.

In terms of the development of entrepreneurial skills in the area opinion was again divided. The economic development officer was optimistic about the work of the Entrepreneurship Action Group, but the careers officers both felt that the funding for projects encouraging entrepreneurship in school was inadequate. The human resources manager I spoke to had been told by an RCT councillor that more money was spent on a one-day cricket match organized by the council than on the World of Work programme.

The issue of the size of enterprises that were eligible to receive development grants was very contentious amongst the respondents. It was agreed by the workers at Engineeringco that an annual turnover of £250,000 was the minimum that would allow a business to be considered eligible for development grants. The same point was made by the health-food-shop proprietor, who said that officials from the Welsh Development Agency had told her that 'We're only interested in things over a quarter of a million'. This lack of support had resulted in the loss of jobs to the area:

They've got to put more grants in the way of small businesses. They really have. I could have taken someone on three years ago, but I didn't because I would have been penalized with all these forms you've got to fill in and everything. I could well have taken someone on. And now with the manufacturing: I get this stuff made in the EU. And if we could get a grant we'd consider making it in Britain, but we can't.

The paperwork surrounding the provision of even the smallest levels of help was a general cause of complaint amongst those who had considered or tried self-employment.

There seemed to be agreement that a more constructive answer might be to encourage many small-scale enterprises, rather than a few large-scale ones. As a human resources manager, herself employed by a large company, said: 'I think that if you want to encourage entrepreneurship it would be brilliant to have millions of tiny little projects that could draw down £1,000 or whatever from the council.' The economic development officer concurred with this view, adding that:

It's redressing the balance really. I would prefer to see more support . . . if every small business in south-east Wales – the majority of small businesses employ twenty-five people or less, and about 80 to 85% of the businesses in south-east Wales employ twenty-five or less – if every one of those recruited one person each next year we wouldn't have an unemployment problem.

In conclusion to this section, what emerged from the interviews was that local people were not highly motivated by the desire to become rich or powerful, which drives many entrepreneurs. It was also generally perceived that there was a lack of historical and cultural experience of creating one's own opportunities, and this perception contributed to a low level of confidence in the ability of local people to create new businesses. However, there were several people in the sample who certainly showed entrepreneurial tendencies and they complained about the poor level of support, particularly for small businesses. The general feeling was that local people were not expected to succeed in business, and the policy of funding foreign companies must surely have contributed to this. The finding from the previous chapter that people were motivated more by guaranteeing their future employment and income security and supporting others in the community, rather than creating a high-growth, high-profit business was confirmed in the interview transcripts.

WORK MOTIVATIONS

The interview respondents cast an interesting light on the issue of work motivations. It became clear that money was by no means the only motivation towards work; in fact, as identified in the section on entrepreneurship, this lack of motivation towards accumulating wealth may account for the poor rate of business start-ups in south Wales. One respondent who had run her own business said: 'I haven't got the drive; I'm not motivated by money.'

However, this remark must be put in the context of the many other remarks that identified the importance of 'a living wage', which tended to mean a breadwinner or household wage of around £400 per week – a figure far higher than that earned by most respondents. The level of wage which is considered acceptable needs to support 'living' not just 'surviving', a distinction made by several interviewees. As one expressed it:

> The thing is when you come home then, and you haven't got enough money to go for a pint or buy a packet of fags, or whatever, and you have worked hard, then you think, 'Well, has it been worth it?' You turn round and you just say to yourself, 'Is it really worth it?'

Many respondents complained about the low level of wages in RCT and surrounding areas, particularly in the factories. One respondent complained that his wife, who was an experienced solderer who 'can do any job in the factory', was still only earning £115 per week.

As identified in the previous chapter, the most satisfied workers in the survey sample were the miners at Tower Colliery. To some extent this may reflect the greater work commitment associated with being a stakeholder, and the fact that they were the best-paid workers in the sample (see table 5.2). However, many interview respondents who had been miners agreed that it was the best type of work and would gladly return to it given the chance. This attitude was typified by the Engineeringco. technician who said: 'If there was a job at Margam [the new pit planned by the Tower cooperative] I'd go back tomorrow.'

When I sought to pin down what it was about the apparently unpleasant and dangerous work of mining that made it so attractive the response was almost invariably 'the camaraderie'. This 'camaraderie', which is a term used frequently in the context of mining, appeared to have three important features: the male banter, the absence of strict monitoring, and the trust that grew out of shared danger. Other respondents explained the appeal of mining by contrasting it to other work they had undertaken, particularly in factories. The constant visibility and monitoring of the factory system was unacceptable to many ex-miners, who had been relatively free to make their own decisions, particularly when working 'underground'. As one miner who had also worked in a factory put it: 'as long as you get the job done by a certain time you're left alone, basically. You can carry on.' The monotony of factory work was also identified by several respondents, as one Tower Colliery employee put it, describing factory work he did not have personal experience of: 'I couldn't work under that regime. It's repetitive isn't it? It's like you're on a conveyor. You're just like bloody robots working there.'

Interestingly, a similar point was made by the matron-manager of a small local nursing home. She identified the superior rewards from working in a small team compared to the large public hospital environment, saying that the satisfaction 'comes home very much quicker to you because there are not so many other people involved . . . therefore there's the ownership; there's the pride in the service you give.' She gave the example of nurses who had left posts as ward sisters in the NHS to work in her nursing home because the non-monetary rewards were higher, although they took reductions in salary.

The lack of trust between workers in a factory setting was also contrasted with the necessarily supportive nature of colliery work. The mines–factory distinction was characterized as comradeship versus 'a dog-eat-dog world', or more generally: 'in the Mines Rescue Service it's more family-orientated. In Sony it's a more strict regime. You have to be there at a certain time, you have to do certain work, no giving and taking anywhere.' An unemployed respondent who had tried self-employment, factory work and mining described his negative experience in the factory:

> I just couldn't stick it. The backbiting and the bitchiness that was going on there it was incredible. You know everybody's looking after No. 1. Now when you was underground everybody looked after each other. You may hate them, hate the person, but you made sure that he was gonna be safe, and if you needed a hand everybody would muck in and give a hand and there was no problems with that.

I interviewed two workers in the caring sector – an auxiliary nurse and the matron of a private-sector nursing home – and one worker in the voluntary sector – the manager of a charity shop. The two caring-sector workers agreed that vocation was an important motivation towards this kind of employment. The nurse, who had spent a long period working in a factory, called her desire to start a nursing career 'a burning ambition', which she managed to achieve after her children started school. She explained her vocation for nursing: 'I just felt that I wanted to help others, you know. And probably more unfortunate than yourself.' She was the most contented worker I spoke to, claiming that she loved her job and that 'I'm very happy. I've got 99 per cent job satisfaction.'

This nurse's prior experience of factory work enabled her to make an interesting comparison between the two types of work in terms of motivation and job satisfaction. She made it clear that her only reason for taking factory work was the money and that it was 'very tedious monotonous work . . . but at the end of the day I was there for the money. I never had no job satisfaction at all.' Although having no personal experience of factory work in the foreign-owned companies she thought that they had a different attitude towards their employees, what she referred to as 'very positive attitudes', meaning that 'they sit alongside you working', which she felt she could not cope with. She had friends who worked in these factories and felt that after a period of adjustment to the different work culture they were fine.

The nursing-home matron-manager was determined to make a distinction between two different motivations on the part of female care workers between those who 'do it as a second income, or come into it when they have had their children' and so need less income than a single earner, and those who 'are training and ultimately take it up as a career'. This distinction seems to mirror that found by Hakim (1996) amongst women in general, and the auxiliary nurse I spoke to certainly seemed to conform to the description of somebody who is motivated towards nursing but has to wait until money is less of an issue so that she can take it up.

When discussing motivations towards nursing the matron-manager brushed aside the issue of vocation, as if it were to be taken for granted. When directly asked: 'Why do you think it is that women are attracted to nursing?', she replied: 'Apart from the obvious down the road of being caring and all the other female issues and the vocational issues, all of those aside', and continued with a discussion of the career–second income distinction discussed above. This response dismisses the importance of vocation and assumes that 'caring' is a natural female skill, in much the same way as the wage-setting structure assumes away these motivations and skills, and consequently fails to reward them (see England, 1984). When pressed further on the issue of vocation and whether men were motivated in the same way as women the matron-manager responded with:

> It's quite an emotive issue. Some yes, some no. But then not all women are motivated for the right reasons. It think it is one of those professions that you could only do on sufferance for a short space of time if you didn't like what you were doing. It's not like a production line in a factory. It's taxing, mentally as well as physically.

The first sentence suggests that she herself feels strongly about this question. Then she assumes that there is a right motivation, presumably an altruistic one, which is not found amongst all men, or, she adds, amongst all women who choose caring work. She then identifies what it is that makes the job difficult, suggesting that these difficulties are tolerable only if one is correctly (perhaps altruistically?) motivated.

In terms of job satisfaction the matron-manager agreed that caring work offers quite different rewards from other kinds of work:

> Certainly, I think it goes without saying. It's a satisfaction from all angles that goes with the job of caring. And I think particularly for those who come in at a later stage, when your ideas are very much more set: unless you really want to do it you wouldn't stick it. I think what goes with it is the discipline that has to go with this kind of work. It's a totally different type of discipline to production work or any kind of office work: it's a dual discipline. It's not only your own standard of work, but you're involved with a person, somebody who has ideas of their own. It's not a piece of paper; you're not churning out machines or whatever. I think it's quite a job!

This respondent introduced and directly addressed the issue of the high numbers of men in management positions within care work, in spite of the massive predominance of women amongst all staff, saying: 'It is not necessarily because they are any brighter, but I think it is maybe that there's a gender issue here. Maybe they feel more comfortable with that.' This appears to tally with the common-sense belief that women are 'naturally' caring but equally 'naturally' lack the motivation to achieve higher positions in an employment hierarchy.

The final caring-sector respondent was the manager of a local charity shop supporting hospices to give respite care to mentally handicapped and terminally ill children. She also felt that the fact that the money she raised in the shop was 'helping children' meant that she had more job satisfaction. Her job satisfaction seemed to result from a balance of knowing that the proceeds from her shop went to a good cause and her ability to meet targets for the shop in terms of income and the standard of the shop. The fact that she had a five-year-old child of her own meant that she felt empathy with the parents of the children supported by the hospice, and it added to her job satisfaction to feel that she was supporting them.

So what conclusions can we draw about work motivations in RCT based on this sample of respondents? It is an important first conclusion that, for workers in RCT, autonomy over one's work is a key requirement of job satisfaction. Secondly, we can conclude that, while money is not the sole motivation of workers, a basic 'living' wage is approximately defined by consensus and any job not offering this will be shunned or avoided. Thirdly, caring work is an important source of employment in the Valleys and requires important skills. However, these skills are undervalued, even by caring workers themselves. It is worth asking whether the public sector in the Valleys should be expanded and funded to create better-paid, higher-skill jobs, much as it is in the Scandinavian economies. In response it is worth noting the findings from the empirical research presented here, that the personal rewards from caring work are high and, because they relate to human contact, are different in kind from those received in other kinds of employment.

LEAKAGES FROM THE RCT ECONOMY

A problem acknowledged by successive commentaries on the economy of the south Wales Valleys is the low level of economic activity (Welsh Office, 1998d; Wales European Taskforce, 1999; Fieldhouse and Hollywood, 1999; Welsh Assembly, 2002a). The proportion of working-age people in employment is too low, and this reduced workforce must then support a larger number of dependants than in other areas. The people outside the workforce are found in a number of different statuses: unemployment, disability and long-term sickness. The following three sections address local views of the three main reasons given for this low level of economic involvement: the leakage of energy into the informal economy; the loss of some of the most talented through migration; the lack of incentive to work because of the poor quality and level of pay received in return for the work that is available. In addition the issue of gender segregation is addressed, since if women are being prevented from reaching their full potential because of their inability to access certain types of employment potential this may also affect the success of a local economy.

The informal economy

The existence, size and nature of the informal economy in any area is always hard to assess, for obvious reasons: 'You're convinced something out there is happening but nobody can sort of pin it down', as one respondent aptly put it. In the Valleys most would agree that this sector is larger than in most areas,[2] but empirical estimates are not available. The informal nature of the interviewing conducted for this book provides useful information that would be unavailable from government statistics or more formal studies. However, only a couple of my respondents were willing to admit that they personally had worked illegally and hence their claims about other people must be treated with caution. It is worth pointing out, though, that the existence of the black economy, which I raised specifically as one of my themes, was taken as a simple fact of life, and that those whose stories seemed less credible were the people who were particularly critical of those who signed on and claimed benefits at the same time and who thus had an incentive to exaggerate the size of this phenomenon. Most respondents were tolerant of the black economy, viewing it as an acceptable survival strategy in difficult circumstances.

Many of the respondents I spoke to volunteered information about the informal economy or 'working on the black' or 'hobbling' as it is more often called. The types of work that were identified as being available 'on the black' included 'back-street repairs', 'on the door of a pub or as a bouncer', 'building sites and the girls who are charging £4 now to clean houses', as well as 'plumbers, chippies, taxi-drivers'. One respondent, who admittedly was strongly opposed to informal economic activity, said: 'The black economy is absolutely booming here: it's not just big, it's huge.' Most respondents thought that the government was well aware of the problem but 'turned a blind eye'.

One respondent was quite frank about his informal work:

> Well, put it this way, this time last year I was a lot better off. I was on the dole last year and I was a lot better off. I could afford a holiday in Spain last year because of what they call 'the black economy' isn't it? Well this year I can just about afford a week in the Isle of Wight because I'm working official . . . I'm seeing somebody on the weekend who wants a smoke detector put in. I could give it to the company and earn nothing, but I'm doing it myself and I'm going to earn about £150 profit. Now there's no tax on that and nobody knows about it . . . So that's hopefully gonna pay for me and my children to go to the Isle of Wight at the end of the month.

Reactions to the existence of an informal economy, and to those who participate in it, appeared polarized amongst respondents. On the one hand some roundly condemned it, like this Mines Rescue worker: 'There's workers and there's shirkers. There's people who will always work and there's people who've been brought up to sponge off the state.' The shopkeeper expressed a similar view. She had told her son that if he signed on for the dole she would make him leave home. She felt it was a question of how you were brought up, and although she had sympathy for those who could not find work, it was tempered by disapproval:

I suppose if I was in that situation I'd be tempted to take the dole as well. It's just that I've been brought up so that you just don't do that. I suppose if I was in that situation I would be tempted, of course I would. It's always tempting to take the easy option. So I do feel sorry for people, but not that sorry.

The contrasting view was that the informal economy represented a form of entrepreneurship: as one technician at Engineeringco. put it: 'We're all entrepreneurial individuals now; after all, it's a market society.' When asked whether Valleys people were self-starters a human resources manager replied:

No, and even those ones that are, I think you'll find have gone into what I'll call politely the grey economy or the black economy, whereas they'll get their money from the state but they might be doing back-street repairs or whatever. They're never going to then become a reputable big company, because the infrastructure isn't there to help them do that anyway.

A more political version of the same view was given by another respondent:

I would call that 'working-class capitalism'. Because these people are taking advantage of the situation and taking money out of the system in the same way as a capitalist would do, without regard for anyone else. So I think of capitalism not just as a rich man's thing but also it goes all the way down the line. In other words putting yourself before other people.

There were various explanations given for the existence of the informal economy. One economic development officer identified the problems of paperwork in the official economy as a major incentive to work informally or to 'just to go out and do things', as she put it. She also identified the group of semi-retired and partially disabled ex-miners as the major grouped involved in informal economic activities:

The other problem we've got here is that, with the decline of the pits, there's an age group and a sector of the male population that did have health problems because of the environment they worked in. But they're not that ill that they can't put those skills to good use. You do have a lot of, not just miners on the coalface, you do have a lot of skilled people. The National Coal Board was renowned for giving excellent apprenticeships. So you've got electricians, carpenters, fitters, and everything that went with it in the professions, and they are out there . . . they are the ones.

Off the record she admitted that her uncle was in fact working on the black as an electrician. Such people have minor health problems, but can still do light work. However, the nature of the benefits system means that to ensure an adequate level of reliable income they have to register as long-term sick. Their skills then enable them to undertake work in the informal economy to supplement their benefits. Another view was of the black economy as a response to exploitation by 'the establishment'. This is why it is so difficult to identify who is involved or to persuade some local people to 'grass somebody up . . . Because the establishment are the enemies of everybody in an area like this.'

The above discussion has focused on the informal economy, but there is also an extensive illegal economy in the Valleys, focusing around the sale of prohibited drugs. Although evidence cannot be found in official figures, one respondent found her own evidence:

> In south Wales there is a thriving drug market. From my previous authority, which is only just over the hill [in Bridgend] from some of our deprived Valley communities, it was amazing how some I would class as the eighteen to twenty-six bracket, their lifestyles are absolutely amazing compared to, well hang on they're not working, they're not in college, they're not on a training course, where's the money coming from?

More information on the Valleys' drugs problems reported in the national media are given in Chapter 2. Aside from the issue of illegality, the informal and illegal economic activity in RCT represents a drain on the local economy, and a full-scale exploration would be of great benefit to policy-makers.

Labour-market mobility

The issue of work mobility in RCT has two apparently contradictory aspects: workers are thought unwilling to travel far to work, because of the tradition of the pit village[3] and the poor cross-valley transport system; those who are willing to move tend to migrate permanently for better prospects in other areas, causing a leakage of talent out of the area. A careers manager mentioned that there was still an unrealistic expectation that work would be found on the doorstep: young people were only prepared to travel to Porth, which is at the convergence of the two Rhondda Valleys. However, this is an easy place to reach by public transport whereas Bridgend, where the new development park has gener-ated many jobs, is, he accepted, difficult to reach by bus. He suggested that in future young people might have to be prepared to travel to Cardiff, which is easily accessible by a train route. Obviously, it was not possible for me to interview successful migrants, but this did not seem to be a popular strategy amongst those I did speak to. Only one respondent mentioned the option of leaving RCT for better employment prospects:

> I'm a single chap, my wife and kids have gone down to Salisbury to live and they're much better off. I'm thinking of going up to Scotland because there is better funding up there for new businesses. I know they're devolved now and everything like that, but what sort of scheme they've got up there for new businesses I've no idea but I'm getting information on that now. And talking to a couple of people that's gone up there, the funding up there is outstanding. They give you the funding and you don't have to pay anything back for five years.

Employment avoidance because of poor incentives

Another source of leakage from the official economy is comprised of people who are refusing to accept jobs because they consider the wages too low. This failure of incentives is widespread, as identified by one local employer, the matron-manager in a private nursing home:

> This is an excuse, or tends to be, that there isn't any work available. I meet it here, particularly with the low-paid, time and time and time again. The number of people who say it is not worth me getting out of bed in the morning because I'll only earn £10 or £15 or £20 more a week than I can get off benefits. With the rise in the minimum working wage I have two care assistants on night duty who have reduced their hours of working and this irks me a great deal.

The same point was made by a shopkeeper: 'Why would they go and work in a factory and earn £120 a week when they can get that on the dole?', or, in the words of another respondent: 'There's no incentive for people to go out and work if they can sit on their backside and let the state pay.'

But the situation looks rather different from the other side, from the perspective of a person who has recently taken on very low-paid work and is now discovering that he is actually worse off:

> I have got a letter written to Mr Tony Blair at the moment, because officially I've been out of work for just under four years. I've had a month's contract here and a month's contract there but . . . now I've started work there's the poll tax beginning, and I've got to pay my own rent, and this, that and the other. And as I've said I am £52 better off working. Now once the CSA catch up with me with the two children I may have to turn round and say I'm sorry I can't work, because they regularly expect a minimum payment of £11.20 I think it is now.

An indication of the low level of wage expectations was given by one respondent who said about his son, 'He can earn £160 a week, which is good money for around here.' The poor absolute level of wages is also exacerbated by some of the contractual arrangements operated by agencies where employees are not paid when factories are closed down at holiday times, reducing incomes further.

These are the views of the local people about how economic incentives fail in their economy. Economists would disagree about whether the problem is on the supply side, where sticky wages result from unrealistic expectations due to an overgenerous welfare system; or on the demand side, where employers fail to offer sufficient incentives. In terms of policy-making, however, the lack of incentive to undertake the employment that is available is a crucial explanation for the persistence of unemployment in the RCT economy and the low level of economic activity and the waste of an important economic resource that this implies.

Gender segregation

The different motivations of men and women in RCT have been indicated in the section on work motivations above. Some of the contributions to that discussion also hint at the nature of the culture of the area and its rigid segregation of men's work from women's work. As described in Chapter 2, south Wales was unusual amongst mining regions for the exclusion of women from the collieries and, since little other paid work was available locally, this meant that women were limited to the domestic sphere. This is reflected today in the low rate of female labour-force participation compared with other areas, although women now represent more than half the workforce. It is also apparent from the lack of confidence amongst women, particularly younger unskilled women, that I noticed while carrying out these interviews.

In the context of the modern labour market, where many of the available jobs are in what were traditionally considered women's areas, such as in the service and caring sectors, and light assembly, there are more opportunities for women than men. While this has been reflected in greater numbers of women working, one respondent hinted that there may be cultural reasons why women would be unwilling to build successful careers within such an economy: 'I think a man who was working, perhaps someone like me working in the mines whose partner would be in an office somewhere earning double the wages, he'd feel a bit threatened by that.' If true generally, this might cause women to limit their ambition within the labour market, in order not to cause trouble at home. Such a point may be extended to explain the low rate of business set-ups, if women are similarly discouraged in the field of self-employment. This may be particularly damaging to the local economy if, as suggested in a quotation cited above, women are actually more successful as entrepreneurs.

The corollary is that men may feel uncomfortable about moving into what are culturally perceived to be women's jobs, a clear example being caring work. The matron-manager considered that 'it's now becoming socially acceptable [for men] to go into the caring professions'. She confirmed this by introducing me to one of her male care assistants who had previously worked for twenty years as an office manager. He considered his switch to the caring sector to be 'the best thing I've ever done'.

The careers officers I spoke to have as part of their remit the attempt to challenge these assumptions about there being a difference between men's work and women's work. They admit that this is an uphill struggle, particularly when stereotypical views of the sexes are so common (for example, one respondent's comment that 'it was more the screwdriver operations on the electronics side, where the shift patterns and the kind of monotonous work that was going on there, the women could cope with far better than the men could'). One careers officer admitted that they still have employers asking to advertise vacancies for a particular sex and said: 'It's still very traditional here in terms of the kinds of subject areas they go into.' The other careers officer also conceded that 'the message isn't going across', although she thought that the persistent problems were at the lower skill end of the labour market:

> It's often easier for people to do the gender swap at the higher professional level, but it isn't as easy to do at the non-skilled or semi-skilled level. Men and women doctors are in roughly equal numbers, in fact I think medical schools are reporting 51 per cent of applicants female, 49 per cent men. And likewise young, female civil engineers: no problem. They had the regular female engineer on the Severn Bridge – she did all the middle section. And I think at the professional level this is the case: the movement is very fluid and it will cross over gender stereotyping. But you move down to the baseline and it's a different story altogether. You can have big projects, big building projects where you have female quantity surveyor, female civil engineer, architect, technician whatever, but you go down to who's actually digging and it's going to be all men, isn't it?

The findings from the questionnaire are particularly illuminating in terms of leakages from the formal economy of RCT, where official data are severely limited. The first point worth noting is that there is appears to be a thriving informal economy, consisting of older, skilled male workers who may be signed on for sickness benefits, and younger unemployed people involved in the sale of illegal drugs. Although only a few respondents reported actual cases of black-economy activity, they all seemed to view it as a normal part of their economy. Most of the 'evidence' amounts to little more than hearsay, but this in itself suggests the need for this major influence on levels of economic activity to be the subject of more determined academic research. An alternative is to develop policies which work on the assumption of its existence and seek to encourage the gradual movement of this activity into the formal sector, for example by introducing a Citizens' Income scheme as discussed in Chapter 8.

One important positive influence on the size of this black economy is the low level of income provided by many of the jobs that are available in RCT. This creates a poverty trap and means that the jobs that are available do not provide sufficient incentive over and above the benefit level. Its existence also suggests that, if benefit levels are reduced or their availability is limited, the result is likely to be more informal and illegal economic activity rather than a greater willingness to take low-paid employment. It is also worth noting that traditional attitudes towards women's employment may prevent women's full and active participation in the economy.

CONCLUSION

To reiterate the point made in the introduction to this chapter, the excerpts from interviews presented here represent personal accounts, which cannot be taken as representative of all the views of people in Rhondda Cynon Taff. Therefore the conclusions that can be taken forward and used to inform policy-making must be treated with caution. These have been collected at the end of the sections above and the links to possible policy initiatives will be made in the final chapter.

7

Tower of Strength, Beacon of Hope: A Case Study of Tower Colliery

If the miners want to keep their pits, let them buy them themselves.
Michael Heseltine, Secretary of State for Trade and Industry, 1992

So far the chapters in this book have presented a picture of Rhondda Cynon Taff including statistical details and cultural background. The previous two chapters presented information drawn from a small-scale survey and related interviewing about local workers' perceptions of work as it is and as they would like it to be. This chapter presents a case study of a particular workplace in the area which was included in the survey: Tower Colliery. As will emerge throughout the chapter, Tower offers a unique example of how work might be organized and has a history and depth of feeling attached to it that cannot be reproduced elsewhere. Yet it also offers lessons and patterns to policy-makers seeking to develop a distinctly Welsh form of employment structure and is thus used as a model of a cooperative form of working that could be shared more widely in other local economies across Wales.

The chapter is based on a variety of sources of information. There is a fair amount of published material, including transcripts of speeches by Tyrone O'Sullivan and newspaper articles, as well as a BBC documentary, *Walking into the Light* and a publication from Tower itself called *Lessons in Vigilance and Freedom* (Francis, 1997). Tyrone O'Sullivan has written (with the support of two others: O'Sullivan, Eve and Edworthy, 2001) his own account of the progress towards buy-out and gives a clear sense of his ideological position which aids the interpretation of events. I have supplemented this with interviews with a number of employees of Tower Colliery including the current NUM chairman, several worker-owners, two members of the management board who were also members of the TEBO (Tower Employees' Buy-Out) team, and some contracted employees. I later spoke to Norman Watson of the Wales Cooperative Centre who acted as financial adviser to the buy-out team, and work by members of the Welsh Institute for Research into Cooperatives has also been helpful. Statistical data are drawn from reports for the DTI and the Treasury as well as information gained from Tower direct.[1]

THE TOWER LEGEND DEMYSTIFIED

The legend of the buy-out of Tower Colliery is a valuable case study because it offers in microcosm the narrative of the working man of the Valleys – except with an unexpectedly happy ending. The narrative includes a hero and heroine – Tyrone O'Sullivan, NUM lodge secretary at Tower for twenty-two years and leader of the buy-out bid, and local Cynon Valley MP Ann Clwyd – a history of double-dealing and deceit, suffering and courage shown by the brawny miner and his wife. It is easy to dismiss this narrative as soap opera, which on one level it is. But one should not allow one's post-ironic sensibilities to overshadow the fact that in the Valleys these sorts of mythologies are believed, and that belief in them generates a tremendous source of passion and energy. The genuine, real-world success of Tower Colliery is the result of channelling that energy and converting it into work. This is a lesson that should be learned by others who expend their energy generating mission statements and bewailing the failure of entrepreneurship in Wales. It is not that the Welsh people are not up to the part but that they are being offered the wrong script.

However attractive and moving the narrative, the role of the academic is to be detached and to provide a factual and, as far as that is possible, objective account of historical events. According to O'Sullivan's own account, the story of the buy-out begins in the resistance to the devastating programme of pit closures in the south Wales coalfield following the 1984/5 miners' strike and the re-election of a Conservative government in 1992. He details the lengthy struggle to resist the combination of pressure and tempting redundancy packages from British Coal, culminating in what he and the fellow union leaders felt to be a humiliating defeat after which it was their responsibility to sign the redundancy agreement. In one of the most moving passages in the book he describes how he cried uncontrollably on the way back from the meeting, and how this emotional crisis led to the idea to buy the mine:

> I'm sure you can imagine that if you are in a car with six miners and one of them starts crying, it really is the others' worst nightmare. These are tough men and they are good men but they cannot handle a man crying . . . Eventually we got to Abercynon and I pulled the car over and just sobbed. I could not believe that we were losing the colliery; even though my father had been killed at Tower, I loved the pit and I loved the people there . . . This was a dreadful day and I hated what they had done to us.

Inevitably they end up in a local pub, joined by their families, reminiscing about good times:

By ten o'clock all the good times had been gone over again and again, but more importantly, this was when the first talk started about buying back the pit. I have to admit that it is Elaine [Tyrone's wife] who tells me about this as by this time I was too drunk to remember.

I have quoted this passage at length in spite of, or perhaps because of, its subjective and emotional content. Employment policy in the Valleys has been created on the assumption of workers as 'rational economic agents', as cogs in a larger industrial machine. But as this extract shows, the 'tough', strong, emotionally controlled miners are driven by human passions, and the success of Tower Colliery is based on the fact that they have found a way of using that passion and the energy it generates to their own advantage rather than in opposition and in 'struggle'.

The campaign to buy back the pit was run by the TEBO team, with Tyrone as chairman and Phil White, NUM chairman at Tower, as the secretary. To make a convincing case to the government and the banks that they should be entrusted with the pit and could pay back the necessary loans, these men who had left school at fifteen and had no business or accountancy training had to draw up a mining plan and a business plan. Their close involvement with the colliery and long experience of mining were found to be more important than formal qualifications. The mining plan was sent to Philip Weekes, ex-chairman of the National Coal Board in south Wales, who approved of it and agreed to act as figurehead and business adviser to the campaign and as the potential first chairman of the revived colliery. Ken Davies, of the mining officials' union NACODS, was another useful addition, as later were Tony Shoot, a surveyor, and Cliff Jones, a former colliery manager. Financial support was provided by the accountants Price Waterhouse, who agreed to work on a *pro bono* basis until the buy-out was successful.

Another key player in the buy-out was Norman Watson of the Wales Cooperative Centre. He had arrived in Wales in 1989 with a brief to enable exactly these sorts of worker buy-outs of ailing companies, a remit he had already successfully fulfilled in many different sorts of companies before the Tower closure plan was announced. He was contacted by the TEBO team a week before the pre-qualifying deadline for bids set by the bankers Rothschild. Trust was cemented by Watson's comment, as reported by Tyrone (O'Sullivan, Eve and Edworthy, 2001: 160), that 'in this day and age you could buy anything, including souls, because this was a country with a Thatcher Government'. That government was, in fact, offering to sell the whole coalfield as a going concern, and so the first stage was to persuade the Welsh Minister John Redwood to allow the miners to buy the single pit – a suggestion that had been unsuccessfully tried already in Yorkshire.

Photo 7.1: The winding gear at Tower Colliery, at the top of the Cynon Valley

Redwood was supportive, leaving the way open for the buy-out of Tower if the financial hurdles could be overcome.

Taking into account the investment of £8,000 redundancy money from all the miners who had decided to participate in the buy-out the TEBO team had £2m in the bank but still needed to raise another £1 million to cover the initial down-payment. Watson ruefully reports that the Cooperative Bank turned them down and they had to resort to Barclays. As a commercial bank taking on a risky venture Barclays' local office required £30,000 as a fee simply for meeting the miners and 8 per cent above base as interest on the proposed loan. Again Watson's contacts and experience were vital: by contacting Leif Mills, the head of the banking union BIFU who knew the Barclays regional director, he was able to have the fee waived and the above-base percentage reduced to 4 per cent. Barclays had no need to worry for the security of their investment: the £1m loan was repaid within the year.

OPERATING IN A COMPETITIVE MARKET

The worker-owners of Tower Colliery have always understood that they find themselves in a highly competitive international market and the experience of the Thatcher years taught them that they could not look to

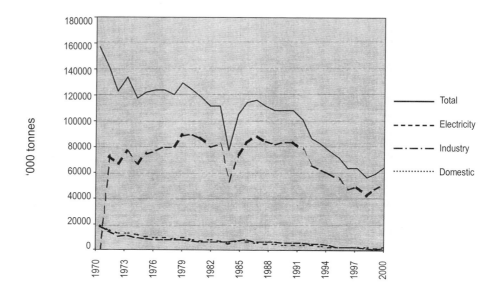

Figure 7.1: Trends in coal consumption, 1970 to 2001
Note: The figure and the data it is based on originate from and remain the sole property of the Department of Trade and Industry, which retains the copyright.

the government for support against its vagaries; government subsidies that are provided are subject to strict European regulation. The market for coal has been hit hard in recent years by the movement towards gas for domestic energy production and by the increase in the level of imports of coal following the denationalization of the industry and its subjection to international competition. Figures 7.1 and 7.2 show trends in coal consumption and production up to 1999.

The latest government assessment of economic prospects for the coal industry dates back to 2001 (Treasury, 2001) and identified the considerable fall in demand for coal due to the expansion of gas-fired power stations for the generation of domestic electricity (electricity generators accounted for nearly 75 per cent of coal consumption in 1999, at 40.5 million tonnes). Total demand for coal fell from 160 million tonnes in 1970 to a mere 60

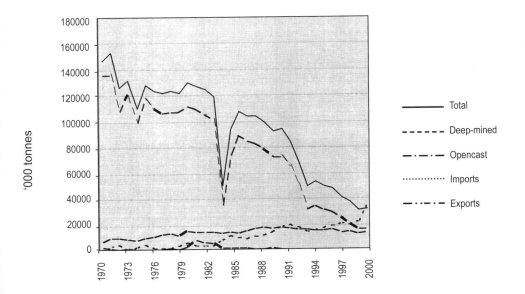

'000 tonnes

Total

Deep-mined

Opencast

Imports

Exports

Figure 7.2: Trends in coal production and imports, 1970 to 1999
Note: The figure and the data it is based on originate from and remain the sole
property of the Department of Trade and Industry, which retains the copyright.

million tonnes by the end of the century. Over the same period imports
increased from zero, in the days of the nationalized coal industry, to 20.8
million tonnes. The balance between deep and opencast mining has also
switched in favour of the latter: deep-mined coal now represents slightly
more than one-third of the total, with slightly less provided by opencast
and the remainder from imports. This contrasts with the situation in 1970
when opencast represented less than 5 per cent of total production.

The poor demand conditions during this period have been combined
with falling international coal prices. International spot prices fell
continuously between 1994 and 1999, as governments retreated from
policies of supporting their domestic industries under pressure from
international trade bodies, allowing countries with cheaper production
costs to drive prices down. Between 1995 and 2000 the average price paid
for coal by major power producers fell by 27.5 per cent, a particularly sharp
fall of 21 per cent occurring during 1997/8.

This is a difficult market in which to operate, displaying all the conditions that challenge businesses: strong competition, weakening demand, falling and fluctuating prices. In response to this in 2000 the Secretary of State for Trade and Industry Stephen Byers announced a government subsidy scheme for the coal industry, especially in response to the difficult market conditions following the privatization of the UK energy market and the sudden switch in demand from coal to gas for electricity generation. According to the Treasury 'the subsidy would be a short-term measure, designed to establish a viable future within a competitive energy market' (Treasury, 2001: 142). Tower has been a successful bidder in this process, which is subject to European Commission approval, and received £3,317,000 in 2002; another £3,776,000 payment is currently being reconciled with the Commission (DTI Coal Operating Aid Scheme figures, from DTI website).

The payment of these subsidies suggests a shift in government thinking away from the political opposition to coal mining which existed during the Conservative administrations and towards its consideration as an essential part of a balanced and secure energy sector. The state of the industry has since been explored by two government surveys, published in 1998 and 2003. Table 7.1 lists the deep-mine collieries that still exist in the UK together with their available coal resources and mineral potential. Tower's resources represent around 6 per cent of the UK total from deep mining; its mineral potential is around 7 per cent of the total.

Tower's output figures are given in Table 7.2; these figures can be compared with the 1995 figure of 480,000 tonnes. Output would have seen a steady rise were it not for geological problems in 1999, including a major gas leak. This explains the failure to meet the budgeted output in that year. Production in 2002 was set to follow the trend and equal around 650,000 tonnes by the end of the year. Tower sells a range of types of anthracite with an average net calorific value of 33,000 J/kg. Seventy per cent of its sales are to industrial customers, including the Aberthaw electricity generation plant (which alone buys 60 per cent of output) and local steel plants; the other 30 per cent is sold for domestic consumption, including contracts with local authorities. Exports account for between 10 and 15 per cent of production with customers in Ireland, France, Belgium, Spain and Germany.

Tower has survived in this market, but it is now facing internal difficulties due to the exhaustion of the currently productive seams. According to IMC, consultants contracted to prepare an assessment of deep-mine coal resources for the DTI, 'the current working area will eventually reach exhaustion, production beyond February 2005 being at significant risk from faulting, steep gradients, and seam thinning'. Work is

Table 7.1: Final reserves and resources statement for UK deep-mine collieries, December 2002 (mT)

Colliery	Reserve	Resource	Total	Mineral potential
Clipstone	0.30	–	0.30	2.40
Daw Mill	26.02	6.38	32.40	43.13
Ellington	3.23	–	3.23	0.27
Harworth	3.33	3.19	6.52	33.55
Kellingley	8.64	26.15	34.79	22.29
Maltby	5.00	6.30	11.30	12.20
Rossington	3.17	7.98	11.15	6.54
Thoresby	6.40	10.36	16.76	10.26
Welbeck	5.73	2.72	8.45	18.06
Hatfield	0.68	9.49	10.17	19.50
Tower	2.60	6.30	8.90	19.00
Aberpergwm	0.48	3.80	4.28	–
Betws	0.57	1.40	1.97	–
Eckrington	0.28	0.29	0.57	–
Hayroyds	0.18	0.05	0.23	–
Thorne	–	–	–	75.33
Total	66.61	84.41	151.02	262.53

Note: 'Reserves' are measured mineral extraction resources for which detailed technical and economic studies have demonstrated that extraction can be justified at the time of determination, and under specific economic conditions; 'resources' are the proportion of the mineral resource that has not been sufficiently appraised to demonstrate them as proven or probable reserves.
Source: DTI, 2003.

Table 7.2: Historical production performance at Tower Colliery (mT)

	1999	2000	2001	2002 (9 months)
Actual output	0.464	0.598	0.642	0.502
Budgeted output	0.610	0.630	0.630	0.486
Difference	–0.146	–0.032	0.012	0.016

Source: DTI, 2003.

ongoing to explore availability in other seams, and a planning submission has been made to sink another shaft at Margam. The DTI report states the following as Tower's long-term plan:

> Tower Colliery Limited are currently undertaking a strategic review of the remaining reserve/resources at the mine. It is recognised that the current area is nearing exhaustion and the feasibility of extending the mine's life beyond this time is being examined. However, it must be borne in mind that access to other seams would represent a major capital investment and such expenditure would be difficult to substantiate in regard to the current state of the market. (DTI, 2003: 207)

Tower is facing a watershed: to develop new resources will require major investment. How will such investment be financed and will it repay itself without destroying the company? Most major investments since the Second World War in deep mines have been made by the government. According to independent consultants IMC, 'there is a unanimous view that financial institutions are risk averse to mining', and this is exacerbated by the instability of the market outlined above. For many of those involved in the buy-out their £8,000 redundancy money has been invested wisely: they have bought themselves well-paid jobs for less than £1,000 a year over the ten years up to February 2005. However, the psychological impact of the closure of the pit is hard to overestimate, especially now that Tower has established its status as the business to buck the trend. Its closure would represent a colossal blow to confidence in the Valleys.

Tower Colliery is clearly a successful, well-run and efficient business. It has been operating in a highly competitive sector for eight years, returning a surplus and paying a dividend in most of those years. It also plays an important role in the local community by its multiplier effect: it is estimated that without it the local economy would lose up to £10m per year (Heath, 2000). To the 239 members of the original cooperative have been added another sixty-one, making a workforce of 300 people, 90 per cent of whom are shareholders. Tower is the only deep mine in Wales employing more than 150 men (Treasury, 2001). All 300 permanent employees have well-paid, relatively secure employment, as well as an additional 100 contracted employees. In December 2002 the *Western Mail* published a list of Wales's top 300 companies. Tower Colliery was number 174 on the list, with a £28m turnover, profits of £2.7m and a 26.8 per cent return on capital. However, it has benefited thus far from accessible reserves that could be exploited without major investment. The next year represents a serious challenge to the colliery and to those who support it. It has proved its efficiency against comparable market players, but it may become a political decision whether or not to support the colliery with public money if it requires major investment in the near future.

VIEW FROM THE COALFACE

For those seeking to develop policies to tackle unemployment in former mining areas it is important to realize that the dominant discourse has been framed by the miners, and that it does not accord with the official version of the pit closures. In other words, miners have their own understanding of how and why the pits were closed, and any employment policies that are drawn up without recognition of this understanding will meet little success. As M. Thomas (1991: 54) writes of the highly contested process of colliery closure, 'It is also important to note that these forms of contestation are not simply important in their own right, but also have significant impact upon subsequent labour market behaviour'.

The official version is that the mines were closed because they were 'unprofitable', 'uncompetitive' and had geological problems. It is clear that the questions of profitability and competitiveness are not as straightforward as they may seem at first. For example, rates of subsidy for coal mining varied widely at this time and those for the UK were some of the lowest amongst its market competitors (see Chapter. 2, note 5). Similarly the level of wages and conditions of work experienced by miners affect both profitability and competitiveness, so that private UK mines not bound by union wage agreements can make higher profits, and foreign mines employing unskilled and sometimes child labour in dangerous conditions can easily out-compete British mines where high levels of safety are enforced.

The feeling on the part of the miners that British Coal was being at best 'economical with the truth' was enhanced by the changing reality presented by these apparently objective statistics. For example, a pamphlet produced by the NCB for an open day at Cwm Colliery in the central south Wales coalfield in 1977 gave the estimated productive life of the pit as 100 years (NCB South Wales Area, 1977), yet less than ten years later in 1986 it ceased production, a casualty of an 'uneconomic industry'. The coincidence of the dates of closures such as that at Cwm with the ending of the 1984/5 Miners' Strike is not lost on local people, who perceive the colliery closure programme of the late 1980s onwards as a political strike-back in punishment for the refusal of the working-class people to accept the political changes of Thatcherism. (Seumas Milne (1995), labour editor for the *Guardian*, presents an account of even murkier dealings during the strike, including a dirty-tricks campaign orchestrated by Stella Rimington, later head of MI5.)

Local people support this position with their own account of the quality and productiveness of their pits. In the case of Tower the official version was very negative: 'According to British Coal the coalface was gassy with a high level of methane that affected production and safety. In addition they maintained that there was no market for the high-quality anthracite that the pit produced' (O'Sullivan, Eve and Edworthy, 2001: 141). This was the picture of Tower presented to the General Colliery Review Meeting in April 1994: a pit that had no market and had geological flaws. So the Tower miners were aware that the case was being made to close the pit, although they were also aware that it was making more than £10m in profit annually during the early 1990s. Their own understanding of the closure as politically motivated, and their inside knowledge of the true value of the mine, persuaded them of the viability of the buy-out bid, a conviction that was strong enough for them to invest £8,000 each in the venture.

To miners in other pits, and by the late 1980s many had experience of several different collieries, as they had transferred from one closed mine to another, the strategy for effecting pit closures became clear. Figures were massaged to indicate unduly pessimistic forecasts, a process that miners referred to as 'fiddling' (M. Thomas, 1991) and that included the purchase of unused equipment and unnecessary and expensive refurbishments to inflate the cost side of the balance sheet. These two examples from interviews reported by Thomas (1991), indicate the view from the coalface:

> In the 12-month after 1984, they decided to install a new railway system to make the transportation of coal more easy – new rails, new roads, new weighbridge. They installed a new control with an estimated cost of £2 million. They decided to open up a new face with new advanced machinery – all to no avail. I don't think that they close a pit overnight as a result of a whim; it must have been on the cards. So why go to the expense of spending all this money? Building up people's hopes, then having them dashed like that. Most of the money was spent since the end of the strike. God knows how many millions it cost.

> They were looking for coal in areas which had been proved to be unsuccessful by the old people in the mine years ago; and they were told not to go to those areas, but they ignored that . . . Management in Llanishen in Cardiff spent all this money in the wrong areas, probably for the right results – to prove to people that Cwm was uneconomical . . . The head surveyor in Cwm had recommended to management that they shouldn't go to that particular area to look for coal, but he was ignored.

It is impossible to validate these claims objectively, but this is less important than the fact that they are strongly believed by local people and influence both the way they are likely to respond to future employment policy-making (with a lack of trust that is discussed further in Chapter 8) and their own survival strategies. For one example, the decision to resist redundancy is undermined by the perceived political nature of the pit closures. According to Thomas, who investigated miners' reactions to the closure of their pit at Cwm,

> Cwm was a modern colliery which produced high-quality coal and it had estimated long-term reserves. The fact that such a pit could be closed had led miners to the conclusion that the future prospects of the remaining pits in the coalfield were poor. (1991: 55)

An interesting light was cast on the role of the British government in the pit closure programme during the negotiations over the Tower buy-out. As stated above, John Redwood, Welsh Secretary, was supportive of the miners' buy-out plans and argued in favour of the bid to the Cabinet. According to one source, he advised the TEBO team not to have anything to do with the British Coal managers. He justified this on the basis that they had failed to make a commercial success of the south Wales coalfield in spite of £139bn of state aid since 1947. However, knowing that working people already suffering hardship were willing to invest £8,000 each in a venture, we might speculate that he was moved to offer this advice because of his own inside knowledge of the real intentions of the British Coal board, whether that was to undermine the bid or to redirect it in the direction of an asset-stripping venture. Suspicions have been raised by several of the people involved, and are repeated in Tyrone's account of the process, that the managers of the colliery wanted to buy the pit themselves, since they knew the extent of its official undervaluation.

There had already been evidence that such a plan was afoot as early as 1993. According to O'Sullivan there was discussion at secret meetings of the Tower managers held at Brecon, just north of the south Wales Valleys, and reported to him by a 'spy in their camp'. They planned to asset-strip the mine by working it heavily for three years without investing in its future. This short-term approach, combined with reduced levels of wages and increased hours for the miners, would generate enormous financial returns. One of the Tower managers I spoke to who had also been a member of the TEBO team put it like this:

> There were some funny things happened when it looked like we was going to get it. There was a couple of assets came out of the woodwork and said 'With our expertise we would like to invest in your company.' They hadn't been there for the first six months when we were battling.

It is unclear from the transcript whether it was actual unaccounted assets that emerged or people who hoped to exploit these, but the suggestion is clear that there was far more value in the company than was calculated in the official accounts, and that others were hoping to capitalize on this dishonest accounting, thinking that the Tower bid would fail. There is no hard evidence for this story, but it does help to explain the enormous pressure that was put on Tower miners to accept redundancy terms, and the speed with which the shutdown proceeded.

O'Sullivan writes:

> During all the negotiations that we had with accountants, lawyers and advisors, the only organization we had to deal with that proved to be unhelpful was British Coal and I can only attribute their behaviour to the fact that they thought that the divine right of ownership was passing to a group of people that they believed had no rights at all. (O'Sullivan, Eve and Edworthy, 2001: 165)

But there is another interpretation. Given that Tower was always seen as a high-productivity pit – and its success since the buy-out has proved this – it is possible that there was a rival plan by former British Coal managers to gain short-term profit from the pit, which may tie in with Redwood's warning to avoid BC involvement. There was certainly enormous pressure to close the pit very rapidly, although any possible plans for a later reopening after a management buy-out were undermined by the enthusiasm that greeted the miners' buy-out bid in all quarters.

The view that the mines were closed for political rather than economic reasons is thus universally held, with most miners and former miners also believing that there were various instances of creative, or rather destructive, accounting in the years leading up to the most intensive period of pit closures. The history of pit closures and political struggle in the Valleys is an essential backdrop to any account of Tower Colliery. The following comment, made by a member of the Tower board, makes clear that the battle at least with the Conservative government has not been resolved, and that the ongoing tension helps to support the confidence of Tower managers and workers:

> The government said it's uneconomical, can't be worked, there's no market, geological problems, poor ventilation, and on and on. After you've done that and you've proved the government wrong, there's something affirming for people here, not totally but perhaps more than just ordinary.

TOWER COLLIERY AS A COOPERATIVE

According to Norman Watson of the Wales Cooperative Centre, Tyrone O'Sullivan does not consider Tower to be a cooperative. He certainly seems rather unwilling to refer to it as such in his own account of the colliery's history (O'Sullivan et al., 2001), although his speeches are littered with references to the importance of cooperation. A member of the Tower management committee who was also part of the TEBO team told me: 'We're not strictly a coop, but the principles are there, where everybody has equal shareholding and rewards, and when the dividends come we share them amongst the people that actually produce the goods and sell them on for us.' The unwillingness to claim the official title of a producer cooperative may relate to the image that cooperatives have in the present economic framework; this same manager told me that most cooperatives were very small-scale and perhaps the Tower managers are concerned that their enterprise should not be seen as on the fringe, since this would adversely affect their economic viability.

Despite this official reluctance, the structure of Tower Colliery does fit the definition of a cooperative offered by the International Cooperative Alliance, which is 'an autonomous association of persons united voluntarily to meet their common economic, social, and cultural needs and aspirations through a jointly-owned and democratically-controlled enterprise'. Tower's articles of association state that decisions are to be made on the basis of one vote per member, with a 3 per cent limit on share ownership per individual member, who must sell his shares on leaving the company.

The International Cooperative Alliance also gives a list of values that cooperatives should share (information from the Cooperative Union Ltd, Manchester). 'Self-help' and 'self-responsibility' are clearly demonstrated by the history of Tower described above. The next three listed values are 'democracy, equality, and equity'. These are the sorts of values that shine through Tyrone's account of Tower and its history. They are also evident in the company's structure. Six members of the board of directors are elected by shareholders; they must work full-time at Tower and must be share-holders. Two of these members retire by rotation every year. They may offer themselves for re-election but others may be nominated to stand against them. There are also three non-executive directors who are appointed by the directors for a two-year term: they are not shareholders of the company. Aside from the board of directors there is a senior management team, led by the colliery manager, the members of which are appointed by the board and run the company on a day-to-day basis. The board holds a weekly operational meeting when the directors are present along with the heads of department and representatives of the four trade unions who have members at the colliery. All members of the cooperative have a single vote in decisions affecting the future of the business according to its articles of association, and they also have equal holiday and pension entitlements.

'Honesty' and 'openness' are harder to assess, although O'Sullivan's decision to move his office alongside the pithead baths and have the connecting door cut in half is a graphic illustration of his determination to stay in touch (Wylie, 2001). One of the Tower managers who had also been a member of the TEBO team told me: 'We try to encourage an open-door policy so that all the information we can possibly give gets down to the ground floor as well.'

The final three values are 'solidarity' along with 'social responsibility' and 'caring for others'. 'Solidarity' is often indicated by the strength of unity in purpose, which was well demonstrated at Tower during the 1984/5 Miners' Strike, when no picket line was necessary (Heath, 2000), although, as the same article reports, solidarity has a slightly different nuance once the former union leaders are the bosses. The 2000 strike indicated that there is now the possibility of conflict between those who were once in solidarity with each other. Its quick resolution (within three days) indicates that the history of trust and comradeship provides a sound basis for 'management' even within a formally cooperative structure.[2]

LESSONS FOR A WELSH ECONOMIC MODEL

The story of the failure of the economy of the Valleys is a story of unproductive, truculent workers who are the victims of an economic tide that has passed them by. There is a sense of helplessness on the part of policy-makers who metaphorically wring their hands when confronted with such a hopeless set of economic circumstances. How then has Tower Colliery managed to remain profitable in a highly competitive market while paying a relatively high level of wages? This section is based on the comments made by workers there during my research project, combined with attitudes expressed by Tyrone in his account of the Tower project (O'Sullivan, Eve and Edworthy, 2001). It attempts to determine what it is about Tower Colliery that has enabled its unexpected success; if these ingredients could be shared with other economic enterprises Tower might be used as a model for a new and distinctively Welsh form of economic organization.

Commitment

An examination of the attitudes of worker-owners at Tower Colliery has interesting implications for a government and its economic planners who constantly reiterate the importance of productivity. As one of them put it to me when I asked about whether his attitude to work was affected by the fact that he owned his own company, 'Yes, because it's our company we work that much harder.' A manager from the colliery who was also a member of the TEBO team discussed the same issue at greater length:

> I think it's a marvellous feeling to own your own place, especially a coal mine, and actually work here. Even though there's 300 of us we still have our rows and arguments like in any family I should imagine. There's very strong debates goes on. The only thing I get worried about sometimes is that we are shareholders but we're only shareholders once a year. We only own the colliery once a year in the AGM of the shareholders' meeting. The rest of the year we come to work as employees. We've given the manager and the management team the right to manage the mine. So they do conflict sometimes, with your shareholders head on and your owners head on and you have some strong debates about issues. But it's our fifth year now, so we must be doing something right.

The movement from employee to owner-worker also leaves the union representatives in a difficult situation. When I asked the present union chairman whether he thought the board now makes its decisions in the interests of the workers or in their own interests he indicated the confusion that this new economic form brings in its wake:

> In the interest of the company, I suppose, as a whole. But it's very difficult to tread the line between being a trade unionist and a full-blown capitalist. It's almost impossible to tread that line. Because that's what we're trying to do here . . . some of the old union officials are now the company directors and they're in a different world and their responsibilities lie in a different direction. Their responsibility really is to the company. That's their legal responsibilities.

This interviewee gave some of the most negative and cynical responses to Tower as a whole. He made a clear distinction between the early days of the return to work, which he describes as euphoric, and the reality shock that the work was actually as hard as ever:

> For the first six months that we were back here there was more or less euphoria. Everybody was happy with everything; you thought you were in El Dorado. But that had long since died the death. Because people have had to face up to reality and the real world instead of living in fairy-tale castles . . . Digruntlement, disillusionment, problems in the marketplace. We're having big problems raising the price of coal; we're having problems holding that

price. And production costs continually rise, and things are not all sweetness and light because of financial circumstances which we can do very little about.

It is interesting to note how seriously he takes the economic side of the question, taking a clear interest in the market situation for coal which would not have been his concern before he became a member of a cooperative. His emphasis on the excessive idealism of the early days was repeated by the two managers I spoke to, who both said that the work itself has not become any easier, and that coal mining is extremely hard, difficult and dangerous work: 'Mining, even with all the technology and the new things in the past twenty or thirty years, it's still hard work, work doesn't become any easier. People still have to work hard.' This is a valuable lesson to the starry-eyed researcher or the economic planner with no experience of manual toil.

Worker involvement is a key theme of management literature. The old system of managers operating surveillance and providing incentives has been replaced by attempts to institute a corporate culture where all share the objectives of the company, and perhaps there is some element of profit-sharing too. This sort of approach was treated with particular scepticism in labour markets with a strong radical tradition, like that of the Valleys, where work culture had always been based on a tradition of 'struggle' between bosses and workers. An ex-miner I spoke to described the effect on his son's workplace – an electrical engineering company – of a US takeover: 'They've taken it over: team spirit, all this. But again the fitters and everybody else are employed as full-time staff; the support workers are employed by agencies and so there's a them-and-us situation.' He felt that the attempt to imply a shared culture was undermined by the fact that different employees had different levels of job security, and terms and conditions. The contrast with the comment made by a support worker at Tower who is not actually a worker-owner is strong. He gave the following judgement of the Tower project: 'I think it's a good thing. They've put their money, their redundancy income, and now they're all working for each other.'

A manager at Tower drew an explicit contrast between what he saw as artificial worker involvement of share-ownership schemes and the genuine involvement of cooperative working:

> The problem I see with workers' involvement, some of the shareholders and share purchase schemes are a scam. The workers don't have any real input. They only own a very small minority and yes they may benefit financially from it but I don't know if it has changed the way that they are treated or even in general discussions about their work: how could they improve, what would be the best for the company, which way do we go?

He continued to explain the consequences of this greater involvement for Tower workers' level of motivation and job satisfaction:

> If they can win their confidence, if they can involve them in everything . . . it's a contentment, it's a job satisfaction. It's no good without any money, I understand that, but I think people are far more responsive to supervision or management where it's not every time 'Do this, do that, do the other' without any explanation. Even to the extent where you can say 'Do this, and why I want you to do it is . . .' I know that sometimes in high-productivity industries nobody's got the time to do that, but I feel that spending a bit of time doing that would be worth it from a productivity point of view rather than the bland instruction 'I'm the boss, you do what you're told. At the end of the week pick up your pay packet and go home and do what you like, and Monday morning come back and we'll start all over again.'

Another Tower manager described the sense of empowerment, specifically as a response to the demoralization of 'the Thatcher years' and the sense of failure that followed the pit closures. Without being naive about the problems they face in a competitive world market, this quotation gives a clear sense of a new realism combined with a sense of hope:

> [Workers at Tower] have some control over their own destiny. World markets can shift, prices and slumps, but it was more controlled than is normal, so you've still got the person who says 'Tower's gonna work and I'm in the workforce for another ten years.' I don't know whether the coal is there, or whether the market's there, but Tower's not gonna close because we failed to work a head.

Job security takes precedence over cash reward

As reported in Chapter 5, workers in the study area have priorities other than income when the issue of job creation is under discussion. This was the case with both managers and miners at Tower, who agreed that security of employment was at least as important as the level of earnings. Fred, an environmental officer, made a joke about how much he loved working at Tower, but his second point makes it clear that his basic concern is for a job that will 'see him out', which for most miners means until retirement or premature illness.

> Fred: We love it here, don't we Dai? [laughter] Up to a point. It'll see me out anyway. I'll be fifty years in August so it'll see me out [coughing].

It is also clear from the following response that the objective of many managers of encouraging employees to take an interest in the market circumstances facing their company, and making the connection between the wages they receive and its competitiveness, can easily be achieved within a cooperative structure:

> George: It's our jobs, like, and if we don't make a success of it it's our jobs, and we don't have them any more . . . Obviously the money is the most important: everybody comes to work to earn money. But it's nice to be the shareholder of a company.

For this respondent, security was at least as important as his level of income. The managers share this sense of priorities:

> The other thing is – it's true like with other things – probably 90 per cent of the workforce, myself included, didn't hold a share in anything before they became shareholders in Tower. And in the first couple of years when dividends were paid people saw that as a boost. It's an extra. It's not the most important. Our commitment from the TEBO days was to form a company that would provide decent terms and conditions for as long as possible, and increase employment opportunities for young people. Saying that, I certainly think there's some satisfaction when people receive a dividend and it's their contribution, it's their work, and it's not the profits going to someone you don't know, somewhere else, never seen on site. So I think that's a benefit. (Manager and member of TEBO team)

Leadership

Another aspect vital to the success of a business is leadership. Again this issue generates a rather paradoxical situation in the case of a cooperative enterprise. It is clear from meeting and listening to Tyrone that he is what is tritely referred to as a 'natural leader', and indeed he led the NUM branch at Tower for twenty-two years before the buy-out, including taking a prominent role in the campaign to save collieries from closure. His leadership skills have been rewarded by the organization Common Purpose, which gives as its aim to 'unlock leadership potential'. Tyrone was awarded their Alchemist Award in 2001 and is attributed with providing 'leadership and vision to the miners'. He was also awarded an honorary degree by the University of Glamorgan in 2001.

Tyrone's view is more prosaic:

> When I was the union secretary I looked out for them [fellow miners] and I still do. I could and did influence their lives then, and I can do so now. They elected me to my position then, and have done so now. The difference is in degree – I can do more for them now. I have to concede that those joining the pit since the

buy-out inevitably view me as the boss but over time they will learn that we are all bosses now. Good management is not rocket science. We have all adapted to it easily. (O'Sullivan, Eve and Edworthy, 2001: 179)

A member of the board I interviewed at Tower was similarly modest about their management achievements, or perhaps unconvinced about the need for advanced training or qualification: for the present Tower board management it is a question of taking the other owners with you in your decision-making, and maintaining trust. Neil described the nature of the trust between management and miners, and how it has changed since the buy-out:

> If you look at the board of directors, out of the six, four were basically workmen before this came along. There's only two who are trained or qualified in senior management positions. The others, like myself, have just worked in the industry x number of years. So it's not a totally them–us situation, but you still have some people, some people always want enemies. In mining that's built up over the years. But it is Tower's [achievement], convincing our own that it's good business sense. I'm sure if there was a total management board of directors, senior qualified people, old British Coal style, and we were doing this now [taking an unpopular financial decision], all hell would let loose. Because everyone would want to know what they were having out of it. But all that's been left behind.

It seems that the miners themselves share this belief in the closeness of working relationships and the lack of distance between management and workers. This is how it was expressed by one of the worker-owners, who described why he liked his work:

> I enjoyed it but we always had the big margin between us and them but here it's not such a big margin. If I want to go and see the chairman I just go. There's no one I can't go and have a chat with . . . It's no big deal . . . Appointments and so on. We're all in the same boat, we're all shareholders and we've all got to make it work.

Such a situation of trust is of enormous benefit to the profitability of a business, and may be the holy grail of management science; at Tower it is a natural consequence of the ownership structure of the business.

In the widespread praise for O'Sullivan himself, and the reflected glory enjoyed by the other members of the management team, it is easy to forget the vital role played by the Wales Cooperative Centre (WCC). The importance of a leadership figure like O'Sullivan in providing inspiration is paramount, but the buy-out was lacking in expertise in the field of cooperative working, and it was here that the contribution of the WCC was crucial. If the cooperative model is to be a success in other areas of the south Wales economy their experience and knowledge will be in great demand.

Innovation in production and management

It is not immediately apparent why having a cooperative structure might lead to innovation in production and management techniques, but an argument could be made that the form is more flexible because of the nature of the selection of the board, and also that having accepted the extremely unusual form of firm organization in the first place, miner-owners would be more willing to be experimental in other areas. Whatever the reason, Tower Colliery has been innovative in developing one of its waste products into a usable source of energy, in a process which has been recognized in an industry Best Practice Brochure by the DTI (DTI, 2000).

During the process of coalification significant quantities of methane are produced. This is generally a hazard in mining – the infamous 'firedamp' that caused so many of the worst mining disasters and that always requires constant vigilance in a colliery. However, this gas also has commercial potential, since it is indistinguishable in quality from conventional natural gas. In 1998 Tower began a project to extract methane from the mine workings and use it for the generation of on-site electricity supplies. Tower now produces $6.5MW_e$ of electricity with a generating efficiency of 95 per cent. In order to be used on site this has to be transformed to the usable voltage of 11,000V to match the infrastructure of the plant. This generation allows Tower to be self-sufficient in electricity. The DTI considers this project to demonstrate best practice because:

> Operating mines to best practice guidelines for CBM [coalbed methane] ensures maximising the safety of miners working at the coal face, minimising influence on the surrounding environment, reducing pollution costs and enabling self-sufficiency in terms of energy requirements. (DTI, 2000: n.p.)

Tower has demonstrated a generally strong commitment to environmental standards which has been recognized by government. Dust and noise nuisance are kept to a minimum and water discharges are carefully monitored. Tip is treated with organic material to ensure the success of later revegetation. Tower Colliery is also developing expertise in the field of energy efficiency in its Energy Services Division. Advice on best practice is offered free to customers to enable them to gain maximum efficiency from their coal with the minimum environmental impact. Tower managers are well aware of the threat posed to their industry by the Kyoto carbon dioxide targets and are keeping abreast of developments in CO_2 capture technology. They are fortunate in terms of the coal industry in that the particular form of anthracite mined in south Wales has low sulphur and low ash content and is therefore relatively non-polluting. The methane plant is also environmentally beneficial since methane is one of the gases that contributes to the greenhouse effect.

The particular kind of relationship between the managers and workers in a cooperative has also worked to the advantage of Tower by allowing innovation in management practice. In 1998 the coalface collapsed. Under British Coal management this might well have led to the closure of the colliery, but because the workers recognized that their livelihood depended on keeping it open they worked together to repair the face, allowing production to continue. A similar situation occurred following the gas leak in 1999. The technical problem was again resolved by the workers, preventing the closure of the face. The productive seam is now five miles or so from the shaft, which could have led to shift problems under British Coal management. However, with the unity possible under cooperative management an agreement was reached to adopt flexible shift patterns, facilitating the distant working. This sort of innovation is possible because miners and managers feel that they are on the same side; it is in both their interests to work together to keep the colliery functioning and protect their investment (for more details see Smith et al., 2002).

The local market and local community

Since the buy-out the Tower management team have worked to establish the colliery as a local business, to keep strong links and support in the community. Part of this linkage has been justified rhetorically by the commitment to keep long-term, well-paid jobs rather than maximizing profits. In addition, Tower has been helped by the strong support it has received, which has led to a situation where all local politicians feel the need to support the project. As noted above Tower exports around 12 per cent of its output. Throughout the UK its coal is sold by Evans and Reid Ltd, a long-standing Cardiff-based firm of coal distributors. In addition, Tower has developed its own local distribution company with a brand – Welsh Dragon Coal – aiming to appeal to community support for the colliery.

Tower has strong links with local authorities in the Valleys, supplying coal direct to more than 100 schools and public buildings through a contract with the Central Purchasing Consortium of Welsh local authorities. Since 1997

**Photo 7.2: Publicity-conscious Tower managers have erected this sign and also
set up a visitor centre**

Tower has been RCT's nominated supplier of solid fuel; the most recent
contract runs for two years from 1 May 2002. The estimated value of the
contract for anthracite is £460,000. RCT Council state that Tower 'have been
awarded the contract on numerous occasions due to their competitiveness
and excellent performance record, providing a value for money service in
terms of price, delivery and technical back-up expertise'. Since the takeover
Tower has engaged in vertical diversification in an attempt to increase the
value added to its coal. This led to the establishment of its own bagging plant
to achieve a direct marketing strategy in the local community.

Tower has also diversified by establishing its own outreach wing called
Tower Energy Services (Tower Colliery, 2000), whose job is to develop an
innovative marketing strategy. Working with a specialist heating
engineering company, Lionheart Heating Services, Tower now offers a
'total energy package' of fuel supply, heating equipment, installation and
maintenance, thus involving it in other marketplaces and increasing value
added. This marketing strategy relies strongly on local loyalty, but the
development of the local market also has environmental advantages, as in
the case of Rhydycar Leisure Centre, whose heating is provided with coal

direct from the Tower plant, just four miles away, thus reducing the environmental impact of long-distance transport.

As identified in the interviews reported in Chapter 6, Welsh workers feel uncomfortable about making profits as individuals, feeling that it is immoral to profit at others' expense. Part of the explanation for Tower's success is that its worker-owners do not believe that their success is personal but that it is for the sake of the community. Community, or camaraderie, has always been a keystone of work in the Valleys and other mining areas (as explained in Chapter 6, this probably has to do with the dangerous nature of the work and the absolute reliance on others for one's survival). When I asked a surface worker at Tower why people like working as miners he explained: 'Well I should think it's because we're all working together here; we're all as one; we're all looking after each other. That's how it should be anyway.' This ideal of support extends beyond the workplace into the wider community, to such an extent that when I asked another miner about the policy of investing money to create jobs he thought I was suggesting that Tower should invest its profits to create jobs for others and said that they were doing what they could to invest in the local community.

The miners to whom I spoke at Tower also shared a commitment to creating secure, well-paid jobs not only for themselves but also for the community as a whole, as described by one member of the management board:

> First and foremost I can honestly say that as a TEBO Team member my first priority was getting my own job back. I believe that it's every individual's right, man or woman's right, to put their family first and to help their children out. That was my first concern. My second concern was, because my valley was decimated by the closure of the coal industry over the last thirty years: high unemployment, crime, drugs, you name it. The valley was becoming like a city area, and my own village. (Keith Morris, manager and member of TEBO team)

I drew attention to the way Keith used the phrase 'my valley', a formulation used by many of the miners. He said proudly 'It's not my valley . . . but I own a part of it!'

The desire of companies to prove their commitment to their local community through sponsorship can often seem artificial, but at Tower it seems more genuine. To maintain the link between the colliery and the local community the colliery established a Visitor Centre at the plant, which tells the stories of mining in the Valleys, the miners' strike, and specifically that of the buy-out. According to the Tower website (*www.tower-colliery.co.uk*) at the opening of the centre:

Tower Chairman Tyrone O' Sullivan said that during the period the workforce were fighting to purchase the pit, the community of Cynon Valley 'fought alongside us'. 'In recognition of that, we decided that any sponsorship we embarked on would be directed into the community to assist various sporting organisations and clubs at grass-roots level.'

Tower Colliery has sponsored a range of sporting and charitable activities including Mountain Ash Girls' Football Club, Aberdare Valleys Athletics Club, Mountain Ash Rugby Club, Cynon Valley Schools Football, Aberdare Park National Road Races, Cwmaman Silver Band, Aberdare Carnival, the Tŷ Hafan children's hospice, and many others. The colliery is now signed up to the government's Sportsmatch initiative. This sponsorship is described as 'safeguarding the good will of the community in appreciation of the support Tower has received during the troubled times of 1994'. It is clearly also a marketing strategy, but in the context of deep identification with mining in the area and the support for Tower as a local success, the community orientation of the colliery rings true.

Respect

The preference for mining work over factory work, with its greater level of supervision and loss of trust between fellow workers, has been reported in Chapter 6. At Tower there seems to be an additional dimension: the respect that miners feel they are shown by the present management in contrast to the attitude of the British Coal 'bosses'. Two members of the Mines Rescue Service discussed with me the distinction between working at the Sony factory and work in the mines. One said of the factory, in a disparaging tone, 'They're more money-orientated. They just wanted to make a profit.' Again this indicates that in the culture of the Valleys, profit-making is definitely a motivation that is perceived as negative. By contrast, 'In the Mines Rescue it's more family orientated. In Sony it's a more strict regime. You have to be there at a certain time, you have to do certain work, no giving and taking anywhere.' A surface worker at Tower told me: 'You're all individuals in a factory' – again this was a negative comment.

So the workers at Tower felt a sense of respect that they did not experience in a factory setting. The following long statement from one of the managers, who had previously been a pit deputy, gives a sense of respect that the experienced, hands-on managers of Tower have for their coalface workers:

I've known this industry from a boy until I became a shareholder, and you would come up against problems from day to day that sometimes even a manager wouldn't be able to answer, but you would get an experienced workman there who had had this problem ten years before and you would ask, perhaps advice is the wrong word, but you would ask 'How did you treat this problem?' Because without the practical skills, and I don't think mining is completely different to anything else, without practical experience, and nobody's got all of that, I don't care if it's the managing director or anybody, to actually speak to the men on the job. Some of the best innovations throughout my lifetime have come about because of suggestions by the workforce, not by some superdon, excuse me for bringing university people into it!

The respect for employees is demonstrated in practical terms in the strong commitment to safety. The company's mission statement is 'To provide employment for as long as possible within a safe and accident free environment and with a disciplined workforce'; the first thing you notice on entering the site is a large board with the bold slogan 'Safety begins here.' Mining is a dangerous business and none of the board, who are mostly ex-miners, is likely to underestimate the importance of safe working conditions. As the safety policy points out, with the workings now so far from the shaft the risk from explosions or geological subsidence is even greater, since it would take the miners much longer to walk out of the drift, as they had to in 1999. The safety slogan at Tower is posted everywhere:

Safety at TOWER means:

Think
Of your
Workmates. It is
Everybody's
Responsibility to work safely

This slogan sums up the camaraderie with its basis in shared risk that is the central aspect of the social side of mining.

Another indication of commitment to both mutual respect and concern for safety is the high level of training at Tower. Before the return to work in 1995 the board insisted on carrying out a thirteen-week assessment of their knowledge of safety procedures and remedial training, which led to a great improvement in the accident rate compared with that prior to the closure in 1994 and a consequent reduction in the employees' liability insurance premium. Tower also runs technical and electrical apprenticeships and has been given the Investors in People Award and National Training Award by the Department for Education, attained in March 1997. Tower was the first mining company to be accredited by BTEC as an NVQ examination centre.

THE COOPERATIVE FORM AS A WELSH EMPLOYMENT PATTERN

Although Tower Colliery is the most renowned it is by no means the only cooperative in Wales. The Wales Institute for Research into Cooperatives is currently carrying out an audit of the social economy in Wales, so that exact numbers are not yet available, but the Wales Cooperative Centre gives plenty of examples of thriving Welsh businesses organized in accordance with cooperative principles (see *www.walescoop.com*).

Tower's charismatic leader Tyrone O'Sullivan clearly understands the role a cooperative work pattern may play in Wales's future. In 2001 he received a standing ovation for the annual Swansea Institute's St David's Day Lecture, which he called 'Welsh Self-Confidence, Community Values, and the Tower Experience'. His presentation contained the usual combination of tales of proud and heroic struggle and inspiring words to others to follow suit. On a similar theme, Tyrone's speech to a conference on the future of Welsh farming recommended they too sell their produce through cooperatives direct to consumers, as 90 per cent of Tower's coal is now sold (*Western Mail*, 2001). When talking to me, one of the management board was more cautious though, emphasizing the huge risk that buying a workplace represents to those who have only their redundancy money to invest. He was concerned that the success of Tower should not be seen as universally applicable and drew attention to the importance of economic realism as well as inspiration:

> Although I do believe other places can do it, the only thing is that the Tower story is more fantasy than fact . . . The [TEBO team] knew the facts about the quality of coal, about what production could be reached, and sometimes we've spoken to people who are a little bit airy-fairy . . . So I would hate for Tower to be an example where people go out and do something and then when you've been made redundant, or put out of work, and somebody asks you to put £5,000, or whatever the figure is, it's not money you can afford to lose. So as long as they know the business, they won't be less experienced in the business world than the TEBO Team was here.

It is inappropriate in a book whose central message is the need to escape the beggarly nature of much employment policy-making of recent decades to make an argument for public subsidy. Independence, and the confidence it brings, is a key part of the success of Tower, and of the future success of the Welsh economy. However, it may be helpful to discuss Tower Colliery from the perspective of public policy. The case was made in Chapter 3 that, in spite of rhetoric espousing free markets, large amounts of public money are spent to maintain incomes in south Wales. When it comes to domestic manufacturing and extractive industries, the argument is made that the outcome must be determined by the economics of the marketplace, not by political decision. However, there are a number of issues that have affected the market facing Tower that are clearly of political, not economic origin:

- the decision to provide a large public subsidy to the nuclear industry because of its national security importance and the inevitability of public funding of its decommissioning;
- the acceptance under world trade rules of widely different standards of employment rights in the EU countries and in those who export to EU countries;
- decisions by EU governments to support their coal-mining industries with subsidies;
- the Kyoto protocol and resulting British targets to reduce carbon dioxide emissions, leading to a turn towards gas and away from coal for electricity generation;
- agreed standards of environmental protection and whether these do or do not permit the opencast method of mining.

A rhetorical commitment to market forces can be used as a fig leaf to cover unpopular or unacceptable political decisions. Ultimately, even our decision to follow pro-market policies is political, even though all the parties that hold seats at Westminster support this decision. However, at the local scale we should remember that it is our right to make these decisions about our future, particularly when public money is involved. There is no market reason why it is acceptable to fund an Asian company to build an electronics factory but not fund the expansion of a colliery. This is a political decision, and in a democracy a decision for us as citizens.

In some ways the most important role Tower Colliery can play in Welsh employment policy is as an icon. In an area that has been in recession for the best part of a century, bar short-term booms during the two world wars, a success story is desperately needed. For people who have suffered so much disappointment and, as they see it, betrayal, to have found something of their own that reflects their values and is also successful is of fundamental importance in rebuilding self-belief and confidence. And the fact that local people do genuinely believe in and value the achievements of Tower indicates that hope has not disappeared entirely.

In an area where so many initiatives have been tried and have failed it is worth exploring Tower closely simply because it is a success story. But what of Tower as a model, what of the reality rather than the myth? The comments quoted above have explored some aspects of Tower as a workplace that may help to explain the success and may be used to guide policy-making throughout RCT. Attitudes towards the workforce by the management are central. The experience of work in the Valleys was an experience of struggle between 'us and them', a phrase which was used repeatedly throughout the interviews. Management is seen as hostile and any chance to gain redress is welcomed, every victory eulogized. At Tower the 'us' have now become 'them', which in some cases led to obvious confusion. From most worker-owners, however, there is respect for those who have successfully taken on the mantle of management, so long as they do not become too distant or unresponsive. This respect is returned by managers who understand the experience and difficulties of the miners, having shared them. This is demonstrated as much in the commitment to safety and training as in the decisions to share surpluses equally. This mutual respect results in an utterly different workplace culture.

Workers at Tower show a high level of commitment to their workplace, which is a necessary consequence of the ownership structure of a cooperative. They can no longer blame outsiders for the failure of their business. They also have a new attitude to job security, an issue which the findings of Chapter 5 indicated was of great salience in RCT. Workers who are their own bosses are responsible on the one hand for their commercial success – and can reap the financial rewards – but must also take responsibility for their own job security. The old argument about the right to a job has now been transmuted into the responsibility of responding to economic forces in a far more direct way than through share-ownership or bonus schemes. This is an extension of the responsibility for each other that mining work always entailed, and this sense of camaraderie, extending to support for the wider community, dominates employment motivations at Tower.

The final ingredient appears to be another that has long been identified in the management literature: leadership. Despite the cooperative nature of the workplace and the sharing of responsibility and decision-making it is hard to imagine Tower as a reality without the dominating presence of Tyrone O'Sullivan. On one level he is an icon, a fact of which he himself is well aware; but he is also an extraordinary person, with impressive personal qualities. Although equality is a basic requirement of cooperative working, without the right people or person 'leading' the enterprise success is always going to be much harder to achieve.

If policy-makers are really looking for a Welsh 'third way' (see Hain, 1999) then they could spend some time assessing the cooperative model as exemplified by Tower Colliery. The discomfort some of the worker-owners felt at times about being bosses themselves and having nobody to confront in times of crisis was clearly outweighed by the pride they felt in owning their own workplace. Perhaps the third way, that was so intellectually evanescent that it appears to have vanished into thin air within a few years of its invention, could have found real form in the cooperative way of working of Tower Colliery. In an economic sector that has always demonstrated the greatest union militancy, workers have become their own bosses and seem to be developing a successful form of inclusive management.

8

Conclusion: An Employment Policy Fit for Rhondda Cynon Taff

A fo ben, bid bont (He who would be a leader, let him be a bridge)

INTRODUCTION

There has been no shortage of models proposed as a solution to Wales's economic problems. According to Lovering 'one of the most striking continuities in Wales is the claim that a new economic era is dawning' (1999: 49), and it is easy to read the history of Welsh employment policy as a process of experimentation with the latest economic and social theories which have refused to embed because they simply did not fit. This has left a huge gulf of trust between policy-makers and the people with whom they need to work in regenerating Wales's depressed regional economies. The first step that should be taken is to rebuild some trust by beginning a process of genuinely seeking the views of local people. I am not talking about the now infamous 'stakeholder dialogue', where one is always left wondering whether the hand that is not clutching the stake might be holding a bunch of garlic, but a humble and human attempt to make contact with the real people who live and would like to work in the Valleys. It is a dreadful indictment of the arrogance of some policy-makers that this recommendation needs to be made.

In an era when the ideology of the free market is so dominant, and where private-sector values and methods of organization are proposed as solutions to the diverse social and economic problems our society faces, it may seem anachronistic even to discuss the nature of regional policy. However, as was made clear in Chapter 3, vast sums of public money are still being spent, so that the commitment to the 'free' market is more apparent than real. If companies are invited to resolve our shared problems, in return for grants and subsidies, this represents placing our trust in others to adjust the failings of the market economy, not allowing it to have free rein. When their remedies fail, whether this is because they are fundamentally misguided or merely inappropriate to the setting where they are put into place, the problems will remain ours, and our money will continue to be spent resolving them.

The Rhondda Heritage Park epitomizes many of the problems of regeneration in RCT. In Chapter 4 I used it as an example of the confusion over work identity there. In a complex sociological analysis of this project Dicks (2000: 247) analyses its failure to fulfil its mutually incompatible objectives of local popular representation and entrepreneurial regeneration. She also makes clear how it typifies many of the problems with bought-in solutions to the area's economic problems, and the fact that, when the bubble has burst and the hype has been exhausted, public money will still be required:

> Local political control is not lost forever where much-vaunted commercial success fails to materialize. In that situation, the public purse continues to pay the bill. Financial control over the Rhondda heritage museum has remained in public hands because the project failed in commercial terms . . . it provides a neat example of the Welsh Office's ultimate failure to wrest the heritage project from 'parochial' hands where the brave new world of enterprise leisure has simply failed to materialize.

The reality of work in the Valleys is concealed by multiple layers of myth-making, whether by proponents of the chimera of the free market or those still wedded to the community-spirited, black-faced miner. I hope I have cleared some of the undergrowth in the foregoing chapters, making a better foundation for the policy recommendations that are presented in the conclusion to this book.

The rest of this chapter proposes some specific measures that could be introduced to improve the employment situation in Wales. The first section suggests a re-evaluation of Wales's resources to challenge the myth of helplessness. The following section expands on the need for genuine dialogue between policy-makers and local workers in Rhondda Cynon Taff. The debate about the balance between indigenous business and inward investment is then presented. Finally, three specific policy recommendations are made, based on the indications that have emerged from the research reported in Chapters 5 and 6.

REVALUING OUR SHARED RESOURCES

Exploring the future prospects for employment in an area like Rhondda Cynon Taff can be a depressing experience. One is greeted by a general air of hopelessness and lack of confidence leavened, at least in the case of the workers themselves, by an irrepressible seam of black humour. The feeling is that everything possible has been tried, that everything has failed, and that we are left, as the Czech proverb has it, pretending to work while they pretend to pay us. This is the view from the ground, and it is depressing. And yet, if we take a step back and look at Wales objectively we can see that it has a huge range of tremendous assets which are not being used to improve the quality of our lives because the global economic structure by which we feel ourselves bound does not value them, and we are accepting that valuation.[1]

It is this gap between the image of a Welsh economy in a permanent and irreversible state of hopeless decline and the reality of a vibrant country with a mass of valuable resources and an intelligent, creative and communicative people that leads me to recommend the need for what I call a Robinson Crusoe approach to policy-making. As a first step towards building a successful economy we need to shake off the shackles that have tied us first to England and later to the competitive global marketplace and take a fresh look at ourselves and our resources. When Robinson Crusoe arrived on his island he felt a sense of despair, but, in the absence of any outside protector, he did what humans have always done to ensure survival in difficult circumstances: he assessed what was available and decided how to make use of these things to increase his well-being. I suggest that we begin to follow this example in Wales, where the response has rather been to expend most of our effort in building one raft after another, all of which have sunk without trace on the merciless seas of international competition.

This brings us to another important point about Robinson Crusoe economics: it is about making a living rather than making a profit. Too much of the rhetoric of economic development is concerned to praise individual success stories, measured largely on the basis of the profits they generate. This message often falls on stony ground precisely because Welsh people are more concerned with quality of life than with profit, and because they feel uncomfortable (as identified in Chapter 6) profiting at another's expense. The commitment to sustainability has been included as a fundamental plank of Welsh Assembly policy-making and will become an unavoidable necessity in economic planning in the twenty-first century, as planetary limits become harder and harder to ignore. Welsh politicians have made a bold step towards a new type of economic planning which puts quality of life and well-being before profit.

It will not be easy to make this switch. During the years of pseudo-colonization Wales and its people have become used to a position of subservience, to carrying out the policy equivalent of stealing the mistress's sugar, of which the combination of the Valleys and west Wales to obtain Objective 1 funding is the most outrageous example. Too often the response to some economic hardship is to bring out the begging-bowl and rattle our collecting-tins in the faces of the Englishmen in suits, and now the Eurocrats. The winning of grants is greeted with delight, as in the story in the *Western Mail* of 10 April 2002 entitled 'Grants Reach a Record High' (Smale, 2002). The report informs us that 'Last year's offers exceed by nearly 50pc the previous record of 181 in 1996–7 and in terms of their total cash value, the offers made are 15pc higher than those made in the previous record year of 1997–8'. Such an attitude suggests a lottery mentality rather than a serious approach to long-term economic development. The report actually ends by reassuring readers that the record demand for grants will lead to an increase in the grant-giving budget so that there is no danger that companies will miss out on the great grant bonanza.

The reliance on grants and the lack of self-reliance were identified as a cultural problem in a Menter a Busnes report from 1994, which addressed specifically the problems of Welsh-speaking business people:

> it's important not to forget the downside which reflects itself today in the continued over-dependence of Welsh speakers on employment in the public sector, in the abiding obsession with Government grants, and the general tendency to look to others to solve local economic problems, instead of asking what more we can do to help ourselves. (Casson et al., 1994)

Although the report addresses itself directly to Welsh-speaking communities its findings in this respect can be applied more widely, particularly in a context where many of those forming the critical opposition to economic policy in the Assembly, as members of Plaid Cymru, either come from Welsh-speaking communities or share their cultural and intellectual outlook. The dependent responses criticized here not only indicate a lack of self-respect inappropriate for a region aspiring to nationhood; they also undermine our faith in our ability to solve our own problems. It is itself a contribution to the unhelpful myth of Welsh helplessness. Brooksbank and Pickernell (2001: 276) acknowledge that the inward-investment strategy

> has created a dependence that Wales can only break by developing its own indigenous companies . . . whether the resources will be available to make this work, especially given the mindset that must have grown amongst the economic development agencies, is debatable. In particular, Wales must decide whether the seemingly continuous need to drip-feed valuable economic development resources to large inward investors is necessary only in the short

run, to gradually wean her off dependency on inward investment. If not, then Wales will remain reliant on inward investment, which is likely to require increasing rather than reducing resources (both financial and otherwise) given the growth in competition countries like Wales now face from Eastern Europe.

My characterization of this psychological dependence on grants may seem rather unfair, but its consequences run deep in the Welsh economic and business structure. A business which has obtained grants in the past, and hopes to obtain them in the future, cannot afford to be too successful, or it might find itself outside the category of desperate cases eligible for economic support. The example of the combination of the Valleys and rural west Wales into a single area to achieve a low enough average GDP to win the race to the bottom with the Mezzogiorno and Andalucia, and thus achieve the dubious status of poorest region in Europe, is the most prominent case of this. It has had two unmistakable consequences in addition to the steady flow of cash. Firstly, those of us who live in this region have had our worst fears confirmed: we are the losers that we always dreaded we might be. Secondly, many Assembly statistics are now produced for this area with no logical or bioregional rationale, confusing its inhabitants even further, undermining our identity as well as our self-esteem, and making life hell for a researcher interested in time-series data. In the west Wales part of the area we reassure each other that we have our spiritual wealth as a priceless substitute for GDP equality; what similar benefits can the losers of the Valleys claim?

As the commentators pointed out in the quotation cited above, grants can have a pernicious effect in terms of perpetuating dependence. A friend of mine who is also an environmental design artist[2] shared with me her findings about regenerating former industrial land. Many projects attract grant funding by promising glamorous, short-term solutions in terms of visual enhancement, while leaving the underlying problems of poor and toxic soil unchanged. These sites are successful as long as the grant lasts, but once it has gone, unless another grant is forthcoming, the veneer of improvement will disappear and the land will revert to its barren state. Successful regeneration requires working with nature to engender positive feedbacks that result in a self-sustaining ecosystem. We both noticed a parallel with economic regeneration, which also needs to engender positive feedbacks to avoid relying on grants in perpetuity.

The environmental regenerators have had to recognize the need to work with nature to ensure that the improvements will become self-sustaining. In the field of economic regeneration we should recognize the similar need to work with culture, as the underlying system directing a local economy. Reading Welsh economic development documents you can sense the frustration of policy-makers for the people of Wales who are so stubbornly refusing to become free-market entrepreneurs. The political battles this has caused have led to an unnecessary demoralization on both sides. How much simpler to see the real value in what we have here in Wales, rather than envying our differently endowed larger neighbour. Once we have found a model that fits local people's attitudes and expectations, and the resources available to us, a cultural feedback system will develop and the local economy will power itself. As FDR famously said, we must do what we can, where we are, with what we have.

I am beginning a chapter of recommendations with this suggestion because without it all the other proposals will fail. The most important first step towards building an economy that works is to carry out a genuine valuation of what we have, and not merely in monetary terms. Before we can evaluate our economy we need to decide what the right indicators are, and it is important that we use a measure that includes quality-of-life considerations rather than the primitive bean-counting approach of GDP. Some initial work to produce an Index of Sustainable Economic Welfare for Wales carried out by researchers in Aberystwyth (see Midmore et al., 2000), is now being taken forward in collaboration with the Welsh Economy Research Unit at Cardiff University, which could contribute to a broader measure of what we are achieving in Wales (see Matthews et al., 2003). It is beyond the scope of this study to propose all the changes in thinking such a re-evaluation would require. However, I have a few suggestions for resources that are blatantly undervalued and underused in present economic planning.

The most basic resource of any people is their land. In Wales our land has not been properly used since the people were exiled to be replaced by sheep during the enclosures of the eighteenth century. This is the most fundamental example of a natural resource being appropriated leaving people with no alternative but to resort to wage-labour or the begging-bowl (the same process that is taking place just now across the developing world). The current crisis in farming demonstrates that this system does not even work in terms of the profit system that created it, never mind in terms of human well-being and environmental quality. Suggestions are made that we replace the CAP subsidy system with payments for environ-mental stewardship (see Policy Commission, 2002; K. Morgan, 2002), a move on from the Big Pit museum to the museumization of our whole countryside. Rather than a working land producing food for local markets, rural people will be transformed into curators, offering themselves for observation by inquisitive visitors from the towns with 'real' jobs and therefore 'real' money to spend. This sort of proposal – the extension of St Fagans nationwide[3] – is the end-point of a mindset that has forgotten what land is for and thinks that food comes from Tesco. It offers a humiliating future for our rural people – what Marsden et al. (2002: figure 2) refer to as 'marginal activities for marginal people' – and, most importantly, a scandalous waste of our most valuable resource.

Welsh agricultural economists have been at the forefront of an argument for a more socially responsive development of our countryside. Marsden et al. (2002) suggest three models for rural development: *the agro-industrial logic*, identifying rural nature as an 'intensive production space'; the *postproductivist model*, celebrating the growth of the countryside itself as a consumption product; and *rural development*, which is a policy for the countryside that is sensitive to local people. In justification of the third model Murdoch, Marsden and Banks (2000: 115) bring the economic sociology concept of embeddedness into play:

> There is an ongoing 'entanglement' . . . between economic and social relations, ensuring that 'even if economic agents in a market economy appear to confront each other as "bare individuals", they still remain always already social actors'. This complex interplay between the economic and social poses problems for the construction and stabilization of purely economic (or fully commoditized) relationships.

They see this model as having its origins in bottom-up initiatives by marginalized rural communities, and by those with ecological concerns. It thus offers a way to reunite social and environmental objectives. Pretty (2002) presents a similar prescription for agricultural policy-making in his poetic and inspiring vision of an alternative future for the rural economy.

The crisis in Welsh farming has led to some interesting alliances. A conference on the future of agriculture at the Royal Welsh Showground in September 2001 saw Tyrone O'Sullivan agreeing with Noel Morgan, NatWest Welsh regional agricultural manager. Unsurprisingly, Tyrone suggested that, like his own fellows at Tower, Welsh farmers should work together cooperatively to solve their problems, by selling direct to local people. More unusually, Noel Morgan agreed, stating that 'farmers cannot rely on other people to save the industry, they have got to stand up and be counted and do something for themselves', and continuing that 'if we cannot sell our commodities without relying on the middlemen taking their cut, as farmers, constantly complain, then the answer is co-operation' (*Western Mail*, 2 October 2001).

The research backs up these ideas, with a report showing that local food distribution creates more employment and keeps more money circulating in the local economy (Norberg-Hodge, Merrifield and Gorelick, 2000; Morgan and Morley, 2002). The link with a cooperative method of distribution is also found in Marsden, Banks and Bristow's (2000; 2002) case studies of successful rural adaptation, especially the Llŷn Beef Co-operative. This association of north Wales beef farmers decided to work together to improve their collective strength in the food chain in 1997. Their gross margin per head is £64 compared with £37 for traditionally finished lowland beef producers. This issue has now been taken up by the Countryside Alliance, who are calling for institutions and individuals to buy local food to support rural life. At the local level farmers in the Valleys are developing their own producer cooperative with the support of Glamorgan NFU's chairman David Williams (Dubé, 2003).

From a Robinson Crusoe perspective a true valuation of land and its productive use is the most fundamental objective of any economy. This is just as true in the Valleys as it is in Wales's agricultural areas; in fact, a short visit to the so-called industrial heartlands will make clear how artificial the rural–urban divide is in this part of Wales. The regeneration of the land of the Valleys from industrial wasteland to a valuable heritage has been 'the jewel in the crown of the Welsh Development Agency despite the hype surrounding inward investment'. The 'generation of expertise in restoring nineteenth-century industrial dereliction to pristine greenness' can be a source of business benefits and of local pride (Cooke and Morgan, 1998: 220).

Our second most seriously undervalued resource is our people. The literature of the Thatcher years makes clear that people in the former mining areas were always seen as part of the problem rather than part of the solution. Japanese companies were invited in partly in the hope that their obedient, docile ways would rub off on the rough, burly workers who were proving so difficult to control. The consequence of thirty-odd years of trying to force square pegs into round holes is a cynical and demoralized work-force. Yet the first thing that strikes you when you engage in social research in the Valleys is how clever the people are. The area is a social scientist's dream, where respondents not only have informed opinions on every imaginable issue, but also enjoy eloquently expressing them. In the Inform-ation Economy where communication skills are so sought after, Welsh workers have a natural advantage. In the Valleys the culture of cooperation and mutual support could also provide a strong basis for economic structures if it were only redefined as 'social capital' rather than 'worker solidarity'. The objective of my research project was to explore what Valleys workers were like; this should be extended and should lead to a genuine valuation of their abilities, rather than the imposition of more pointless training programmes in irrelevant skills that they so universally despise.

A step towards this re-evaluation has been taken at Tower, where the managers have themselves been 'workers' and they have a respect for

Photo 8.1: Daniel Morris of Maerdy Farm, Maerdy, Rhondda Fach: growing up in the Valleys offers much in terms of access to the countryside

those who carry out manual work in the colliery today. This attitude is summed up in the following comment from a current Tower manager:

> What bothers me, although I don't have any vast knowledge of industry outside mining, but what bothers me, people always want to talk to you about what they've invested in a new computer, what they've invested in a new machine. I mean surely the biggest asset any company has is its employees, is its workforce. I'm not saying everybody is happy here every day of the week, we have our quarrels and we have our disagreements, that is mining. But I can't understand why the brains of industry give me the impression that employees are just a subsidiary. I'm convinced that you can spend money on machines and equipment but if you haven't got the workforce with the will and the contentment and the knowledge that there's some future for them, then you don't get the best results, whatever you invest in.

It is a cliché of histories of the Valleys, and one not lost on the Tower board, that 'Wales is built on coal', but intriguingly this abundant resource plays a minor part in considerations of our economic future. A new valuation of our national resources would have to place it high on the list and would make a priority of finding ways of addressing the problems of the greenhouse gases that its combustion produces. The Coalfields Communities Campaign (CCC), unsurprisingly, has 'consistently argued that coal still has an important role to play in a secure, sustainable and diverse energy policy'. The campaign argues against 'an energy market rigged in favour of other fuels', but without providing details of what constitutes the present unfairness. A case could certainly be made that, as our primary indigenous fuel, coal should be treated as a strategic resource rather than subjected to the vagaries of a market that is seeking profits rather than the well-being or security of citizens. Coal faces greater challenges in an era of concern about the emission of greenhouse gases, but such an argument makes no sense when so much of the coal burned to generate power in the UK is imported. Tyrone O'Sullivan's intervention in this debate is as predictable as that of the CCC. Discussing a deal between Tower Colliery and the Aberthaw power station he criticized the lack of attention paid to the coal industry: 'He said there was no logic to a government policy that destroyed its energy source, then relied on overseas imports. Lack of support for coal mining meant energy needs must come from outside. "It's like storing the family silver in the house next door", he said' (R. Jones, 2001).

The energy sources of the future – wind, wave, and small-scale hydro – are also all being developed in Wales. Friends of the Earth Cymru note (NATTA, 2002) that

Wales has abundant natural energy resources that can be harnessed by renewable energy technologies to generate electricity, hot water and hydrogen fuel. Indeed, Wales has some of the highest tidal ranges in the world and the UK has about a third of Europe's wind energy resource.

The report makes another point of much relevance to a study which focuses on employment policies: 'Most renewables create more jobs per unit energy than fossil fuel or nuclear power, and in a more flexible and widely distributed pattern across urban and rural areas.'

Energy has been identified as a key strategic area of the Welsh economy and an Energy Review is currently under way. Christine Gwyther, chair of the Assembly's Economic Development Committee, notes in her foreword to the report on renewable energy that:

Wales is well-endowed with energy resources and has a track record in manufacturing and engineering – both vital to energy production. As a modern economy, we have learned in recent years to embrace new technologies and to work with companies and investors from all over the world. We are therefore well placed to play an active part in the changes necessary to achieve a global shift from the reliance on fossil fuels, to combat global warming and develop renewable resources. There are unprecedented opportunities to develop new technologies, for research and innovation, and for Wales to place itself at the forefront of these developments.

This is an important realization so far as it goes. So far the exploitation of Wales's renewable energy resources has followed the same pattern as the exploitation of her coal – with entrepreneurs taking the profits and the local people paying the price – and with the same consequences: hostility and opposition by local people who experience the side-effects of the industry but without any gain for themselves. It must be a basic priority for economic planners to ensure that the value from renewable energy is used to benefit the people of Wales. The renewable energy review includes such a commitment, requiring that the National Assembly should 'find mechanisms whereby renewables developments can provide immediate and tangible benefits to the local communities in which they are located'. An encouraging example of such a development is the Dyfi Eco-Valley windfarm project near Machynlleth, where villagers have bought a £1,000 share in the wind turbine that now provides their electricity.

Local opposition is often led by those who enjoy the Welsh scenery for only a few weeks of the year, or whose livelihoods depend on such people. D. J. Williams (2003) characterizes many of the opponents to the development of wind-power as confusing the concept 'environment' with the concept 'view' and points out that quaintness has not served rural Welsh people well in the past. From a broader green perspective wind farms, far from being a blot on the landscape, represent a source of pride and economic hope. We should not allow our natural advantage in this technological area of the future to be blighted by the lobbying of interest groups or vocal individuals.

And finally the resource for which Wales is perhaps most famous: water. The flooding of Welsh valleys – especially Treweryn – to provide water for the industrial heartlands of England's Midlands and north-west is a touchstone of nationalist resentment in Wales (see, for example, G. Evans, 1956; Tickell, 1995). And yet no attempt has been made to provide a modern assessment of this key asset. If treated as a strategic resource rather than a free good it might provide a valuable source of income to the Welsh economy. The likely scarcity of rainfall through the United Kingdom as a result of changing weather patterns consequent upon global warming suggests an increase in the value of water. The sector also provides an interesting case study for the mutualization of the economy: the water supplied to Welsh consumers has, since January 2001, been provided by a company unique in the utility sector, the not-for-profit group Glas Cymru (Taylor, 2001). The relationship between this company's directors and Wales's Assembly members (who have rights of inspection over its activities) may provide a model for the provision of basic services in the future which better suits the mutualist aspirations of Welsh people (see Mayo and Moore, 2001). In spite of concerns about the failure of the Glas Cymru model to address issues of ownership and control, it appears to be a move in the right direction. It is no coincidence that this model is being developed in this country and in this sector: I will pursue this theme of mutual or associationist economic structures further in a later section.

So here we have four sources of tremendous economic benefit – the land, the people, energy and water – which are presently either underused, used inefficiently or used to generate private profits rather than increasing the well-being of Welsh citizens. If the Robinson Crusoe perspective were adopted many more resources would receive their genuine valuation and Wales would cease to look like a hopeless economic case. Valuing our people and our resources and changing our objective from global competition for profits to cooperation by local people for a better quality of life is the first recommendation for a better future for the people of the Valleys and the rest of Wales.

THE IMPORTANCE OF RESPONDING TO LOCAL ASPIRATIONS

Employment policy in Wales, as well as the success of this early industrial economy that preceded it, has been almost exclusively the result of external endeavour and external priorities, to such an extent that the 'internal colonialism' model developed by Hechter (1975) finds resonance with economic historians. With this history it is hardly surprising that the people who actually carry out the jobs are not committed and greet each new policy measure with cynical amusement. The point has been made repeatedly throughout this book, and has influenced the method followed during the research reported, that employment policies will not be effective unless they are supported by those they are designed for, the idea now given the term 'ownership' in the policy-making jargon. This view was shared by the economic development officer I spoke with:

> The only way that we are going to make anything work in the long term and give it sustainability is by getting ownership by local people. Again they have even more of a vital role to play in making it work and making it happen than the council or the WDA, or the tec, or the Assembly or all of us thrown in together.

In their introduction to a collection of essays exploring the employment relationship in Europe, Gallie and colleagues (1998: 17) draw attention to the need to respond to local conditions and cultural variations in the development of employment policies: 'Given our emphasis upon the significance of the "societal" at the national level, we would not suggest that a standard set of solutions can be simply located and applied independently of national and local contexts.'

Too often employment policies in Wales have been second-hand policies developed in an alien cultural setting, whether it be Essex or Seoul. The dissatisfying response from the Welsh economy to international conditions at the start of the third millennium needs to be addressed.

> But it must be addressed in the context of a strategy of empowerment, not the imposition of ideas and values from outside. Effective cultural and economic change must therefore be seen as coming from within the culture, through a process of reinvention and reassertion of its core values in its economic life. (Casson et al., 1994: 19)

In the case of economic policy for the Valleys it is crucial that policy-making takes into account the history and culture of the area. Rather than criticizing and further demoralizing the local workforce for its failure to adapt, policy-makers should recognize that different local economies respond differently to the same economic pressures and that 'the inherited physical and human capital of an area and its geographical location play a crucial part. The result is that some places prove to be better than others in adapting to shifts in the scale and organization of production' (Beatty, Fothergill and Lawless, 1997: 2041).

The interviews I reported in Chapter 6 give some indication of the level of mistrust local workers feel for policy-makers. There is a sense of betrayal, that foreign-based companies receive grants while local people are not supported, a view espoused by the present union leader at Tower:

> They've got the same policy as the Thatcher government in terms of that. They just leave people to fend for theirselves. They've got to sink or swim, unless they're a multinational. If you're a locally based company like ourselves, employing local people, putting a medium amount of money into the community through wages, they don't care if you do sink or swim. They'd make noises, I suppose, if we was under threat of closure. They'd make sympathetic noises and they'd come round and visit but that would be about it. But if it's BMW they'll give them 200 million or 200 billion if they had it.

A Tower manager described his approach to decision-making, which included the humility to listen to workers themselves and to involve them in the process:

You're still the top guy, if you want to be, as manager . . . not all the advice you get will be right, but as long as the people believe that at least you're prepared to listen. And even if, after listening, you want to do your own thing, at least you've reasoned it out and you can say we're not doing that because of this . . . I think in this country there is still people at the top level who believe they've got the answers to everything and the rest of us must follow that. Personally I don't believe that is true and I believe Tower has moved some way to prove that it's not true.

In the introduction I suggested that part of the reason for the continuing failure of the RCT economy to move with the times relates to its very successful adaptation to the forms and requirements of Britain's industrial economy. The supporting ideology of the New Economy is another development of evolutionary theory – social Darwinism. Economic planners who have presided over the fifty years of recession in the south Wales coalfield have espoused the 'survival of the fittest' as their mission state-ment. The weakest should go to the wall to allow the strongest to survive. This view of Darwin's theories (whether or not they can ever be applicable in a social context) is misguided on two accounts. Firstly, it fails to include in the picture Darwin's conviction that evolution required diversity, so that as environmental conditions changed there were alternative species that might find a chance for survival in the new conditions. Secondly, it misdefines the word 'fittest' to mean strongest, as though species which obeyed the health educationalist's dictate to jog regularly were the most likely to be successful. In fact Darwin used the word in the sense of 'most appropriate'. Hence a true social Darwinist perspective on the economic life of RCT would suggest the need to stimulate a diverse range of economic forms and then to encourage those that best suited the needs and abilities of the local people. It is from this perspective that I suggest the cooperative model as 'fitter' in the Valleys context than the competitive, capitalist model.

There is also recognition that policy-making needs to acknowledge the importance of society or 'community'. According to Giddens this concern is a central one in terms of employment policy under the third way espoused by many New Labour politicians (see e.g. Blair, 1997; Hain, 1999):

> Since the revival of civic culture is a basic ambition of third way politics, the active involvement of government in the social economy makes sense. Indeed some have presented the choice before us in stark terms, given the problematic status of full employment: either greater participation in the social economy or facing the growth of 'outlaw cultures'. (Giddens, 1998: 127)

It is possible to interpret the substantial informal economy of RCT as just such an 'outlaw culture'. To counteract such a tendency Giddens suggests greater participation in the 'social economy'; this is a policy proposal that is supported by the findings of this research. In this chapter it is discussed under two headings, first in terms of a cooperative pattern of working as exemplified by Tower Colliery, and second in terms of the non-profit sector.

Research into the social impact of volunteering (see the full review in Cato, 2000b: Chapter 5) suggests that expanding the social economy might have positive spillover effects in the community by strengthening the institutions of civil society. Wilson and Musick (1997) found a strong link between individuals' work motivations and their motivation towards involvement in these community institutions:

> There is evidence in these results to suggest that giving people decent jobs might go a long way toward ensuring a socially active population. People whose work is empowering will be active in their community. People whose ego is boosted and not deflated by their work are more willing to give of themselves outside work. There is also evidence in these results that public-sector workers are a reservoir of volunteer labor. If public spending cuts reduce the size of the public sector and workers transfer to work environments more hostile to volunteer work, this does not bode well for the health of the third sector. (Wilson and Musick, 1997: 269)

Thus boosting the social economy in Wales, as suggested below, may have beneficial social effects beyond the narrow policy area of employment.

It is also likely to create an economic form that is fitter for the culture of the Valleys than competitive, global capitalism, which has so clearly failed to thrive there. Given the findings reported in Chapters 5 and 6 about local people's perceptions of and attitudes towards work this is unsurprising. Local people stated that their priorities for job creation were job security and a decent level of wages – inward-investment job creation has been unable to provide either of these. The concept of 'capital anchoring' is being developed (by the Wales Institute for Research into Cooperatives, amongst others: see Arthur et al., 2003) to attempt to tackle the first, by converting firms that may be vulnerable to closure or transfer overseas within the globalization model to local worker ownership, thus tying them and their assets in to the local community. Developments along these lines are well advanced in Canada, where over 230 new types of economic instrument to support social economy activity have been developed since 1984 (Mendell, 2000). The level of wages can also be addressed by the cooperative model, which changes the wage-setting agenda and puts workers in control of their own economic future. Local workers' enthusiasm for jobs that strengthen the community and that are genuinely useful can also be matched by increasing the employment contribution of the social economy.

Some data, now rather old, suggest that creating jobs in the social economy may also be good value for money. A report published by the International Common Ownership Movement in 1986 states that local initiatives to create employment through Cooperative Development Agencies and local authorities in the UK as a whole in 1983–4 created 2,000 new jobs at an average cost of £1,500 per job. This compares favourably with a cost per job created by regional development agencies of £3,510, and an estimate of £7,000 for keeping a person in unemployment (ICOM and Taylor, 1986).

Another exploration of responses available to local economic planners in the era of globalization (Jessop, 2000) also emphasizes the role of the social economy. Jessop is critical of inward investment, which he terms a 'weak strategy', resulting as it does in the gaining of advantage by some areas only because of the balancing loss of other areas. The 'strong strategies' he explores involve the embedding of economic activity, primarily through innovation. Although preferable, such a strategy can have only a short life expectancy, until the innovation spills over to other areas which then compete in the same sector. Jessop suggests that the social economy offers a means of holding the value derived from economic developments in the local area, plugging the leaks and creating a virtuous cycle of benefits.

The document discussing the strategy for the investment of Objective 1 money, granted to the 'West Wales and the Valleys' area from the European Social Fund (Wales European Taskforce, 1999; hereafter 'SPD'), encapsulates the debate about the future economic development of these areas. The strategy appears to be based on two seemingly inconsistent principles: encouraging competitiveness and entrepreneurship, while at the same time reinforcing communities and sustainability. Achieving both these objectives may require squaring the circle, although some pointers towards a form of entrepreneurship that may not be inconsistent with strong social links, and in the specific context of Wales's culture and history, are offered below.

The popular perception of the likely benefits of Objective 1 is in stark contrast to the up-beat account presented in the SPD. Some of those I spoke to were cynical, and felt that it was unlikely that the money would reach them. As a self-employed fitter of burglar alarms who was seeking capital to set up a business himself put it, 'Now this is the problem: it's not gonna come down to the grass-roots. It's not gonna come down to the people that really do need it.' Planners were also criticized in terms of their speed and efficiency in developing strategy: according to the human resources manager I spoke to: 'There's been no like, "Well, here's the forms, this is the strategy, now get on with it!" I can see this going on for a couple more years, and in the last year they'll be trying to spend seven years' money.'

The perspective from economic planners themselves was hardly more encouraging. The economic development officer I spoke to admitted that many of the professionals involved in developing economic strategy were seeking to maximize the outcome for their organization, rather than prioritizing the well-being of citizens in the designated area:

> I'm still sensing political manoeuvrings, like the WDA thinking 'Oh, hang on, there's an opportunity here in the way these funds have got to be managed, for a lead body to develop a thematic approach across the whole of the Objective 1 region.' And you can see the WDA thinking 'We want to do community regeneration; we want to do business support.' They'll take it all in and put in a bid. It shouldn't be about that. It shouldn't be about strengthening their position. It should be about what's needed . . . it looks like the demise of the tecs is going to be in 2002. All of a sudden now it's like 'There's a hatchet looming, we've got to find a role for ourselves to ensure our survival. And we should be overseeing the strategic delivery of post-16 training.' And they are muscling in. It's just watching the eagles and the jostling and who's talking to who.

This sort of empire-building has been identified as an explanation for the failure of economic development in depressed areas: because the planners share a culture and background they tend to look favourably on the creation of employment of their own type, and to neglect the lower-skilled workers who are the intended recipients of help. According to an account of economic development with young people in Northern Ireland:

> Apart from some noticeable exceptions they do not generate innovative programmes that are based on the self-assessed needs of young people. They do, however, provide short-term benefits for agencies and adults involved in the business of working with and providing services to young people and the communities they live in. (Fleming and Keenan, 2000)

I did find some evidence of this kind of thinking amongst my interviewees, particularly the careers officers I spoke to, one of whom said the following in connection with their submission for Objective 1 funding:

> We've come up with things like a mobile facility that can out-reach to young people and go to the more distant communities. So Social Services will put in for a very large chunk – it's anticipated that theirs will be a large part of the bid . . . in our case it's certainly going to knock on that way because we'll probably put in for certain activities we're going to do that will mean we'll need to recruit half-a-dozen new careers advisers, and maybe five more support or administrative staff to do it. So you could say that directly if our money comes through it will create those jobs in every unit that has put in a submission. So

presumably Social Services will increase their numbers – that's inevitable – but those are the public-sector jobs we have anyway. I don't know how you could say it will affect, say, the building industry. And it would be very difficult to monitor anyway exactly how many jobs it had created.

This comment relates to the social projects that will be funded, but much of the money will be spent on infrastructural developments, where a related problem occurs. The contract-based nature of the building industry ensures that many workers will be brought in on short contracts, probably from booming areas of the UK economy so that the job-creation potential of the projects is seriously undermined. According to one respondent who had seen this happen during the LG project at Newport,

> If you need a specialist project and the only people who can do it are from Germany then you're going to have to bring them in. You can't wait until you've trained local people to do it if it's needed straightaway now as part of the project.

The second major recommendation to come out of this research project is the importance of rebuilding connections between policy-makers and those who will be affected by the policies they implement. A wide gulf of trust grew up between Valleys workers and policy-makers during the years of the Thatcher governments, and the Assembly administration has not gone far enough in closing it. An important step forward would be genuine and inclusive consultation with local people, rather than another raft of message-driven, freshly created policy initiatives, which local workers will only treat with distrust.

INWARD INVESTMENT OR INDIGENOUS ENTREPRENEURS?

Since the establishment of the Welsh Assembly in 1999 the debate over economic policy has been characterized as that between 'inward invest-ment' and 'indigenous business', and it appears that the balance of economic policy is shifting towards 'indigenous business'. The Welsh Affairs Select Committee (WAC, 1998) concluded that:

> There seems to be a growing consensus that the key to future economic growth in Wales is in developing indigenous industry . . . Encouraging indigenous businesses to expand, and new businesses to start up, is the only realistic way of creating new jobs and increasing prosperity in rural Wales. (paras. 22–3)

It is a criticism frequently made of the Welsh economy that it demonstrates no strong tradition of entrepreneurship. This is explained on the basis of historical factors such as the importance of the highly oligopolistic coal and steel industries and the resulting concentration on highly firm-specific skills (K. Morgan, 1987: 40–1). Researchers have found a similar low level of enterprise in other coalfield areas (see, for example, Leeds Metropolitan University, 2002). The Welsh Office (1998d) economic development document *Pathway to Prosperity* highlights 'the importance of entrepreneurship to a successful economy' and proposes the establishment of an Entrepreneurship Action Plan Steering Group as part of a plan 'to develop a stronger entrepreneurial culture to produce a step change in entrepreneurial activity in Wales'. The Steering Group's initial report identifies one of the issues to be faced as the fact that 'the Welsh are not a race of self-starters in business. A drive towards entrepreneurialism is lacking throughout the country so that the lead invariably has to be given by one or other official body.' This unattributed quotation seems to reinforce an unhelpful stereotype, although it is backed up by a poll figure of 57 per cent for the proportion of Welsh people who thought entre-preneurs should be admired, compared with 73 per cent for Germany and 91 per cent for the USA (comparative UK figures are not given).

Evidence as to the entrepreneurialism or otherwise of Welsh citizens is sparse, however, and the view seems to be supported more by repetition than by empirical fact (at least in the sector of SMEs registered for VAT, government figures presented in table 3.5 indicate a higher rate of activity in RCT than the UK average). A notable exception is the thoughtful report by Menter a Busnes (Casson et al., 1994), which explores cultural and historical influences on atttitudes towards entrepreneurialism in Wales (although itself noting 'the absence of detailed research') and recommends encouraging an 'associative' as contrasted with 'competitive' form of entrepreneurship. This suggestion is backed up by anthropological analysis of Welsh culture in the Welsh-speaking heartlands (Trosset, 1993) which draws attention to the disapproval shown to those who push themselves forward, contrasted with the strong approval given to those who act on behalf of the group:

> In Welsh-speaking Wales, I found, social honor means behaving in the correct way (not acting superior to anyone else), holding the correct values (loyalty to Wales and one's home community, rather than 'getting ahead in the world'), and demonstrating one's authenticity with respect to the traits held to define Welsh ethnicity. (Trosset, 1993: 77)

This cultural assessment of the type of enterprise likely to meet success within a Welsh cultural framework merits further exploration, perhaps as part of a wider programme of research investigating cultural attitudes towards employment generation amongst Welsh people.

Another such factor worthy of empirical exploration is that identified by Val Feld, who was, before her untimely death, chair of the Assembly's Economic Development Committee (Feld, 1999). She suggested that the nature of Wales's economic history – with a predominance of extractive, foreign-owned industries – has created a negative association with the idea of 'entrepreneurship'. In Wales 'entrepreneurship' has been equated with 'exploitation', with a parallel conviction that being economically successful must mean 'doing others down'. While these assertions have a superficial appeal, policy-makers would certainly benefit from empirical evidence as to their applicability or otherwise.

In the absence of such evidence the stereotype persists, evoking a proposed solution to the problem of these 'cultural attitudes' which 'fall behind other nations' in the form of a well-funded national programme to encourage entrepreneurs, backed up by introducing 'entrepreneurship education at all levels of the education and training system' and encouraging everyone to play their part in 'creating the culture that values and celebrates entrepreneurship in Welsh society' (EAPSG, 1999: 7). To tackle the recognized failure of entrepreneurship in some of Britain's most depressed local economies the Chancellor has introduced a policy for Enterprise Zones, which would offer tax breaks to those starting businesses there. Rhondda Cynon Taff is one such area. While this is an acknowledgement of the difficulties faced by potential creators of businesses in an area experiencing permanent depression, it fails to tackle the fundamental economic, social and cultural obstacles.

The concept of 'entrepreneurship' remains poorly defined, and as such it is hard to establish what role it should play in Wales's economic future. There is, however, an understandable association of the concept with neo-liberal economic policies that have traditionally found little resonance in Wales. The assumption of the benefits of entrepreneurship might be one that policy-makers might choose to challenge as the kind of policy 'hand-me-downs' Cynog Dafis referred to in a debate in the Assembly on its strategic plan 'A Better Wales' held on 10 October 1999.[4] Such a strategy also faces growing competition from eastern Europe, which will soon become internal competition within the single market following the admission of the largest and strongest central and eastern European countries into the EU in 2004. In terms of global competition, Wales has little hope in the competition for the lowest wages against countries with huge and increasingly skilled labour forces, such as China and India.

In the view of the local workers I spoke to such competition can mean only one thing: lower levels of wages in Wales. These suspicions are supported by recent assertions by Digby Jones, chair of the Confederation of British Industry, that British workers will need to be considering wage levels on a par with those of Brazilian and Chinese workers if they can hope to continue to find employment in the globally competitive market-place. A member of the Tower board saw what he considered the destructive economic policy towards the Valleys as a preparation for just this sort of competition:

> The way I look at it, you can knock a house down, smash a house down, in a couple of hours. But to build a house takes six or seven months. I think we've had such a hiding over the past eighteen or nineteen years, and I believe it's because the Conservatives believed that to compete with the Third World you've got to have Third World wages here. I think that's basically what it's all about.

An alternative vision for the Welsh economy is of a self-sustaining, self-provisioning local economy, operating with trade subsidiarity such that we begin by producing goods locally, and only look further afield for those we cannot obtain from our own town, county or nation (see Cato, 2003 for more detail). This vision runs counter to the inevitability of global com-petition that is a frequent refrain from policy-makers, although this inevit-ability is less well supported by academic research (see McQuaig, 1998). Such a vision was presented to Wales as the BBC Wales Lecture in May 2002 by Caroline Lucas, Green MEP for South-East England. As a former policy adviser to Oxfam, she sees this as a solution for depressed economies in the South of England as well as the less successful regional economies of developed nations, both of which, according to Lucas, are losers in the global trade system that works to the benefit of global cor-porations. Lucas outlined this alternative vision as follows:

> Over a period of time, there would be a gradual transition away from depend-ence on international export markets (with every country trying to compete with each other, leading to a downward spiral of social and environmental standards) towards the provision of as many goods and services as feasible and appropriate nationally. Long distance trade is then reduced to supplying what cannot come from within one country or geographical grouping of countries. This has the developmental advantage of enabling poorer countries to protect their own food security by being able to refuse to have their own food economies undercut by imports from the North; it has the environmental advantage of no longer transporting so many goods over unnecessary distances. And it has the democratic advantage of enabling an increase in local control of the economy, and of offering the potential at least for its benefits to be shared out more fairly. (Lucas, 2002)

It appears that Lucas's call has been heeded. Developments towards localizing Welsh food procured by local authorities were discussed more fully in Chapter 4. The call for the links between strengthening the local economy, improving the quality of children's nutrition and preserving the countryside are now uniting in the developing policy of supplying locally grown, organic food for school meals (see Williamson, 2003).

My third recommendation is that policy-makers reassess the scale of the economy they are seeking to support. This relates to both the previous recommendations. Like the first, it requires a re-evaluation of the attitude Wales should take towards its place in the globalized economy. Like the second it requires the inclusion of the attitudes and culture of the people who actually form the society the economy is embedded within. This third recommendation requires policy-makers to move towards stimulating a locally focused economy, providing for local needs, based around local businesses and fitting in with the local culture.

A MODEL FOR INDIGENOUS ECONOMIC SUCCESS?

In establishing an authentic, home-grown employment policy Welsh planners need a success story, which perhaps explains the popularity of Tower Colliery across the whole spectrum of political opinion: support has been received from all of Wales's political parties, who vie for photo opportunities at the pit (see Llewelyn Jones, 1998). The responses I gleaned from local people to the Tower make clear the almost universal support and enthusiasm in an area where most other developments are met with cynicism. Since hope is the commodity most in demand in the Valleys' economy it would be wise for policy-makers to draw what lessons they can from the Tower experience, and to attempt to reproduce as much of its pattern as is transferable to other businesses in the area.

It was identified in Chapter 6 that the interviewees had an ambivalent attitude towards self-employment and towards money in general (for more details on these Welsh attitudes see the anthropological study of Welsh culture by Trosset, 1993). This has been identified as stemming from the experience of enterprise as being imposed by outsiders. Casson et al. (1994) identify the almost exclusive role played in entrepreneurial activity in Wales by English industrialists, leading to a sense of mistrust and disillusion with entrepreneurialism in general, particularly at a time when Wales is moving towards seeing itself as a new nation, and has achieved a degree of economic independence under the Welsh Assembly. The so-called radical tradition in Wales, which is particularly strong in the south Wales Valleys, also acts as an impediment to the establishment of an entrepreneurial culture and was stronger in south Wales than anywhere else in the UK.

Several respondents stated that the competitive ethos had been, and still was, a handicap to economic development: as the human resources manager I spoke to put it, 'I definitely think the cooperative ethos works better.' However, a sense of solidarity can also work to encourage individuals to be successful to reduce the burden they place on others: an economic development officer told me that 'the dependency culture is changing to "Well if I feel better in myself I'm not going to be such a drain on everyone around me and we will drag ourselves up by our bootstraps"'. The point has been made in Chapter 4 that Welsh culture may well be better suited to employment creation that uses this combination of self-reliance and mutual support rather than a competitive and individualist ethos. Working with the grain of the people and their culture is a preferable strategy to that followed for too long in Welsh economic planning of trying to transform the ways of thinking of residents of the Rhondda, identified by Dicks (2000: 31). She describes a representational strategy for Rhondda people as proletarian, an identity that is then portrayed as a 'burden to enterprise culture'.

This evidence as to the nature of Welsh culture indicates the importance of developing what I have called elsewhere a form of 'associative entrepreneurship' (see Cato, 2000a). Cooke and Morgan also called for a movement towards an 'associational economy' (1999), although their concept is based more at the level of institutions. They contrast the response to the failure of dominant industries in the Ruhr to that in Massachusetts. Their characterization of the failings of regional planning in the latter case are, as they point out, depressingly familiar:

> Massachusetts boasts a broad range of programmes and services to workers and firms that are aimed at increasing the competitiveness of the state's workforce and industrial firms. These programmes are not particularly well-coordinated and involve a variety of state agencies and departments. Some are targeted to the state's high-tech firms, some to the state's 'mature industries'. Some focus on financing assistance, some on education and training and some on the development of new co-operative research and development ventures. (Cooke and Morgan, 1998; quoting Sabel et al., 1989: 398)

As an alternative they laud the Danish system, although until Wales becomes an independent economy it cannot be used as a model. The features of the system they suggest importing are three: the learning culture in the economy and wider society; the importance of trust resulting from a collective order; and the need for democratic and inclusive institutions. I would add a fourth requirement without which these will fail: a closing of the gap between the institutions and the people they serve. A genuine understanding of Wales's cultures and communities is a

Photo 8.2: Abercwmboi, Cynon Valley, in the rain. The terraced houses stretch into the distance like an exercise in perspective

necessary foundation to the development of a democratic process and to people's trust in their institutions.

Developing successful businesses is important for the regeneration of any economy, but in the Valleys the objectives may need to be community-focused rather than individualist, and the management structure may need to be more inclusive and established along cooperative lines. Cooperative businesses that prioritize making a living above making a profit and that involve their workers in workplace decisions or are even wholly owned by their workers would be a far better 'fit' with the local culture than the individualist entrepreneurial model propagated by government agencies. They would have the additional advantages of creating positive social spillovers, as identified in Chapter 7, and could guarantee the local control and anchoring of capital, preventing the footlooseness of international corporations, identified in Chapter 3 as a major reason for the loss of support for the inward-investment employment strategy. Such a cooperative model that found resonance with the local culture could be the means of 'turning on the tiny economic engines' (in the words of Mohammed Yunus, founder of the Grameen Community Bank in Bangladesh) whose inability to function has been a major reason for the continued economic failure of the Valleys. Finally, the long history of 'struggle' and of 'us and them' which has characterized work relations in the culture would be ended by the merging of workers and managers within the cooperative structure. The evidence from Tower is that this process is a complex one, but that its outcomes are very positive. At Tower the distinction between 'us' and 'them' has all but disappeared, and Tower's achievements can be offered as proof of the success that follows when both sides are learning to pull in the same direction.

EXPANDING THE NON-PROFIT SECTOR IN WALES

Critical accounts of the Welsh economy concur that the overdependence on the public sector has been a serious weakness, particularly following the decline in nationalized industry and the cutting back of the provision of state services. According to one account, this dependence results partly from cultural factors:

> Rather than seeing both private and public employment as equally legitimate domains there has been a popular tendency to equate esteem and worth with service to the community . . . This may be described as the result of the predominance of an other-regarding rather than a self-regarding value system. (Casson et al., 1994: 15).

The evidence from the social valuation of occupations carried out by a sample of workers in RCT and reported in Chapter 5 suggests that this culture is still thriving in the Valleys. Respondents uniformly valued nurses, midwives and dustmen more highly than chief executives or factory workers. This may be one of the reasons why the private sector is failing to create jobs to replace those lost in former nationalized industries. The dependence on externally created jobs has been replaced by a dependence on grant-funded employment, with a 'grant entrepreneurialism' (Arthur et al., 2004) replacing private-sector enterprise. However, this very value system may be turned to advantage in an era when such attitudes could provide a useful basis for the development of the third or non-profit sector, which is undergoing significant expansion in most developed societies, and when the 'social economy', of which the non-profit sector forms a part, is drawing increasing attention from policy-makers. In Chapter 7 I suggest the cooperative ownership form as one policy that fits

Table 8.1: Comparison of number of registered charities and their income, in UK regions, 1997

Region	No. of charities	Income (£m) p.a.	Charities/ '000 population	Income per capita per annum (£)
Wales	8000	160	2.74	54.79
Scotland	25500	1400	4.97	272.90
N. Ireland	5000	400	3.05	243.90

Source: Pharoah (1998).

this local culture (a point developed further below), but another might be the fostering of the voluntary sector. The responses of local workers towards caring work, reported in Chapter 6, suggest that this would be a popular step in Rhondda Cynon Taff.

In spite of the 'other-regarding' cultural tendency identified above, spending on the non-profit sector has typically been low in Wales compared with the other nations of the UK (see table 8.1). Given the traditional hostility of the left wing to voluntary activity, and the dominance of this political ideology in Wales, this is perhaps unsurprising. Kendall and Knapp (1996: 156) quote one of their Welsh interviewees as follows:

> You have some very statist local authorities who have . . . a total grasp of power of the area and a very monolithic approach to life. Meaning that, if a service is worth running or something's worth doing, then the council [local authority] should do it and if it's not, then it's not worth spending money on anyway.

Other interviewees identified a 'cosy' or 'symbiotic' relationship between local politicians and a number of mainstream voluntary organizations who formed cliques so that the direction of funding was fixed and change was hard to effect.

In terms of the employment-generating potential of this sector in Wales, the figures reproduced in table 8.2 (from Vincent, 1998) are illuminating. They indicate that far fewer paid jobs are provided by the voluntary sector in Wales, although the number of volunteers is actually higher, relative to the size of the population, than in the other regions. Thus the employee: volunteer ratio of the sector in Wales is low, suggesting that the sector may be starved of cash but could generate employment if funding were made available. Figures for the funding of the sector by local and national government in the different regions (table 8.3) show a similar picture, with Wales having the lowest per capita level of central-government funding;

Table 8.2: Paid and voluntary work in the voluntary sector in UK regions, 1996 (000s)

Region	No. of employees	No. of volunteers	Empl./vol. ratio
Scotland	34	700	4.9
Wales	10	700	1.4
Northern Ireland	30	131	22.9
England	244	1469	16.6

Source: Vincent, 1998.

Table 8.3: Levels of central and local government expenditure on the voluntary sector, 1996

Region	Direct central government funding		Local government funding	
	£m	per capita	£m	per capita
Scotland	25.6	4.99	94.2	18.37
Wales	13.7	4.72	22.1	7.58
Northern Ireland	85.7	52.45	5.8	3.53
England	283.5	5.77	1,254.2	25.55

Source: Vincent, 1998.

Northern Ireland has a lower level of local-government expenditure, but only because of the particular political history of that region.

The disparity in rates of employment relative to voluntary activity in the non-profit sector, and in the levels of funding provided to it, may reflect the ideological bias resulting from a left-wing political tradition, which, as mentioned above, views the voluntary sector as ideally a historical anachronism which should wither away in the socialist state. While the inadequacies of the socialism that has been achieved in Scotland and Wales may make a continuing present and future for voluntary caring inevitable, politicians may be unwilling to accept the need for its role, far less to recognize it by providing funding for genuine employment in this sector. As outlined in the following section, in the Welsh context it has been the Liberal Democrats who have been strongest in their support for the 'third sector'.

Before coming to Wales Alun Michael, the inaugural First Secretary of the Welsh Assembly, was a keen advocate of voluntary activity which he called 'the essential act of citizenship' (Michael, 1998). He indicated his continuing commitment to community projects in the debate on the social economy:[5] 'There are three golden threads of partnership set in place and endorsed by the Assembly, with business, local government and the voluntary sector. We must not downplay the contribution of any of those three because they are all important.' As a whole, however, the Assembly debate on the issue indicates limited thinking about the social economy, which is perceived as almost synonymous with the voluntary sector and as a bridge to something else, namely 'real employment' in the private or public sector. For example, Alun Michael comments:

> During my time in youth and community work, I have seen people contribute initially by making a cup of coffee or helping in a low-key way. They then realise that they have a contribution to make. They gather self-confidence and make a significant contribution, even offer leadership in the community. In many cases, they go on to gain employment and become qualified in a way that would have been beyond their wildest dreams had it not been for the opportunities provided by the voluntary sector.

This is a different view of the non-profit sector from that outlined in much of the literature on the social economy (Kendall and Knapp, 1996; Salamon and Anheier, 1996, Knight, Smerdon and Pharoah, 1998), where it is seen as a sector that will grow as a result of a shrinking public sector and the failure of the private sector to provide many vital services. Indeed, the view of the social economy held by Assembly members presupposes by definition that it will not generate job creation since 'It provides superb value for money because it relies so much on volunteers who give up their time freely but do a job that has economic worth' (Jenny Randerson). A first policy proposal in this area must be that the Assembly conducts comparative research into the social economies of other countries and broadens its conception of the definition of this sector. There is some suggestion that the Economic Policy Division of the Welsh Assembly is moving in this direction, with its recent commissioning of research to investigate the business support needs of social-economy enterprises. However, the ethos of competition that pervades the latest policy document, *A Winning Wales*, seems to conflict directly with the motivation and values of the social economy.

Funding for social-economy projects is also likely to be increasingly available in view of the rapid growth in ethical investment. Financial institutions such as the Ecology Building Society, the Family Charities Ethical Trust and Triodos Bank are seeing rapid expansion as concern for ethical investment grows. The latter saw its balance sheet and profits increase by almost a third in 1999 and its loan portfolio grow by more than half. Its managing director, Glen Saunders, expresses his frustration with 'the government's failure to address social finance issues', and Triodos, as a 'social bank', aims to fill the gap by lending only to borrowers who are 'socially, ethically and environmentally sound' (Cowe, 2000). These ethical banks and building societies are obliged to invest in socially valuable and sustainable projects, which will itself provide a stimulus to the social economy. The perception of the social economy that emerges from the Assembly debate, by contrast, is of a sector that will be dependent on grants in perpetuity.

The 'tradition of self-help' is considered as a building-block of community regeneration, although no empirical work has been undertaken to explore whether it still exists in the competitive economic climate of the new century. The research I conducted for this book suggests that the social value of work is important to those who undertake it. The results of the survey conducted in RCT also indicate that workers there are committed to their communities and value types of employment that have a high social value, as opposed to high financial rewards. This seems a strong empirical base for proposing that encouraging community regeneration might be a policy worth pursuing, given the support of local people.

Participation will be key to the success of community regeneration. Fleming and Keenan (2000) make the following point:

> Carley and Christie (1993) argue that regeneration without participation is unsustainable in that experience tells us that initiatives fail unless the community is a full partner. Often there is a requirement for community consultation but this is invariably carried out in the most tokenistic and divisive way . . . Again the main beneficiaries of the regeneration process are the businesses and professionals who commute in to an area daily (and back to the suburbs at night).

There seems to be an awareness of this amongst economic planners, one of whom told me that 'Community regeneration is more about local ownership, again changing the culture from somebody will come along and sort it out for us.' She considered that the issue had traditionally been misconceived:

> To me it's about totally rethinking what goes on in local communities. Community enterprises traditionally have been good ideas that are continually a drain on the grant system to keep them going. I would rather look at a community enterprise as a local service provided by local people that is not available through the private sector or national networks. For instance, I would very much like to see that local neighbourhoods, like village centres, have . . . local fresh fruit and veg., a local baker, a local butcher – fresh things, local things. So that they're tackling health issues, they're tackling community, talking to each other, rather than everybody get in a car and drive ten miles to

the local superstore which provides them with everything and they come home and their local village centre is dead.

This is a far more vibrant view of community development than that found in the SPD and one far more akin to the innovative ideas coming out of the Green movement (see, for example, Rajan, 1993; Douthwaite, 1996). Such radical empowering strategies for community development are also being encouraged by the European Commission's Integra programme. Examples include the Action for Urban Regeneration project based in Genk, Belgium, which is fostering self-employment in an old industrial and mining area; and the HARP method for assessing the potential of those in marginal economic situations, rather than focusing on their problems, which was developed in Newcastle, UK.

A recommendation in terms of community regeneration is that community members should be funded to undertake exchange visits to other locally based regeneration projects in Europe. The local economies of RCT would benefit from an exchange of information between successful projects, and this would encourage confidence in the local community. Although exchanges take place between policy-makers, this tends to disempower rather than empower the members of the community itself.

There are already examples of successful community regeneration in RCT, and these should be used as inspiration; an example is the following described by an economic development officer:

> There are quite a few very, very exciting groups that have sprung up now in RCT. Yesterday I was talking to Penrhiwceiber Community Revival Group who are looking at what they want to do to completely revive Penrhiwceiber. They were looking at the old colliery site: it's allocated for employment, but what kind of employment? What kind of units? How was that going to fit in with other things they wanted to do with the school, with the community centre and everything else? And it was great. Not only did I have two consultants sitting at the table from Cardiff who'd come up with ideas, I had two people from the actual community who'd come up with them. And I thought 'This is more like it. This is more what community regeneration is all about.'

TACKLING THE FAILURE OF INCENTIVES

Regenerating an economy that is depressed and has been depressed for a long period is essentially a bootstrap problem. All forms of energy that might generate some economic success have failed, at the psychological level, in terms of confidence and incentives, at the cultural level, in terms of entrepreneurial skills, and fundamentally at the economy level in terms of money. This section proposes solutions to two of these problems with the failure of incentives that prevents the regeneration of the economy of RCT. The first is the removal of the risk of loss of income to potential entrepreneurs via the introduction of a Citizens' Income. The second is a more radical proposal to inject more money actively into the economy and, by restricting its use to the specific local authority area of RCT, to prevent its being drawn out to a wider global economy where more interest could be earned in return.

As identified by several of the interviewees reported in Chapter 6, risk aversion is an important barrier to entrepreneurial activity in RCT. The willingness to take risks has been frequently cited as the key trait of the entrepreneur (Casson, 1991; 1993). It is equally clear that confidence is an essential prerequisite for such risk-taking behaviour: according to *Pathway to Prosperity*, 'Wales has the talent needed for commercial success in today's highly competitive global markets. What is often lacking is the confidence and ambition to exploit these talents to the full' (Welsh Office, 1998d: para. 5.1). The issue of ambition may be resolved by consideration of what that ambition is programmed to achieve, as already addressed, but the issue of confidence should not be neglected. Although the willingness to take risks is identified as a prerequisite for entre-preneurial success in *The Entrepreneurship Action Plan for Wales* (EAPSG, 1999), no policies are suggested to tackle its absence amongst workers, particularly in the Valleys. This was identified amongst the local workers whose responses are reported in Chapter 6, where it is also linked to the narrowly focused policy of attracting 'foreigners' to create jobs. This has been interpreted as a lack of confidence in the ability of local people to create jobs for themselves, and may therefore have had a negative impact on entrepreneurial potential (this point is developed further in Cato, 2001a).

Financial insecurity is an added discouragement to risk-taking, which could be addressed by guaranteeing entrepreneurs a basic income in the form of a Citizens' Income scheme. This policy (for further theoretical and technical details see Atkinson, 1995; Parker, 1989; van Parijs, 1995) is favoured by proponents of the so-called 'new economics' who see it as a means of delinking income from employment in advanced industrial economies where, typically, fewer than two-thirds of the population have a job (Williams and Windebank, 1998). Instead, under the Citizens' Income scheme every citizen would receive a basic income as a social entitlement, without the need for job-seeking or means-testing. The policy is favoured on the suggestion that 'those presently unemployed would be freed to engage in activity, whether paid or unpaid, to improve their own well-being and as an outlet for their creative potentials and/or entrepreneurial spirit, and the "poverty trap" would be abolished' (Williams and Windebank, 1998).

Several of the interview respondents linked this idea immediately to the Enterprise Allowance scheme which ran during the 1980s. A similar scheme is currently running called Work-Based Learning: those with a convincing self-employment plan can receive £10 extra on top of their benefit for a period of six months. The economic development officer I spoke to said: 'I think if you are going to provide an Enterprise Allowance, if you like, but a bit more worth having than what's currently available, then that would be a good idea.' While the Citizens' Income could support new business people in a similar way, although fixed at a more realistic level to provide real support, it would also have a general impact on the economy, as identified by the small shopkeeper in my sample:

> I think that's excellent. It's a green idea. I think everybody in the country should get a basic wage. For instance, if I've got it right they add it together and tax the lot. And also you should penalize employers because they're taking people on the side . . . They're all doing it. So if you made it illegal and checked employers out: I think it's a fantastic idea! . . . And they'd pay tax if they got over a certain limit. But you'd have to give it to everyone including the pensioners . . . I think it's an excellent idea. It's the only way forward, really.

Given the high levels of economic inactivity in Wales, one economic commentator has written that 'coaxing the economically inactive back into employment is the biggest challenge facing the Welsh Assembly' (O'Leary et al., 2003). A Citizens' Income (CI) scheme could also act as a carrot to encourage these 'inactive' individuals into the labour market (see Mayo, 1996). The problems of the benefit trap, high levels of sickness and invalidity benefit, and the informal economy were identified in Chapter 2 as major explanations for the low level of economic activity in RCT, which is itself a major reason for the low level of GDP. A Citizens' Income could act as a bridge from benefit into work: since the income is guaranteed, earning in the official economy does not affect it, which would provide an incentive to work for those who currently prefer the security of benefits – a security that is removed by a decision to take employment. The Working Families Tax Credit is intended as just such a policy measure: according to Val Feld, formerly chair of the Welsh Assembly's Economic Development Committee, 'It provides a bridge from benefit into work' (debate on social economy, 3 November 1999). However, it is distinct from the CI proposal since it involves an earnings taper and has restrictive eligibility criteria.

Another similar policy proposal is being implemented by the Wales Cooperative Centre under the rubric 'Enterprise Rehearsal Project', which 'allows people to test out a business idea while still claiming benefits'. This scheme, covering a period of about six months and run in collaboration with the Job Centre and Benefits Agency,

> is designed to release the entrepreneur in people who are not currently in paid employment. It provides a safety net whilst a business idea is being tested out and allows people to begin to build an order book before 'signing off' benefits and achieving fully self-employed status.

The Citizens' Income could, via its operation as a bridge from unemployment, expand the opportunities of RCT workers who, in a depressed local economy, have such poor prospects within the present benefit structure. A study focusing on the opportunities in the labour market for miners who were made redundant during the 1980s (Fieldhouse and Hollywood, 1999: 499) drew the following conclusion:

> The results of this paper indicate poor employment prospects for ex-miners and their families. The mechanisms of the benefits system and the lack of alternative employment for miners has led to a situation whereby the most rational option for miners is to register as sick or to take early retirement. This effectively disenfranchises those ex-miners from the job market and compounds their lack of employment prospects, since being registered as permanently sick makes them ineligible for restart schemes and job clubs, thus making it hard for those who withdraw to re-enter into employment.

While the present benefits system reduces the flexibility of those without work to improve their situation, a Citizens' Income scheme would do the opposite: by guaranteeing their basic needs it would expand their employment horizons. In addition, at the level of the local economy as a whole, energy that is currently wasted could be reincorporated to the benefit of the entire community.

Respondents from RCT saw the link between economic inactivity and a Citizens' Income scheme. The economic development officer saw this as an ideal policy to tackle the failure of incentives:

> It would give them basic stability but would also take away the cushion of comfort that discourages them from coming off benefits and getting themselves a job. Because, let's face it, most people who are getting a raft of benefits would say 'Well, if I took a job there I would be working all those hours and only bringing home £10 a week more: why should I?'

The human resources manager I spoke to identified how the encouragement of those in the black economy into the official economy might make the CI an economically efficient policy measure:

> They would be able to keep going and keep the local people working. I suppose if you did the figures it would work out, because so much money is being lost through the black economy if they stopped it the money could all go towards paying people a proper wage, couldn't it? And then they'd spend the money.

Many respondents felt that informal economic activity represents an important drain of talent and energy out of the economy; the CI could provide the incentive for this energy to be retrieved in this area where punitive policies such as hotlines to report on neighbours have proved unsuccessful.

The most forceful criticism commonly raised against the Citizens' Income is that such a policy would be unaffordable. It is hard to assess this proposal in isolation from other tax and benefit changes, and from its direct and indirect consequences on economic activity. However, a costing produced for the Green Party (Lord, 2001) suggests a net cost, taking into account only changes to tax allowances and administration costs, of £71.81bn.[6] Since this is based on national figures it includes areas of the country where very few people are presently receiving benefits, suggesting that a pilot study in a depressed regional economy would be relatively less costly. A costed proposal to phase in CI along with other green taxes while removing employment-related taxes suggests that government revenue could reach surplus within ten years (Robertson, 1999).

The second economic criticism is that CI would encourage idleness. However, this is again based on an assumption that financial rewards are the only motivation towards employment, an assumption which is undermined by the findings reported in theoretical work reported in Cato, 2000b (Chapters 4, 5 and 6). If people have other motivations towards unemployment, and the responses reported in Chapters 5 and 6 of this book suggest that workers in RCT certainly do, then they would tend to continue to work even if they received a Citizens' Income. Indeed, given that their basic needs were already covered, they might be inclined to work for a lower rate, particularly if they felt that the work had social value and offered a greater level of job satisfaction. Hence the Citizens' Income might also stimulate the social economy.

Most discussion of the impact of a Citizens' Income is at the theoretical level, although the Netherlands government has commissioned formal research and proposals (Stroeken, 1996). The only currently existing form of citizens' dividend is that operated by the state of Alaska, known as the Alaska Permanent Fund Corporation. Each citizen who had been in Alaska for more than a year received $1850.28 per annum from the Dividend Program in 2001. This fund is based on stocks and shares and so the rate had fallen to $1540.76 in 2002. The scheme is based on investments of oil revenues for the common good of Alaska citizens and has been running since 1982 (see *www.apfc.org/alaska*).

The idea of a Citizens' Income in the form of a negative income tax was tested in the USA from 1967 onwards by President Johnson's Commission on Guaranteed Incomes, which carried out a number of pilot projects to explore its impact on work incentives. The results were somewhat unexpected:

> a number of politicians believed that the very idea of guaranteeing an annual income would seriously undermine the work ethic and produce a generation of Americans unwilling to work at all. While the commission's recommendations languished, the federal government did carry out a number of pilot projects to test the viability of providing a guaranteed annual income. To his [Johnson's] surprise, the government found that it did not appreciably reduce the incentive to work, as many politicians had feared. (Rifkin, 1995: 262)

Studies of the negative income tax were conducted in four contrasting parts of the USA: in urban areas in New Jersey and Pennsylvania from 1968 to 1972; in rural areas in Iowa and North Carolina from 1969 to 1973; in Gary, Indiana from 1971 to 1974; and in Seattle and Denver from 1970 to 1978. The results showed that, on average, the men investigated worked only 6 per cent less than when they were not receiving the guaranteed income payment; women cut their work rather more, leading to an average reduction in work hours of 9 per cent. The conclusion from the Seattle-Denver experiment was that:

> Cash assistance programs would not cause a massive withdrawal of workers from the labor force, as many have feared. When combined with jobs, they would result in increased work effort. Any reduction in work effort caused by cash assistance would be more than offset by the increased employment opportunities provided in public service jobs.

In addition, there were significant but unmeasurable increases in well-being and the development of individuals' creative abilities (Sheahen, 2003).

In conclusion to a discussion of basic income in connection with informal employment, Williams and Windebank (1998) suggest that the only way forward is to test the policy in a number of pilot areas: 'What is perhaps required, therefore. . . is for pilot projects of various types of basic income scheme to be run so as to evaluate their impact on economic and social life . . . There is an urgent need . . . for such pilot projects to be conducted.' A detailed proposal for the introduction of such a scheme is being considered by the City Council of Dordrecht in The Netherlands. The proposal of this book is that Rhondda Cynon Taff should also introduce such a pilot scheme.

On a more practical level, part of the failure of Welsh entreprenership can be explained by its past absence: in this field, as much research has shown, the aphorism that 'nothing succeeds like success' is appropriate. Two interlinked reasons explain the hypothesized 'inheritability' of enterprise: the acquisition of family capital, and the sharing of entrepreneurial skills within familial and social networks. Blanchflower and Oswald (1998) found that the availability of personal wealth eases the process of acquiring investment capital. Dunn and Holtz-Eakin (2000) concur, but, in an analysis based on US data, find that the role of financial capital is rather weak, and that the role of cultural capital, in the form of entrepreneurial skills, is much stronger, particularly between fathers and sons. A review article covering research into self-employment in five national labour markets (Le, 1999) found that the employment status of the father and the availability of financial capital were generally strong predictors of self-employment.

Capital is a necessary prerequisite for entrepreneurship and in this area, too, imaginative policies are required if the Valleys' economies are to be revived. In 1999 the Assembly proposed the creation of a new Enterprise Development Bank 'to channel venture capital into particular community enterprises' (Mike German, 3 November 1999), in particular grants from Europe under the Objective 1 provisions. This was intended to be independently managed but has come to life as Finance Wales, a wholly owned subsidiary of the WDA (see Welsh Assembly report on the WDA, 2001). Again an opportunity was missed to create a financing structure outside the stranglehold of the public finance bodies.

Support has also been given to the development of credit unions: according to Alun Michael, 'Developing credit unions . . . creates a driver in the local economy as well as providing an opportunity for people to come together and support each other.' As the latter quotation implies, the development of such alternative finance is still perceived as a fringe activity, an alternative for those who cannot compete to attract external bank-based capital. However, the Assembly is at least taking this sector seriously in terms of providing services to deprived communities: in July 2000 Edwina Hart announced a contribution to the Credit Union movement of nearly half a million pounds for that year (Assembly website).

Research demonstrates that the international financial system encourages the draining of financial resources from depressed areas with consequent loss of financial and broader economic returns. In Ireland, Patrick Honohan of the Economic and Social Research Institute in Dublin explains that 'financial institutions lend to borrowers who look as if they have plans that will result in a cash flow sufficient to repay the loan. By definition, such borrowers are less plentiful in depressed regions' (quoted in Douthwaite, 1996: 122). Even in depressed areas money is saved by those in employment, but the banking system draws this money out of the local economy. In Ireland farmers lent approximately £943 million to banks in 1993, for which they received some £10 million in interest. However, farmers borrowing the same amount would have been required to pay some £113 million in interest, resulting in a net loss to the rural community of some £100 million (Douthwaite, 1996: 125). Reducing this leakage of capital out of the local economy should be a priority of the Assembly's development bodies, rather than merely being a channel of grant aid.

An interesting model of a development bank in a depressed economy is that of the Grameen Bank in Bangladesh. It lends to only the very poorest borrowers and does not demand collateral; instead, the group members – lenders and borrowers – ensure that loans are repaid. Because of the community-based nature of the bank, social and economic pressure can be brought to bear on those who threaten not to repay, and support and advice can be offered when needed. Since its inception in 1983 Grameen Bank has spread rapidly: it is now established in 39,000 villages and lends to 2.4 million borrowers (Yunus, 1999). This is distinct from a charitable development programme; Grameen is a profit-making institution. While developed in a very different setting, the poor of Bangladesh face many similar difficulties in attracting finance to entrepreneurs in any depressed economy: they lack collateral, cannot offer large returns, and are beyond the reach of the large financial institutions (P. Smith, 1999). Yunus (1999: 13) sums up the developmental advantage of such a community bank as follows:

> The poor are poor not because they are lazy or untrained but because they cannot keep the returns on their labour. Self-employment may be the only solution. Microcredit views each person as a potential entrepreneur and turns on the tiny economic engines of a rejected portion of society.

An econometric study of three such 'micro-credit' programmes in Bangladesh, including Grameen Bank, found that they have positive impacts on income, production and employment, and that the growth in self-employment tends to be from the waged employment sector, implying an employment multiplier effect (Khandker, Samad and Khan, 1998).

The local nature of Grameen banking activities would also be appropriate to the RCT setting. The industrial village proposal (Welsh Office, 1998d) sought to build on the feeling of community identity deriving from the pit villages. Developing Grameen-style community banks could provide a focus for the activities of these industrial villages. One of the local people I interviewed expressed strong support for keeping the access to finance local:

> I went to a seminar by the Chief Executive of Rhondda Cynon Taff . . . and he was saying that what they're going to do in Rhondda Cynon Taff is to get permission to have a strategy so that anybody locally who wants to draw down funding doesn't have to apply to the Assembly they only have to apply to Rhondda Cynon Taff, which sounds like a great idea. (Human resources manager)

A more direct policy for making capital available specifically for local businesses, and one that ties in with the need for 'capital anchoring' discussed above, is the creation of local currencies. The rapid decline in the proportion of money in circulation that has been created by the government rather than by private-sector banks has been identified by some radical economists as the source of continued economic depression in areas of a national economy – whether functional or geographical – where the money will fail to yield high returns (see Douthwaite, 1999; Rowbotham, 1999; Hutchinson et al., 2002). An early day motion by Austin Mitchell (EDM1515: Using the Public Credit) makes a similar point:

> That this House . . . urges the Government to redress the balance back to the people by instructing the Bank of England to create credit on an experimental basis to be used exclusively to finance specific public investment in projects, schools, hospitals or transport . . . and further urges the Treasury to review and report on the benefits and procedures for using the public credit to achieve higher economic growth and full employment in an economy where both have suffered as the burden of debt, private and public, have increased.

In response to the failure of effective demand in RCT the local authority could create money locally, restricted for use within its own geographical boundary. By accepting the currency in payment of some proportion of the council tax the authority could underpin its value. In contrast to the pound sterling this local currency could not be extracted into the global economy since it would only have legitimacy within RCT.

A proposal along these lines designed specifically to revitalize the depressed economies of south Wales was recently funded under the Objective 1 scheme. The Institute for Community Currencies is a partnership between Time Banks UK, Valleys Kids (based in RCT) and the University of Wales College, Newport. The group proposes to create new community currencies in the south Wales Valleys and use the extra liquidity to invest in projects that have insufficient collateral or profitability to gain funding from commercial banks. The Institute aims to establish sixteen pilot Community Time Banks spread across the six local authority areas of the Valleys, laying the foundation for a Valleys currency. This is a practical response to the leakages of money from the local economies of south Wales that have led to persistent low levels of economic acitivity.

CONCLUSION

So, we have reached the end of the line. I hope it has been an informative and interesting journey, at least insofar as the need to present facts and figures has allowed. I hope I have convinced you that the Valleys of south Wales have the hope of a bright and successful future to match their inspiring past. In closing I would like to place the responsibility for ensuring that the people of the Valleys enjoy the future they deserve squarely on the shoulders of their politicians and policy-makers. On many occasions in the past, for the sake of expediency or for sheer lack of imagination, the employment policies implemented in the area have been misguided and inappropriate. I hope the ideas presented in this book will be at least greeted with open minds, rather than being rejected without consideration as politically impossible. For too long the blame for the area's economic failings has been placed on its people. I hope if I have achieved anything in these 250-odd pages it is to relieve them of this most undeserved burden. The people of the Valleys won my respect and my affection. I only hope that in the future they will find the leaders and policy-makers they deserve.

Notes

1   J. A. Owen (1977) notes that when King George and Queen Mary visited the Dowlais ironworks on 27 June 1912 the sleeper mill was making components for the Uganda Railway, while the solid plate and fish plate mills were making items for the Union of South Africa. Sanyal (1930) identifies the dependence of Indian railways on south Welsh production, although it is often identified as 'English'.

2   The story of the Insoles, one Cardiff-based coal-shipping family, is typical. Their major fortune was made after they agreed a contract selling Rhondda steam coal to the merchant marine, including the Royal Mail Steam Packet Co. and the Peninsula and Orient Steam Navigation Company (R. Watson, 1997). See also Phillips (1994), sect. 3.2, 'Rhondda Coal across the World'; and table 2 in J. Williams (1980).

3   A couple of times while applying for funding for this research I have been made aware of the ignorance of the nature of working people's lives by the middle-class people who make decisions about them. During an interview with one grant-making body I tried to justify my decision to consult local workers to ensure that they might not be forced to do jobs they detested. The very debonair and neatly groomed man who chaired the panel looked at me pityingly and told me that he sometimes did not want to come into work in the morning. He did not know that I had worked in the office next door to his, which was in a Georgian building in Oxford with a leafy garden attached, but the contrast with the life of Valleys workers, to which he was sublimely indifferent, filled me with rage. More recently, my application for a funding grant was rejected on the basis that 'Whilst the idea of "participatory employment policy-making" is quite interesting, it is open to accusations of being somewhat utopian'. In my response I pointed out that even in medieval Europe, according to a Muttenberg ordinance, 'every one must be pleased with his work' (Kropotkin, 1902: 160).

4   By Kevin Morgan, chair of the Penrhys Multi-Departmental Forum and director of Cardiff University's Regeneration Institute.

5   For details of the incorporation of earlier pagan earth-goddess cults into the fabric of Celtic Christianity see French, 2001.

6   Details of Welsh Assembly debates can be found on the Assembly's website at *www.wales.gov.uk/assemblydata*.

7   According to the definition in the *Penguin Dictionary of Philosophy* (Mautner, 1997: 592),

The Vienna Circle was a group of analytical philosophers of a scientific and mathematical turn of mind . . . Their aim was a unity of science expressed in a common language to be reached by a logical analysis and, hence, a clarification of the statements made in the various sciences.

[8]   Three points about my personal history seem pertinent to an assessment of the likely biases in my research. First, I am a woman with three children and I grew up at a time when second-wave feminism was a strongly influential ideology on young women in the UK. This seems to have affected my view of the research process and my recognition of the nature of gender-based power relationships in our society and economy. Secondly, I have family connections with the area I chose to study. My grandfather was born and brought up in Dowlais, the centre of the Merthyr steel-making industry at that time. My first visit to the area was a trip he arranged for us when I was twenty-three, in 1986. Despite my best attempts to cast an objective eye on the Valleys it would be dishonest to deny that I had an emotional response to the area: a positive attraction to the landscape and people, and a revulsion against the decay I saw. It is similarly important that my Welsh relatives, like the majority of Valleys people, were staunch socialists, condemning my grandfather as a 'class traitor' for voting Conservative in 1979. These strongly held beliefs have had an influence on my ideological outlook, which explains my enthusiasm for the Tower Colliery venture. Finally, I have been active for some years in the Green Party, including standing for election at various levels. This is indicative of my personal commitment to issues of sustainability, justice and emancipation. While I have striven to achieve objectivity and to represent all sides fairly, the reader may use this information about me to assess when I have inadvertently adopted a partial perspective.

[9]   At a recent women's meeting I attended one woman identified that this is a particularly female way of speaking and perhaps thinking. Rather than following a series of points in a straight line towards a target conclusion, women add relevant and supportive points around a central theme in a process she referred to as 'plaiting a conversation' (Lindy Brett, personal communication, July 2002).

Notes to Chapter 2

[1]   The Coalfield Communities Campaign was set up in February 1985 by twenty-two local authorities whose citizens had been affected by pit closures. Since then it has provided social and economic research on the consequences of the pit closure programme as well as lobbying for government support with regeneration work.

[2]   The calculations (based on data in Beatty, Fothergill and Lawless, 1997: table 3) are made as follows:

Coalmining job losses in north and south Wales, 1981–91
    24,300
Total job losses in coalmining in UK, 1981–91
    159,600
Percentage of job losses in Welsh coalfields
    15.2%

Funding made available for regeneration of English coalfields
   45m
Funding made available for regeneration of Welsh coalfields
   £1.157m
(Figures from *www.coalfields-regen.org.uk*)
Proportion of total funding earmarked for Wales
   2.57%

3   These are the last available figures at this level of disaggregation, since only censuses and the five-yearly intercensal surveys provide data on county-district-level unemployment. Most of the figures in this chapter that relate to this level or smaller (i.e. the ward-level figures) are now, inevitably, somewhat out of date, as we approach the publication of the ward-level data from the following 2001 census. The first release data have been used where data at the unitary-authority level is sufficiently fine-grained.

4   This generic title is not limited to the area under study here but covers in addition the Neath, Ogwr and Lliw Valleys to the west and the Rhymney, Merthyr and Gwent Valleys to the east.

5   The Welsh Index of Multiple Deprivation 2000 is based on administrative information at the small-area level for all boroughs in Wales. It is derived from a range of indicators for different aspects of poverty including income levels, employment rates, data on health, education, housing and access to services, as well as an indicator of child poverty. The two indicators reported in the table below concern income and employment. The income indicator is based on overlapping counts of people in receipt of means-tested benefits, presented as a percentage of the total population living in such families, in other words the rate of the population (including children) reliant on means-tested benefits. The employment indicator is an indication of employment deprivation, rather than claimant counts, as an attempt to include consideration of 'hidden unemployment'. The domain seeks to measure enforced exclusion from work, whether for reasons of lack of job availability or through sickness. This indicator is also based on non-overlapping counts of the unemployed and those on certain types of government employment scheme, combined with those on Incapacity Benefit or Severe Disablement Allowance, as a proportion of the economically active combined with the registered sick. For further details see

   http://www.lgdu-wales.gov.uk/html/eng/our_projects/eng_wimd.htm

Indicators of deprivation for all wards in the study area, 1998/9

Electoral division name	Index of multiple deprivation score	Rank of index of multiple deprivation	Income domain score	Rank of income domain	Employment domain score	Rank of employment domain
Aberaman North	33.62	148	34.59	173	23.36	128
Aberaman South	46.95	61	40.21	79	28.04	48
Abercynon	34.52	131	35.34	158	22.31	152
Aberdare East	25.41	274	29.85	294	21.61	176
Aberdare West/ Llwydcoed	21.60	362	27.35	364	20.38	218

Electoral division name	Index of multiple deprivation score	Rank of index of multiple deprivation	Income domain score	Rank of income domain	Employment domain score	Rank of employment domain
Beddau	14.04	569	21.91	517	13.06	538
Brynna	10.76	664	19.18	595	10.87	652
Church Village	12.65	617	22.31	508	14.21	485
Cilfynydd	26.09	259	28.25	334	17.76	301
Cwmbach	37.02	112	36.56	137	26.66	63
Cwm Clydach	53.56	36	37.99	107	30.38	26
Cymmer	47.33	56	41.28	66	27.02	60
Ferndale	36.49	117	28.32	332	24.41	94
Gilfach Goch	52.46	39	38.09	105	27.70	53
Glyncoch	57.71	26	52.62	17	29.61	32
Graig	22.71	330	28.11	338	17.85	296
Hawthorn	19.11	414	28.67	319	16.28	372
Hirwaun	32.61	156	33.63	197	25.31	85
Llanharan	19.15	412	29.70	297	15.55	398
Llanharry	29.40	208	32.00	234	18.34	283
Llantrisant Town	5.05	822	15.45	691	10.55	663
Llantwit Fardre	4.17	836	9.03	822	7.57	794
Llwynypia	55.30	29	40.75	74	30.84	22
Maerdy	68.43	5	46.04	35	34.77	6
Mountain Ash East	28.08	234	27.90	345	21.96	163
Mountain Ash West	51.67	42	43.64	52	28.58	41
Penrhiwceiber	54.01	31	45.20	41	25.49	77
Pentre	31.86	171	27.71	348	24.74	91
Pen-y-graig	45.57	71	36.23	140	28.01	49
Pen-y-waun	73.34	2	59.68	9	35.75	4
Pont-y-clun	7.61	760	16.01	679	12.19	578
Pontypridd Town	5.83	802	15.75	684	10.36	676
Porth	30.14	199	28.81	314	24.09	105
Rhigos	31.60	173	31.95	235	23.51	123
Rhondda	22.03	346	23.82	463	16.52	359
Rhydfelen Central/Ilan	52.94	38	52.64	16	27.05	59
Rhydfelen Lower	30.78	190	38.07	106	20.38	216
Taffs Well	9.04	711	20.90	549	10.50	669
Talbot Green	17.75	456	26.59	385	18.62	270
Ton-teg	4.50	832	11.46	782	10.07	685
Tonypandy	35.15	124	30.26	281	23.83	113
Tonyrefail East	33.98	140	33.46	199	23.65	118
Tonyrefail West	46.22	67	36.11	143	28.10	47
Trallwng	13.04	600	24.12	453	13.75	503
Trealaw	46.99	60	37.46	115	28.89	40
Treforest	11.31	650	10.58	796	7.66	786
Treherbert	53.84	33	39.66	85	31.03	20
Treorchy	29.30	211	28.75	316	24.14	102
Tylorstown	64.66	11	45.95	36	32.03	13
Tyn-y-nant	22.17	342	30.07	288	18.02	292
Ynyshir	47.05	59	37.35	119	28.11	46
Ynysybwl	22.54	333	24.97	435	18.15	288
Ystrad	37.23	110	32.22	224	25.28	86

[6]   Average rates of subsidy per tonne of production over the period 1979–87 in the UK and its major competitor countries in the European Community were

as follows: Belgium – £28.28; France – £18.70; UK – £15.26; FR Germany – £14.70. The average subsidy figure for the UK is artificially inflated by the huge effective subsidy created by the strike in 1984: for further details see Wass and Mainwaring (1989: 181). European competitors may not be as strict at enforcing European competition regulations as are UK authorities: the Commission had to investigate unauthorized aid paid to Charbonnages de France in 2000 and in the same year issued a formal notice to the German government concerning concealed aid to Saarbergwerke AG and Preussag Anthrazit Gmbh (Treasury, 2001).

[7]   See Welsh Assembly debate on the economy, 7 July 1999.

Notes to Chapter 3

[1]   This chapter presents the latest available data provided by the Welsh Assembly. As mentioned in the text, data for the amounts of money granted to private-sector companies by development agencies are not published.

[2]   The calculation is based on data for Wales's twenty-two unitary authorities taken from *Digest of Welsh Local Area Statistics* (Welsh Assembly, 2003) for 2001, tables 7.9 (employment in foreign-owned plants) and 1.3 (populations). The index numbers are as follows:

Unitary authority	Index
Anglesey	0.636942
Gwynedd	0.43656
Conwy	0.103234
Denbigh	0.730252
Flint	1.658383
Wrexham	2.049652
Powys	0.269019
Ceredigion	0.150408
Pembroke	0.3762
Carmarthenshire	0.766555
Swansea	0.545706
Neath	1.433197
Bridgend	1.936713
Vale of Glamorgan	1.614964
Cardiff	0.436223
RCT	0.928258
Merthyr	0.961493
Caerphilly	1.186171
Blaenau Gwent	1.78091
Torfaen	1.557784
Monmouth	0.633414
Newport	1.860338

³ The calculations of the LQs for the standard statistical regions used for compiling UK statistics are presented in the following tables, the first for manufacturing projects, the second for non-manufacturing projects.

I. Manufacturing projects

Region (1)	N projects (2)	Size of labour force (000s) (3)	2 ÷ 3 × 100 (4)	LQ (col. 4/ average) (5)
North-East	49	1157	4.24	2.03
North-West	20	3216	0.62	0.30
Yorks/Humbs.	50	2397	2.09	1.0
East Midlands	16	2082	0.77	0.37
West Midlands	85	2548	3.34	1.60
East	19	2771	0.69	0.33
London	30	3706	0.81	0.39
South-East	42	4173	1.00	0.48
South-West	26	2460	1.06	0.51
Wales	72	1290	5.58	2.67
Scotland	57	2488	2.29	1.10
Northern Ireland	19	739	2.57	1.23
Total/Average	485	29027	2.09	

II. Non-manufacturing projects

Region (1)	N projects (2)	Size of labour force (000s) (3)	2 ÷ 3 × 100 (4)	LQ (col. 4/ average) (5)
North-East	41	1157	3.54	1.08
North-West	67	3216	2.08	0.64
Yorks/Humbs.	27	2397	1.13	0.34
East Midlands	22	2082	1.06	0.32
West Midlands	99	2548	3.89	1.18
East	78	2771	2.81	0.86
London	356	3706	9.61	2.93
South-East	42	4173	5.92	1.80
South-West	26	2460	2.15	0.66
Wales	72	1290	1.86	0.57
Scotland	57	2488	3.05	0.93
Northern Ireland	19	739	2.30	0.70
Total/average	1107	29027	3.28	

4 Of course the same point can be made here about the inevitable relationship between these two variables, given that Assisted Area status is based on the level of GDP per head. The assumption of GDP as a useful measure of economic or social well-being is itself increasingly contested (see Mayo, 1997) and especially in the context of areas such as Wales that have high levels of other quality-of-life indicators (see Midmore, et al., 2000).

5 According to the Department of Trade and Industry Regional Selective Assistance is paid in instalments against project progress, including job numbers. So monitoring does take place, but it is hard to see what enforcement measures could be taken against foreign-based companies.

6 The calculation that follows should be treated with great caution and is only intended as a rough indication of the sorts of sums involved.

Annual loss in south Wales coalfield 1979/80–1983/4	£32,800,000[a]
Proportion of SW miners employed in Mid Glam.	59.4%
Annual loss attributable to Mid Glam. pits	£19,480,000
Direct manpower employed in Mid Glam. 1979–84 av.	12,000[b]
Annual cost of keeping a mining job	£1,623.60
Cost of an unemployed person p.a.*	£6,300[c]

*This includes the cost to the state in lost taxation (63%) as well as the cost of welfare benefits (see Fraser and Sinfield, 1985).

Sources: [a] Mainwaring and Wass, 1992: 157; [b] Mortimer, 1989: 4; [c] Fraser and Sinfield, 1985.

The calculation assumes that all areas made equivalent losses. The proportion of workers employed in Mid Glamorgan is arrived at by dividing Mortimer's figure for Mid Glamorgan by Mainwaring and Wass's figure for the whole of the south Wales coalfield. Some discrepancy between the two figures is likely.

7 Data from minutes of the Economic Development Committee, 10 July 2002, *www.wales.gov.uk*. Criteria for determining the 'Welshness' of a company include having the registered office or head office in Wales; being owned, managed and controlled in Wales; and not being a subsidiary or division of an English or overseas-owned group.

Notes to Chapter 4

1 After I published an argument along these lines on the Internet I was helpfully informed about the working conditions in MFI factories by a specific whistle-blowing pressure group called Manufacturers Fighting Injustice (MFI). Apparently the sofa was probably manufactured in a factory in Runcorn.

2 A recent example along similar lines is provided in an ethnographic study of undertaking, including a scene where the author buries his father (Lynch, 1997).

3 The opera, *Tower*, written by Alun Hoddinott, which toured Wales

complete with male voice choirs, is a classic piece of image-making. The coal-dusted hero, Tyrone O'Sullivan, is quoted as follows: 'We were ordinary men . . . We wanted jobs . . . We bought a pit.'

[4]   Comments along these lines were made in Parliament on 7 May 2002 during a debate introduced by Llew Smith on the subject of racism in Welsh politics. Don Touhig also related the debate to Welsh nationalism, as did Wayne David, who said (Hansard, col. 62WH):

> I congratulate my hon. friend the Member for Blaenau Gwent [Llew Smith] on his forthright contribution. The strong strand of racism and xenophobia in Plaid Cymru's history is well tabulated. We have only to look at some of the writings of Saunders Lewis, the founder of Plaid Cymru, to recognize the truth of that . . . Saunders Lewis had sympathies for Mussolini, Franco and Hitler. Other elements in Plaid Cymru had sympathies. [Interruption] Opposition Members should not betray some of their pedigree by interrupting in the way in which they are. If they stopped to listen for a moment, they might learn something. That goes for Scottish as well as Welsh nationalists.

[5]   The day I spent reading Michele Lamont's book *The Dignity of Working Men* in the National Library in Aberystwyth an exhibition commemorating Paul Robeson was being set up there.

[6]   Judgement of the Court of Justice in Case C-513/99: a municipality which organizes a tender procedure for the operation of an urban bus service is entitled to take account of ecological considerations concerning the bus fleet offered. This judgement is interpreted as offering scope to include consideration of ecological factors in the case of other goods and services by local authorities.

Notes to Chapter 5

[1]   The data were drawn from the Welsh Assembly statistics website: economics statistics tables 15.3, 15.5 and 15.6. Variables analysed were: percentage of pupils in last year of compulsory schooling 2000/1 with five or more GCSE A*-C grades; GDP index in £ per head compared with the whole of UK; and the percentage employment rate.

[2]   The responses to the questions designed to obtain demographic data were mostly recoded as dichotomous variables, with respondents in the active category, e.g. having undertaken training, assigned the value '1'. In the case of the question regarding the sex of the respondent, men were assigned the value '1'. Information on academic and technical qualifications is presented for purposes of comparison, although it is not possible to impute comparative numerical values to the different kinds of qualifications. The health question, which merely asked respondents to describe their health, was recoded into a four-category schema ranging from 1 for 'excellent' to 4 for 'poor'. Most of the demographic variables could not be included in the analysis, since the number of responses was so low that once the group was split cell sizes would become too small for significant results to be possible.

The question ascertaining respondents' income asked them to identify their income bracket from a series of five ranging from < £100 to £400+ per week. The income brackets were assigned in terms of weekly and annual earnings, so that £100 per week was approximated to £5,000 per annum. This allowed simple comparison of earnings of those who were paid either wages or salaries. In order to make the data comparable between full-time and part-time workers, the variable reported in the results section is 'pay per hour', which was obtained by dividing the mean value of the weekly earnings category by the number of hours worked by each respondent per week. The responses to the questions using 7-point scales were entered as simple values. However, the recoding of the rank-based question concerning rationales for job creation was more complex. Workers were asked to choose three rationales and rank them in order of importance. Their first choice was awarded 3 points, the second 2 points, and the third 1 point. As mentioned in the text, a significant minority of respondents found this question confusing, and there were a corresponding number of missing values. Other respondents had simply ticked three boxes. To avoid losing more cases, where this had happened I assigned all three rationales a score of '2'.

3   The ISCO classification is internationally comparative and this category is clearly important in the context of less developed economies, where many people are employed in primary industries. In the context of a highly industrial area of a developed economy it is inevitably a marginal category.

4   This was a disappointing outcome, given that teachers form such a significant proportion of public-sector workers in this country. Several tentative explanations may be offered: the increase in paperwork required of teachers under the National Curriculum arrangements may have made them loath to fill in 'another questionnaire'; my first major research visit coincided with an outbreak of meningitis, which occupied much of teachers' time; and my visits tended to be at times when university teaching terms had finished, which may well coincide with busy beginning- and end-of-term times for school staff.

5   It would be misleading to assume a public–private bias in support for the questionnaire, since the other two private-sector companies were very supportive, one even allowing staff time off for me to make a presentation to them and then discuss their responses to the questionnaire. This led to three very interesting 'focus group' discussions reported in Chapter 6.

6   The mean health values are clustered around '2', indicating 'good', with slightly lower values demonstrated by the workers at Minitaki, Sunnyside and Hillside. Surprisingly, given the nature of the work, the miners at Tower Colliery have the highest health value, although this may indicate a 'toughness' and unwillingness to admit health problems, since it is a self-assessed value. This attitude is typified by one miner who claimed on his questionnaire to have 'a body like a Greek god'!

7   The high level of perceived job security at Tower is rather remarkable, given the history of massive job losses amongst miners in the study area. One interpretation is that the miners at Tower feel in some sense in control of their future, so that this adds to their perception of security; alternatively, one could hypothesize that, with such a bleak past, they might have a particularly low expectation about how much employment security to expect.

[8]   Using both r and ρ provides more robust results than a single measure of correlation, and for some of the tests significance differs between the two. Intuitively this is clear, since the Pearson's correlation coefficient is taking all the values as separate points and measuring their individual variation from a hypothetical perfect correlation; Spearman's correlation coefficient, by contrast, is based on the ranking, so that the actual magnitude of values that might or might not correlate has no impact.

Notes to Chapter 6

[1]   This interview was conducted three months before the first Assembly elections were held in May 1999. It already hints at the wish for the Assembly to be autonomous, which was later reflected in the overthrow of the first leader, Alun Michael, who was perceived to be a puppet of the Blair administration in London, and his replacement by Rhodri Morgan.

[2]   See Alun Cairns's question to the Economic Development Minister Rhodri Morgan in the Welsh Assembly debate on the economy, 7 July 1999.

[3]   One of the managers at Tower Colliery unwittingly gave evidence that this attitude persists in his comment that 'We would say for a pit in the south Wales valleys we're fairly cosmopolitan, because the workforce comes from about thirty miles away'.

Notes to Chapter 7

[1]   The names of people I interviewed have been changed to protect their anonymity.

[2]   Neurological research suggests a novel reward from cooperative endeavours that might be available to the workers at Tower Colliery. Rilling and colleagues from Emory University, Atlanta (2002) conducted an experiment on women based on the Prisoners' Dilemma game while carrying out an MRI scan of their brains. They found that the pleasure centres received stimulation if they chose a cooperative strategy, suggesting that there may be fundamental psychological rewards available within a cooperative workplace.

Notes to Chapter 8

[1]   Some light is cast on this issue of Welsh resources by the recent refurbishment of the National Library in Aberystwyth. A decision has been taken to incorporate the Welsh material slate in the new paths that are being laid, but the slate has been bought from the Welsh Slate company, based in London, whose impressive website (*www.welshslate.com*) suggests the sort of costs incurred and

implies that the company is a subsidiary of the Alfred McAlpine group. A direct relationship between the suppliers of slate and the builders would have meant more money moving directly to the Welsh slate industry; instead a gesture has been made in the direction of a product that appears to be Welsh, but the economic reality is little different from the history of extraction of Welsh natural resources and value beyond the benefit of Welsh people.

2   Stephanie Findlay, personal communication.

3   The Museum of Welsh Life at St Fagans, near Cardiff is 100 acres of parkland dedicated to reconstructing Wales's history from Celtic times to the present day.

4   See the National Assembly website: *www.wales.gov.uk/assemblydata*.

5   Extracts presented in this section are from the debate on the social economy, 3 November 1999; *www.wales.gov.uk/assemblydata*.

6   The table below presents estimates for the costs of CI in the UK in 2000 taken from Lord, 2001. The figure given for the Accommodation Allowance is an estimate of an initial transitional figure averaged out over the whole population; exact figures would depend on local housing markets and levels of need.

Age	CI costings (£)	£bn saved p.a.	£bn spent p.a.
0–11	8.5m @ £20.20 p.w.		8.93
11–16	4.5m @ £25.90 p.w.		6.06
16–19	2.7m @ £30.95 p.w.		4.35
20–60	30.2m @ £52–20 p.w.		81.97
60+	12m @ £75 p.w.		46.80
Disability supplement	2m @ £25 p.w.		2.60
Accomm. Allowance*	46m @ £22 p.w.		52.62
Gross cost of Citizen's Income			203.33
Payments which would cease			
Social Security payments+		93.81	
Housing subsidies+		3.77	
Tax allowances			
Starting rate	£4385 x 1m x 10%	0.44	
	£2000 x 0.5m x 10%	0.10	
Basic rate	£4385 x 22m x 22%	21.22	
	£2000 x 8m x 22%	3.52	
Higher rate	£4385 x 2m x 40%	3.51	
	£2000 x 1m x 40%	0.80	
Administration costs saved		4.35	131.52
Net cost of Citizen's Income			71.81

7   See debate on the economy on the Welsh Assembly website, *www.wales.gov.uk*

References

Amin, A. and Thrift, N. (1994), 'Holding down the Global', in A. Amin and N. Thrift (eds), *Globalization, Institutions and Regional Development in Europe* (Oxford: Oxford University Press), pp. 257–60.

Apffel-Marglin, F. (1998), *The Spirit of Regeneration: Andean Culture Confronting Western Notions of Development* (London: Zed).

Arthur, L., Cato, M. S. and Smith, R. (2004), 'Developing an Operational Definition of the Social Economy', *Journal of Cooperative Studies*, forthcoming.

Atkinson, A. B. (1995), *Public Economics in Action: The Basic Income/Flat Tax Proposal* (Oxford: Clarendon Press).

Baber, C. and Thomas, D. (1980), 'The Glamorgan Economy, 1914–1945', in A. H. John and G. Williams (eds), *Glamorgan County History*, v. *Industrial Glamorgan from 1700 to 1970* (Cardiff: University of Wales Press), pp. 519–80.

Banks, J. and Marsden, T. (2000), 'Integrating Agri-Environment Policy, Farming Systems and Rural Development: Tir Cymen in Wales', *Sociologia Ruralis*, 40/4: 466–80.

Baudrillard, J. (1975), *For a Critique of the Political Economy of the Sign* (St Louis, Mo: Telos).

—— (1988), *Selected Writings*, ed. M. Poster (Stanford, Calif.: Stanford University Press).

Bauman, Z. (1998), *Work, Consumerism and the New Poor* (Buckingham: Open University Press).

BBC Manchester (1998), *File on Four*, programme on inward investment broadcast on 10 November (Manchester: BBC).

Beatty, C. and Fothergill, S. (1996), 'Labour Market Adjustment in Areas of Chronic Industrial Decline: The Case of the UK Coalfields', *Regional Studies*, 30/7: 627–40.

——, Fothergill, S., Gore, A., and Green, A. (2002), *The Real Level of Unemployment 2002* (Sheffield: Sheffield Hallam University, Centre for Regional Economic and Social Research).

——, —— and Lawless, P. (1997), 'Geographical Variation in the Labour-Market Adjustment Process: The UK Coalfields 1981–91', *Environment and Planning A*, 29: 2041–60.

Beck, U. (1992), *Risk Society* (London: Sage).

—— (1999), *Schöne neue Arbeitswelt*, translated as *Brave New World of Work* (Cambridge: Polity Press, 2000).

Becker, G. S. (1986), *An Economic Analysis of the Family* (Dublin: Economic and Social Research Institute).

—— (1991), *A Treatise on the Family* (Cambridge, Mass.: Harvard University Press).

Becker, Gary S. (1975), *Human Capital*, 2nd edn (Chicago: Chicago University Press).

Beddoe, D. (1995), 'Munitionettes, Maids and Mams: Women in Wales, 1914–1939', in A. V. John (ed.), *Our Mothers' Land: Chapters in Welsh Women's History, 1830–1939* (Cardiff: University of Wales Press), pp. 189–207.

Begg, I. (1995), 'Factor Mobility and Regional Disparities in the European Union', *Oxford Review of Economic Policy*, 11/2: 96–112.

Bell, D. (1973), *The Coming of Post-Industrial Society* (New York: Basic Books).

Bewley, T. (1995), 'A Depressed Labor Market as Explained by Participants', *AEA Papers and Proceedings*, 85/2: 250–4.

Blair, T. (1998), *The Third Way: A New Politics for a New Century* (London: Fabian Society).

Blanchflower, D. and Oswald, A. (1998), 'What Makes an Entrepreneur? Evidence on Inheritance and Capital Constraints', *Journal of Labor Economics*, 16/2: 26–60.

Bosworth, D., Dawkins, P. and Stromback, T. (1996), *The Economics of the Labour Market* (Harlow: Longman).

Boyns, T., Thomas, D. and Baber, C. (1980), 'The Iron, Steel and Tinplate Industries, 1750–1914', ch. 3 in A. H. John and G. Williams (eds), *Glamorgan County History*, v. *Industrial Glamorgan* (Cardiff: University of Wales Press), pp. 97–154.

Brand, S., Hill, S. and Munday, M. (2000), 'Assessing the Impacts of Foreign Manufacturing on Regional Economies: The Cases of Wales, Scotland and the West Midlands', *Regional Studies*, 34/4: 343–56.

Brooksbank, D. J. and Pickernell, D. G. (2001), 'Changing the Name of the Game: RSA, Indigenous and Inward Investors and the National Assembly for Wales', *Regional Studies*, 351/3: 271–7.

Bryman, A. and Cramer, D. (1997), *Quantitative Data Analysis with SPSS for Windows: A Guide for Social Scientists* (London: Routledge).

Burchell, B. (1994), 'The Effects of Labour-Market Position, Job Insecurity and Unemployment on Psychological Health', ch. 6 in D. Gallie and C. Marsh (eds), *The Experience of Unemployment* (Oxford: Oxford University Press), pp. 188–212.

Cacioppe, R. and Mock, P. (1984), 'A Comparison of the Quality of Work Experience in Government and Private Organizations', *Human Relations*, 37: 923–40.

Carley, M. and Christie, I. (1993), *Managing Sustainable Development* (London: Earthscan).

Casson, M. C. (1991), *The Entrepreneur: An Economic Theory* (Farnborough: Gregg Revivals).

—— (1993), 'Cultural Determinants of Economic Performance', *Journal of Comparative Economics*, 17: 418–42.

——, Cooke, P., Merfyn Jones, R. and Williams, C. H. (1994), *Quiet Revolution? Language, Culture and Economy in the Nineties* (Aberystwyth: Menter a Busnes).

Cato, M. S. (1998), 'Is Social Worth a Compensating Differential', paper presented to the research seminar, Economics Department, Aberystwyth University.

——— (2000a), 'A New Economic Development Model for the New Wales', *Contemporary Wales*, 13: 68–93.

——— (2000b), *Employment Motivations and Unemployment Policy, with a Special Focus on the Rhondda Cynon Taff Labour Market*, Ph.D. thesis (Aberystwyth).

——— (2001a), 'Inward Investment and Economic Regeneration: Listening to Workers in Rhondda Cynon Taff', *Local Economy*, 16/3, 198–220.

——— (2001b), 'Sen and Sustainability: Poverty, Consumer Pressure, and the Future of the Planet', paper presented at the 2001 Conference on Feminist Economics, Oslo, 22–4 June.

——— (2003), *Trade Subsidiarity: Localising Production for the Benefit of People and Planet* (Aberystwyth: Green Audit).

Clark, A. E. (1997), 'Job Satisfaction and Gender: Why are Women so Happy at Work?', *Labour Economics*, 4: 341–72.

Clifford, J. and Marcus, G. E. (1986) (eds), *Writing Culture: The Poetics and Politics of Ethnography* (Berkeley: University of California Press).

Coalfield Communities Campaign (Wales) (2001), *The Welsh Coalfields: Problems and Regeneration in the Former Mining Communities of North and South Wales* (Cwmbran: CCC).

Coalfields Taskforce Report (1998), *Making the Difference* (London: HMSO).

Cooke, P. N. and Morgan, K. (1998), *The Associational Economy: Firms, Regions and Innovation* (Oxford: Oxford University Press).

Cowe, R. (2000), 'Lending an ear to social services', *Guardian*, 12 April.

Daly, H. E. (1992), *Steady-State Economics*, 2nd edn (London: Earthscan).

Davies, G. and Thomas, I. (1976), *Overseas Investment in Wales* (Swansea: Christopher Davies).

Derrida, J. (1967), *L'Ecriture et la différence*; trans. as *Writing and Difference* (London: Routledge and Kegan Paul, 1978).

Desai, P. and Riddlestone, S. (2002), *Bioregional Solutions for Living on one Planet* (Totnes: Green Books).

DETR (1998) (with DTI, DCMS and DFEE), *Making the Difference: A New Start for England's Coalfield Communities: The Government's Response to the Coalfields Taskforce Report* (London: HMSO).

DfEE (1998) (Department for Education and Employment), *The Learning Age: A Renaissance for a New Britain* (London: HMSO).

Dickens, R., Gregg, P. and Wadsworth, J. (2000), 'New Labour and the Labour Market', *Oxford Review of Economic Policy*, 16/1: 95–113.

Dicks, B. (1996), 'Regeneration and Representation in the Rhondda: The Story of the Rhondda Heritage Park', *Contemporary Wales*, 9: 56–73.

——— (2000), *Heritage, Place and Community* (Cardiff: University of Wales Press).

Disney, R., Goodman, A., Gosling, A. and Trinder, C. (1999), *Public Pay in Britain in the 1990s* (London: Institute for Fiscal Studies).

——— and Webb, S. (1991), 'Why are There So Many Long-Term Sick in Britain?', *Economic Journal*, 101: 252–62.

Douthwaite, R. (1992), *The Growth Illusion: How Economic Growth has Enriched the Few, Impoverished the Many, and Endangered the Planet* (Bideford: Green Books).

——— (1996), *Short Circuit: Strengthening Local Economies for Security in an Uncertain World* (Totnes: Green Books).

—— (1999), *The Ecology of Money*, Schumacher Briefing 4 (Totnes: Green Books).

Driffield, N. (1998), 'Indirect Regional Impact of Inward Investment', in S. Hill and B. Morgan (eds), *Inward Investment, Business Finance, and Regional Development* (Basingstoke: Macmillan).

—— (1999), 'Indirect Employment Effects of Foreign Direct Investment into the UK', *Bulletin of Economic Research*, 51/3: 207–21.

Drinkwater, S. (1997), 'The Welsh Economy: A Statistical Profile', *Contemporary Wales*, 10: 219–41.

DTI (2000) (Department of Trade and Industry), *Use of Extracted Coalbed Methane for Power Production at Tower Colliery*, Best Practice Brochure from the Cleaner Coal Technology Programme (London: SO).

—— (2003) (Department of Trade and Industry), *Review of the Remaining Reserves at Deep Mines* (dti website).

Dubé, S. (2003), 'Co-operative Plan Aims to Provide for Local Customers', *Western Mail*, 16 June, online at *icWales.icnetwork.co.uk*.

Dunn, T. and Holtz-Eakin, D. (2000), 'Financial Capital, Human Capital, and the Transition to Self-Employment: Evidence from Intergenerational Links', *Journal of Labor Economics*, 18/2: 282–303.

EAPSG (Entrepreneurship Action Plan Steering Group) (1999), *Entrepreneurship Action Plan for Wales: Offering a Helping Hand to Future Welsh Stars* (Cardiff: EAPSG).

Eliot, G. (1901) *Adam Bede* (Edinburgh: Blackwood).

Employment Intelligence Unit (1991), *Valleys Skills* (Cardiff: Employment Department Office for Wales).

England, P. (1984), 'Wage Appreciation and Depreciation: A Test of Neoclassical Economic Explanations of Occupational Sex Segregation', *Social Forces*, 63/3: 726–49.

—— (1993), 'The Separative Self: Androcentric Bias in Neoclassical Assumptions', in M. A. Ferber and J. Nelson (eds), *Beyond Economic Man: Feminist Theory and Economics* (London: University of Chicago Press), pp. 37–53.

Equal Opportunities Commission Wales (n.d.), *Educational Reforms and Gender Equality in Welsh Schools* (Cardiff: EOC Wales).

European Commission (1997a), *Community Involvement in Urban Regeneration: Added Value and Changing Values* (Luxemburg: European Commission).

—— (1997b), *Fighting Long-Term Unemployment* (Luxemburg: Commission of the European Communities).

—— (1998), *Social Action Programme 1998–2000* (Luxemburg: European Commission).

Evans, G. (1956), *Save Cwm Tryweryn for Wales* (Swansea: Gwasg John Penry).

Evans, J. (1994), *How Real is my Valley: Postmodernism and the South Wales Valleys* (Pontypridd: Underground Press).

Feld, V. (1999), 'Small Businesses and the Assembly', paper presented at the Conference on Entrepreneurship and Small Businesses in the Media: Past, Present and Future, School of Management and Business, Aberystwyth, 8 October.

Ferner, A. (1998), 'Multinationals, "Relocation" and Employment in Europe', in J. Gual (ed.), *Job Creation: The Role of Labour-Market Institutions* (London: Edward Elgar), pp. 165–96.

Fevre, R. (1987a), 'Redundancy and the Labour Market: The Role of "Readaptation Benefits"', ch. 4 in R. Lee (ed.), *Redundancy, Layoffs and Plant Closures: Their Character, Causes and Consequences* (London: Croom Helm), pp. 62–83.

—— (1987b), 'The Social Creation of Unemployment', *Planet: The Welsh Internationalist*, October/November: 14–20.

—— (1987c), *Wales is Closed* (Nottingham: Spokesman).

Fieldhouse, E. and Hollywood, E. (1999), 'Life after Mining: Hidden Unemployment and Changing Patterns of Economics Acitivity amongst Miners in England and Wales, 1981–1991', *Work, Employment and Society*, 13/3: 483–502.

Fleming, J. and Keenan, E. (2000), 'Youth on the Margins in Northern Ireland, England, and Ukraine', *European Journal of Social Work*, 3/2: 165–77.

Flick, U. (2002), 'Qualitative Research – State of the Art', *Social Science Information*, 41/4: 5–24.

Forrester, V. (1999), *The Economic Horror* (Cambridge: Polity Press); orginal French edition published 1996.

Fothergill, S. and Witt, S. (1990), *The Privatisation of British Coal* (Barnsley: Coalfields Communities Campaign).

Foucault, M. (1969), *L'Archéologie du savoir* (Paris: Gallimard); trans. as *The Archaeology of Knowledge* (London: Tavistock, 1972).

Fox Keller, E. (1985), *Reflections on Gender and Science* (New Haven, Conn.: Yale University Press).

Francis, H. (1997), *The Tower Story: Lessons in Vigilance and Freedom* (Cynon Valley: Tower Colliery).

Frank, R. H. (1985), *Choosing the Right Pond: Human Behaviour and the Quest for Status* (Oxford: Oxford University Press).

Fraser, N. and Sinfield, A. (1985), 'The Cost of High Unemployment', *Social Policy and Administration*, 19/2: 92–9.

Freeman, R. (1996), 'The Limits of Wage Flexibility to Curing Unemployment', *Oxford Review of Economic Policy*, 11/1: 63–72.

French, C. (2001), *The Celtic Goddess: Great Queen or Demon Witch?* (Edinburgh: Floris Books).

Frey, B. S. (1997), *Not Just for the Money* (Cheltenham: Edward Elgar).

Friedman, M. (1975), *Unemployment vs. Inflation: An Evaluation of the Phillips Curve* (London: Institute for Economic Affairs); reprinted in *Monetarist Economics* (Oxford: Basil Blackwell, 1991), pp. 75–9.

Gallie, D. and Vogler, C. (1998), 'Labour-Market Deprivation, Welfare and Collectivism', ch. 10 in D. Gallie and C. Marsh (eds), *The Experience of Unemployment* (Oxford: Oxford University Press), pp. 299–336.

——, White, M., Cheng, Y. and Tomlinson, M. (1998), 'Work, Restructuring and Social Regulation', introduction to *Restructuring the Employment Relationship* (Oxford: Oxford University Press).

—— (eds) *Restructuring the Employment Relationship* (Oxford: Oxford University Press).

Gellner, E. (1983), *Nations and Nationalism* (Oxford: Blackwell).

Gershuny, J. (1998), 'The Psychological Consequences of Unemployment: An Assessment of the Jahoda Thesis', ch. 7 in D. Gallie and C. Marsh (eds), *The Experience of Unemployment* (Oxford: Oxford University Press), pp. 211–30.

Giddens, A. (1998), *The Third Way: The Renewal of Social Democracy* (Cambridge: Polity Press).

Glyn, A. (1996), 'The Assessment: Unemployment and Inequality', *Oxford Review of Economic Policy*, 11/1: 1–25.

Goldsmith, E. and Mander, J. (1996), *The Case Against the Global Economy* (San Francisco: Sierra Club).

Gorz, A. (1999), *Reclaiming Work: Beyond the Wage-Based Society* (Cambridge: Polity Press); original French edition published 1997.

Grabiner, Lord (2000), *Report on the Black Economy* (London: The Stationery Office).

Granovetter, M. (1985), 'Economic Action and Social Structure: The Problem of Embededdness', *American Journal of Sociology*, 91: 481–510.

—— (2001), 'A Theoretical Agenda for Economic Sociology', in M. F. Grillen, R. Collins, P. England and M. Meyer (eds), *Economy Sociology at the Millennium* (New York: Russell Sage Foundation).

Grant, R. (1991), *Cynon Valley in the Age of Iron* (Aberdare: Cynon Valley Borough Council).

Gray, A. (1999), 'The New Deal and Welfare Reform: Opportunity, Punishment or Deterrence?, *Employment Studies Paper 28* (Hatfield: University of Hertfordshire).

Gray, M. (1996), 'Penrhys: The Archaeology of a Pilgrimage', *Morgannwg*, 40: 10–32.

Gregg, P., Knight, G. and Wadsworth, J. (1999), 'Heaven Knows I'm Miserable Now: Job Insecurity in the British Labour Market', ch. 3 of E. Heery and J. Salmon (eds), *The Insecure Workforce* (London: Routledge), pp. 39–56.

Habermas, J. (1987), *The Theory of Communicative Action* (Cambridge: Polity Press).

Hain, P. (1999), *A Welsh Third Way* (London: Tribune Publications).

Hakim, C. (1996), *Key Issues in Women's Work: Female Heterogeneity and the Polarisation of Women's Employment* (London: Athlone Press).

—— (1998), *Social Change and Innovation in the Labour Market* (Oxford: Oxford University Press).

Harris, C. C. (1987), *Redundancy and Recession in South Wales* (Oxford: Blackwell).

Harvey, D. (1989), *The Condition of Postmodernity* (Oxford: Blackwell).

Heath, T. (2000), 'Strike Closes Pit Run by Miners in "Silly" Dispute', *Guardian*, 12 April.

Hechter, M. (1975), *Internal Colonialism: The Celtic Fringe in British National Development 1536–1966* (London: Routledge and Kegan Paul).

Higgs, G. and White, S. (1997), 'A Comparison of Community-Level Indices in Measuring Disadvantage', *Contemporary Wales*, 10: 126–69.

Hill, S. and Keegan, J. (1993), *Made in Wales: An Analysis of Welsh Manufacturing Performance* (Cardiff: CBI Wales).

—— and Roberts, A. (1993), 'Why Wales? The Competitive Advantage', in Institute of Welsh Affairs (ed.), *Welsh Economic Review Special Issue: Inward Investment in Wales* (Cardiff: Welsh Economy Research Unit), 18–22.

—— and —— (1998), 'Investment, Local Linkages and Regional Development', in S. Hill and B. Morgan (eds), *Inward Investment, Business Finance, and Regional Development* (Basingstoke: Macmillan), 30–47.

Hines, C. (1993), *The New Protectionism: Protecting the Future against Free Trade* (London: Earthscan).

—— (2000), *Localization: A Global Manifesto* (London: Earthscan).

—— and Lang, T. (1996), 'In Favor of a New Protectionism', in J. Mander and E. Goldsmith (eds), *The Case against the Global Economy, and for a Turn toward the Local* (San Francisco: Sierra Club Books), pp. 485–93.

Hirst, P. and Thompson, G. (1996), *Globalisation in Question* (Cambridge: Polity Press).

Holmes, P., Lynch, H. and Molho, I. (1991), 'An Econometric Analysis of the Growth in Numbers Claiming Invalidity Benefit: An Overview', *Journal of Social Policy*, 20: 87–105.

Hudson, R. (1994), 'East Meets West: The Regional Implications within the European Union of Political and Economic Change in Eastern Europe', *European Urban and Regional Studies*, 1/1: 79–83.

Huggins, R. (2001), 'Embedding Inward Investment through Workforce Development: Experiences in Wales', *Environment and Planning C*, 19/6: 833–48.

Hughes, D. (2002) 'Judge Names and Shames Schoolboy Racist and Sentences him to 18 Months' Detention', *Western Mail*, 20 February.

Hutchinson, F., Mellor, M. and Olsen, W. (2002), *The Politics of Money: Towards Sustainability and Economic Democracy* (London: Pluto).

ICOM and Taylor, A. (1986), *Worker Cooperatives and the Social Economy* (Manchester: ICOM).

ILO (1990), *International Standard Classification of Occupation: ISCO–88*, Geneva: ILO.

Institute of Welsh Affairs (1993), *Welsh Economic Review Special Issue: Inward Investment in Wales* (Cardiff: Welsh Economy Research Unit).

Jackman, R. (1995), 'Regional Policy in an Enlarged Europe', *Oxford Review of Economic Policy*, 11/2: 113–25.

Jahoda, M. (1982), *Employment and Unemployment: A Social-Psychological Analysis* (Cambridge: University Press).

——, Lazarsfeld, P. and Zeizel, H. (1933), *Marienthal: The Sociology of an Unemployed Community* (London: Tavistock).

James, A., Hockey, J. L. and Dawson, A. H. (1997) (eds), *After Writing Culture: Epistemology and Praxis in Contemporary Anthropology* (London: Routledge).

James, L. (1996), 'Greenham Common: The Development of Feminist Security Ideas in Britain in the 1980s', Ph.D. thesis (Birmingham).

—— (1998), 'Identity in Research: Feminism, Methodology and Analysis', paper presented at the conference Linking Theory and Practice: Issues in the Politics of Identity, University of Wales, Aberystwyth, 9–11 September.

Jessop, B. (2000), 'Globalisation, Entrepreneurial Cities and the Social Economy', in P. Hamel, H. Lustiger-Thaler and M. Mayer (eds), *Urban Movements in a Global World* (London: Routledge), pp. 81–100.

John, A. (1995), 'Introduction', in A. V. John (ed.), *Our Mothers' Land: Chapters in Welsh Women's History, 1830–1939* (Cardiff: University of Wales Press), pp. 1–16.

John, A. H., Williams, G. and Williams, M. F. (1980), *Glamorgan County History* (Cardiff: Glamorgan County History Trust).

Jones, D. (1995), 'Counting the Cost of Coal: Women's Lives in the Rhondda, 1881–1918', in A. V. John (ed.), *Our Mothers' Land: Chapters in Welsh Women's History, 1830–1939* (Cardiff: University of Wales Press), pp. 109–33.

Jones, R. (2001), 'O'Sullivan Welcomes Tower Deal', *Western Mail*, 12 September.

Kelly, A. (2000), 'The Welsh Development Agency was Right to Support the Inward Investment by LG at Imperial Par, Newport in Gwent, Notwithstanding LG's Dependency on the Stability of the South Korean Economy from where the Company's Origin Stems', thesis, Planning Department, Oxford Brookes University.

Kendall, J. and Knapp, M. (1996), *The Voluntary Sector in the United Kingdom* (Manchester: Manchester University Press).

Khandker, S. R., Samad, H. A. and Khan, Z. H. (1998), 'Income and Employment Effects of Micro-Credit Programmes: Village-Level Evidence from Bangladesh', *Journal of Development Studies*, 35/2: 96–124.

Klein, N. (2000), *No Logo: No Space, No Choice, No Jobs, Taking Aim at the Brand Bullies* (London: Flamingo).

Klemencic, M. M. (1995), 'Experiences of Spatioeconomic Restructuring in Slovenia', ch. 2 in M. Tykkyläinen (ed.), *Local and Regional Development during the 1990s Transition in Eastern Europe* (Aldershot: Avebury), p. 263.

Knight, B., Smerdon, M. and Pharoah, C. (1998), *Building Civil Society: Current Initiatives in Voluntary Action: A Special Edition of the Non-Profit Sector to Mark the 50th Anniversary of the Publication of 'Voluntary Action' by Sir William Beveridge* (West Malling: Charities Aid Foundation).

Kropotkin, P. (1902/1939), *Mutual Aid* (Harmondsworth: Pelican).

Krueger, A. B. and Summers, L. H. (1988), 'Efficiency Wages and the Inter-Industry Wage Structure', *Econometrica*, 56/2: 259–93.

Kuhn, T. S. (1962), *The Structure of Scientific Revolutions* (Cambridge, Mass.: Harvard University Press).

Lamont, M. (2000), *The Dignity of Working Men: Morality and the Boundaries of Race, Class and Immigration* (New York: Russell Sage Foundation).

Lang, P. (1994), *Lets Work: Rebuilding the Local Economy* (Bristol: Grover).

Latour, B. (1987), *Science in Action* (Cambridge, Mass.: Harvard University Press).

—— (1999), *Pandora's Hope: Essays on the Reality of Science Studies* (Cambridge, Mass.: Harvard University Press).

Lauristin, M. and Vihalemm, P. (1993), 'The Baltics: West of the East, East of the West', in S. Hoyer, E. Lauk, and P. Vihalemm (eds), *Towards a Civic Society: The Baltic Media's Long Road to Freedom* (Tartu: Baltic Association for Media Research), pp. 13–14.

—— and —— (1997) (eds), *Return to the Western World: Cultural and Political Perspectives on the Estonian Post-Communist Transition* (Tartu: Tartu University Press).

Lawson, H. (1989), 'Introduction to Stories about Science', in H. Lawson and L. Appignanesi (eds), *Dismantling Truth: Reality in the Postmodern World* (London: Weidenfeld and Nicolson), pp. 79–81.

Lawson, T. (1994), 'Why are so Many Economists so Opposed to Methodology?', *Journal of Economic Methodology*, 1/1: 105–34.

—— (1997), *Economics and Reality* (London: Routledge).

Layard, R., Nickell, S. and Jackman, R. (1991), *Unemployment: Macroeconomic Performance and the Labour Market* (Oxford: Oxford University Press).

Le, A. T. (1999), 'Empirical Studies of Self-Employment', *Review of Economic Surveys*, 13/4: 381–416.

Lee, R. M. (1987), *Redundancy, Lay-offs and Plant Closures: Their Character, Causes and Consequences* (London: Croom Helm).

Leeds Metropolitan University (2002), *The Selby Coalfield Impact Study* (Leeds: European Regional Business and Economic Development Unit).

Lewis, E. D. (1959), *The Rhondda Valleys* (Cardiff: University College Cardiff Press).

Lindbeck, A. (1996), 'The West European Employment Problem', *Weltwirtschaftliches Archiv*, 132/4: 609–37.

Llewelyn Jones, R. (1998), 'Pride of the South Wales Coal Field', in *Rhondda Cynon Taff 1998 Economic Survey* (Cardiff: Western Mail), 11.

Lord, C. (2001), *A Guide to the Citizens' Income*, online at *www.greenparty.org.uk*

Lovering, J. (1999), 'Celebrating Globalization and Misreading the Welsh Economy: The "New Regionalism"' in Wales', *Contemporary Wales*, 11: 12–60.

Lucas, C. (2001), *Stopping the Great Food Swap: Relocalising Europe's Food Supply* (Brussels: European Parliament).

—— (2002), 'Re-localising the Global Economy', BBC Wales Lecture, 1 May 2002, *www.cf.ac.uk/cplan/ri/lectures/lucas.html*

Lucas, R. E. B. (1977), 'Hedonic Wage Equations and Psychic Wages in the Returns to Schooling', *American Economic Review*, 674: 549–58.

Lynch, T. (1997), *The Undertaking: Life Studies from the Dismal Trade* (London: Jonathan Cape).

Lyon, D. (1994), *Postmodernity* (Buckingham: Open University Press).

Lyons, B. and McCloughan, P. (1998), 'Uncle Sam's Ireland', in S. Hill and B. Morgan (eds), *Inward Investment, Business Finance, and Regional Development* (Basingstoke: Macmillan), pp. 100–15.

Lyotard, J.-F. (1967), *La Condition postmoderne*; trans. as *The Postmodern Condition: A Report on Knowledge* (Manchester: Manchester University Press, 1984).

McQuaig, L. (1998), *The Cult of Impotence: Selling the Myth of Powerlessness in the Global Economy* (Toronto: Viking).

Mainwaring, L. (1995), 'Catching Up and Falling Behind', *Contemporary Wales*, 8: 9–28.

—— and Wass, V. (1989), 'Colliery Closures and Productivity Gains in the South Wales Coalfield 1982/83–1989/90', *Contemporary Wales*, 5: 157–63.

Marglin, S. A. and Marglin, F. A. (1990), *Dominating Knowledge: Development, Culture, and Resistance* (Oxford: Clarendon Press).

—— and —— (1996), *Decolonizing Knowledge: From Development to Dialogue* (Oxford: Clarendon Press).

Marin, A. and Psacharopolous, G. (1982), 'The Reward for Risk in the Labor Market: Evidence from the United Kingdom and a Reconciliation with Other Studies', *Journal of Political Economy*, 90: 827–53.

Marsden, D. (1975), *Workless: Some Unemployed Men and their Families* (Harmondsworth: Penguin).

Marsden, T., Banks, J. and Bristow, G. (2000), 'Food Supply Chain Approaches: Exploring their Role in Rural Development', *Sociologia Ruralis*, 40/4: 424–38.

——, —— and —— (2002), 'The Social Management of Rural Nature: Understanding Agrarian-Based Rural Development', *Environment and Planning A*, 34/5: 809–26.

——, Murdoch, J. and Morgan, K. (2000), 'Sustainable Agriculture, Food Supply Chains and Regional Development', *International Planning Studies*, 14/3: 295–302.

Matthews, J., Munday, M. and Roberts, A. (2003), 'Project Report: A Welsh Index of Sustainable Economic Welfare', *Welsh Economic Review*, 15/1: 33–6.

Mautner, T. (1997) (ed.), *Penguin Dictionary of Philosophy* (Harmondsworth: Penguin).

Mayo, E. (1997), 'More Isn't Necessarily Better', working paper (London: New Economics Foundation).

—— and Moore, H. (2001), *The Mutual State: How Local Communities Can Run Public Services* (London: New Economics Foundation).

Mendell, M. (2000), 'Local Finance in a Global Economy', in P. Hamel, H. Lustiger-Thaler and M. Mayer (eds), *Urban Movements in a Global World* (London: Routledge), pp. 101–21.

Meredith, C. (1988), *Shifts* (Bridgend: Seren).

MGCC (Mid Glamorgan County Council) (1989), *Mid Glamorgan: Issues for the 1990s* (Clydach Vale: Policy Research and European Affairs Unit).

—— (1995), *Rhondda, Cynon, Taff Insight: A Profile of Rhondda, Cynon, Taff County Borough* (Clydach Vale: Mid Glamorgan Policy Research and European Affairs Unit).

Michael, A. (1998), 'Volunteering and Community Action: Building the Future Together', *RSA Journal*, 2/4: 60–7.

Mid Glamorgan Careers Ltd (1996), *Corporate Plan 1997–2000* (Pontypridd: MGCL).

Mid Glamorgan tec (1997), *Labour Market Assessment 1997–1998* (n.p.: Mid Glamorgan tec).

Midgley, M. (2001), *Science and Poetry* (London: Routledge).

Midmore, P. (1999a), 'Rural Economic Development: A Research Agenda for the National Assembly for Wales', *Contemporary Wales*, 11: 101–9.

—— (1999b), 'Globalization and the Rural Economy', inaugural lecture given in the Old Hall, Aberystwyth University, 1 December.

——, Matthews, J. and Christie, M. (2000), 'Monitoring Sustainable Development in Wales: A Pilot Index of Sustainable Economic Welfare', Working Paper No. 11 (Aberystwyth: Welsh Institute of Rural Studies).

Milne, S. (1995), *The Enemy Within: The Secret War Against the Miners* (London: Pan).

Mincer, J. (1974), *Schooling, Experience, and Earnings* (New York: National Bureau for Economic Research).

—— (1991), 'Human Capital, Technology and the Wage Structure: What Do Time Series Show?', NBER Working Paper no. 3581; repr. in *Collected Essays of Jacob Mincer*, i. *Studies in Human Capital* (Aldershot: Edward Elgar).

—— (1997) 'The Production of Human Capital and the Life Cycle of Earnings', *Journal of Labour Economics*, 15/1: 526–47.

Morgan, A. (1983), *The Growth of a Welsh Coal Mining Community: Rhondda 1860–1914* (Treforest: Welsh History Resources Unit).

Morgan, B. (1993), 'Inward Investment: The Economic Impact', in Institute of Welsh Affairs (ed.), *Welsh Economic Review Special Issue: Inward Investment in Wales* (Cardiff: Welsh Economy Research Unit), pp. 13–17.

—— (1998), 'Regional Issues in Inward Investment and Endogenous Growth', in S. Hill and B. Morgan (eds), *Inward Investment, Business Finance, and Regional Development* (Basingstoke: Macmillan), pp. 13–17.

—— (1999), *Welsh Assembly Elections: 6 May 1999*, House of Commons Research Paper 99/51 (London: TSO).

Morgan, K. (1987), 'High Technology Industry and Regional Development: For Wales see Greater Boston?', *Contemporary Wales*, 1: 39–51.

—— (2002), 'The New Regeneration Narrative: Local Development in a Multi-Level Polity', *Local Economy*, 17/3: 191–9.

—— and Morley, A. (2002), *Relocalising the Food Chain: The Role of Creative Public Procurement* (Cardiff: Regeneration Institute).

——, Sayer, A. and Sklair, L. (1988), *Microcircuits of Capital: 'Sunrise' Industry and Uneven Development* (Cambridge: Polity Press).

Morris, J. (1993), 'Who, What and Where? The Nature of Foreign Direct Investment in Wales', in Institute of Welsh Affairs (ed.), *Welsh Economic Review Special Issue: Inward Investment in Wales* (Cardiff: Welsh Economy Research Unit), pp. 4–12.

—— and Mansfield, R. (1988), 'Economic Regeneration in Industrial South Wales', *Contemporary Wales*, 2: 63–82.

——, Munday, M. and Wilkinson, C. (1993), *Working for the Japanese: The Economic and Social Consequences of Japanese Investment* (London: Athlone).

—— and Wilkinson, B. (1995), 'Poverty and Prosperity in Wales: Polarization and Los Angelisization', *Contemporary Wales*, 8: 29–45.

Mortimer, P. (1989), *The Coal Industry in Mid Glamorgan 1947–1989: A Statistical Collection* (Clydach Vale: MGCC Policy Research and European Affairs Unit).

—— and Davies, P. (1988), *Mid Glamorgan: A Coalfield Area Profile* (Clydach Vale: MGCC Economic Policy and Research).

Munday, M. (2003), 'Review of the Welsh Economy', presented at the Welsh Economy Research Unit Eleventh Annual Conference: Sustainable Development in Wales: Theory, Practice and Measurement, Cardiff Business School, 14 May.

—— and Peel, M. (1997), 'The Comparative Performance of Foreign-Owned and Domestic Manufacturing Firms during Recession: Some Descriptive Evidence from Wales', *Contemporary Wales*, 10: 50–79.

—— and Roberts, A. (2001), 'Assessing the Regional Transactions of Foreign Manufacturers in Wales: Issues and Determinants', *Tijdschrift voor economische en sociale geografie*, 92/2: 202–16.

—— and Wilkinson, B. (1993), 'The Social Consequences of Inward Investment: Recent Survey Evidence from Japanese Manufacturing in Wales', in Institute of Welsh Affairs (ed.), *Welsh Economic Review Special Issue: Inward Investment in Wales* (Cardiff: Welsh Economy Research Unit), pp. 40–5.

Murdoch, J., Marsden, T. and Banks, J. (2000), 'Quality, Nature and Embeddedness: Some Theoretical Considerations in the Context of the Food Sector', *Economic Geography*, 76/2: 107–25.

Nader, L. (2001), 'Anthropology! Distinguished Lecture 2000', *American Anthropologist*, 103/3: 609–20.

NAO (2003) (National Audit Office), *The Department of Trade and Industry: Regional Grants in England* (London: TSO).

NCB (National Coal Board) South Wales Area (1977), *Welcome to Cwm* (Cardiff: NCB).

NATTA (2002), Network for Alternative Technology and Technological Assessment, 'FoE Cymru – Renewables at 30% by 2010?', *NATTA Newsletter*, November/December.

Nelson, J. (1993), 'Value-Free or Valueless? Notes on the Pursuit of Detachment in Economics', *History of Political Economy*, 25/1: 121–46.

—— (1995a), 'Feminism and Economics', *Journal of Economic Perspectives*, 9/2: 131–48.

—— (1995b), *Feminism, Objectivity and Economics* (London: Routledge).

Ngugi wa Thiongo (1986), *Decolonising the Mind: The Politics of Language in African Literature* (London: Currey).

Norberg-Hodge, H., Merrifield, T. and Gorelick, S. (2002), *Bringing the Food Economy Home: Local Alternatives to Global Agribusiness* (London: Zed).

Oakley, A. (1981), *Subject Women* (London: Martin Robertson).

OECD (1994a), *The Jobs Study: Evidence and Explanations*, i. *Labour Market Trends and Underlying Forces* (Paris: OECD).

—— (1994b), *The Jobs Study: Evidence and Explanations*, ii. *The Adjustment Potential of the Labour Market* (Paris: OECD).

—— (1997), 'Is Job Insecurity on the Increase in OECD Countries?', *Employment Outlook* (Paris: OECD), ch. 5, pp. 129–58.

O'Sullivan, T., Eve, J. and Edworthy, A. (2001), *Tower of Strength: The Story of Tyrone O'Sullivan and Tower Colliery* (Edinburgh: Mainstream).

O'Leary, H., Murphy, P., Jones, M. and Blackaby, D. (2003), 'Inactivity and Unemployment in Wales: A Contribution to the Policy Debate', *Welsh Economic Review*, 15/1: 28–32.

ONS (1998), Office for National Statistics, *Regional Trends*, 33 (London: TSO).

—— (2002), Office for National Statistics, *Regional Trends*, 37 (London: TSO).

Owen, G. (1993), 'Inward Investment and the Training and Enterprise Councils', in Institute of Welsh Affairs (ed.), *Welsh Economic Review Special Issue: Inward Investment in Wales* (Cardiff: Welsh Economy Research Unit), pp. 30–1.

Owen, J. A. (1977), *The History of the Dowlais Ironworks 1759–1936* (Risca: Starling Press).

Pahl, J. (1989), *Money and Marriage* (Basingstoke: Macmillan).

Pain, N. (2000), *Inward Investment, Technological Change and Growth: The Impact of Multinationals* (London: National Institute for Economic and Social Research).

Parker, H. (1989), *Instead of the Dole* (London: Routledge).

Pavlinek, P. and Smith, A. (1998), 'Internationalization and Embeddedness in the East-Central European Transition: The Contrasting Geographies of Inward Investment in the Czech and Slovak Republics', *Regional Studies*, 32: 619–38.

Pearson, E. (2002), 'English Man Commits Suicide after Racial Abuse from Welsh', *South Wales Echo*, 12 March.

Pharoah, C. (1998), 'Recent Data on the Size, Scope, Income and Expenditure of the Voluntary Sector', ch. 1 in C. Pharoah and M. Smerdon (eds), *Dimensions of the Voluntary Sector* (West Malling: Charities Aid Foundation), pp. 13–23.

Phelps, N. A., MacKinnon, D., Stone, I. and Braidford, P. (2003), 'Embedding the Multinationals? Institutions and the Development of Overseas Manufacturing Affiliates in Wales and the North East', *Regional Studies*, 37/1: 27–40.

Philips, D. (1994), *Rhondda: The Story of a Coal Community* (Pontypridd: Mid Glamorgan County Council Educational Support Unit).

Pike, A. (1999), 'The Politics of Factory Closures and Task Forces in the North East Region of England', *Regional Studies*, 33/6: 567–86.

Pilgrim Trust (1938), *Men without Work* (London: 1938).

Policy Commission (2002), *Farming and Food: A Sustainable Future* (London: Cabinet Office).

Preston, J. (1997), *Feyerabend: Philosophy, Science and Society* (Cambridge: Polity Press).

Pretty, J. (2002), *Agri-Culture: Reconnecting People, Land and Nature* (London: Earthscan).

Pride, E. (1975), *Rhondda My Valley Brave* (Risca: Starling Press).

Rajan, V. (1993), *Rebuilding Communities: Experiences and Experiments in Europe* (Totnes: Green Books).

RCTBC (Rhondda Cynon Taff Borough Council) (1996), *Economic Development Statement 1996–1997* (Abercynon: Navigation Park).

—— (1998), *Economic Development Statement 1998–99 Datganiad Datblygu Economaidd* (Abercynon: Navigation Park).

Rees, T. (1988), 'Changing Patterns of Women's Work in Wales: Some Myths Explored', *Contemporary Wales*, 2: 119–30.

Reinarman, C. (1987), *American States of Mind* (New Haven, Conn.: Yale University Press).

Rifkin, J. (1995), *The End of Work: The Decline of the Global Labor Force and the Dawn of the Post-Market Era* (New York: Putnam).

Rilling, J. K., Gutman, D. A., Zeh, T. R., Pagnoni, G., Berns, G. S. and Kilts, C. D. (2002), 'A Neural Basis for Social Cooperation', *Neuron*, 35: 395–405.

Roberts, A. (1994), 'The Causes and Consequences of Inward Investment: The Welsh Experience', *Contemporary Wales*, 6: 73–86.

Roberts, B. (1994), 'Welsh Identity in a Former Mining Valley: Social Images and Imagined Communities', *Contemporary Wales*, 5: 77–96.

Robertson, J. (1999), 'A Green Taxation and Benefits System', in M. S. Cato and M. Kennett (eds.), *Green Economics: Beyond Supply and Demand to Meeting People's Needs* (Aberystwyth: Green Audit), pp. 65–77.

Romer, P. M. (1986), 'Increasing Returns and Long-Run Growth', *Journal of Political Economy*, 94: 1002–37.

—— (1990), *Human Capital and Growth: Theory and Revenue*, Carnegie-Rochester Conference Survey on Public Policy, no. 32: 251–86.

Rowbotham, M. (1999), *The Grip of Death: A Study of Modern Money, Debt Slavery and Destructive Economics* (Charlbury: Jon Carpenter).

Roy, A. (1998), 'Out of the City: Japanese Financial Sector FDI in the UK Regions', paper presented at the Third Annual Postgraduate Economics Conference, Leeds, 13 November.

Sabel, C., Herrigel, G., Dees, R. and Kazis, R. (1989), 'Regional Prosperities Compared: Massachusetts and Baden-Württemberg in the 1980s', *Economy and Society*, 18: 374–403.

Sahara, N. (1993), 'Japanese Manufacturing Investment: Toyota at Deeside', in Institute of Welsh Affairs (ed.), *Welsh Economic Review Special Issue: Inward Investment in Wales* (Cardiff: Welsh Economy Research Unit), pp. 23–5.

Said, E. (1994), *Culture and Imperialism* (London: Vintage).

Sakho, H. (1998), 'Expatriate Managers: Skilled Workers of the Globe or Guardians of Global Corporate Values', paper presented at the Third Annual Postgraduate Economics Conference, Leeds, 13 Nov.

Salamon, L. M. and Anheier, H. K. (1996), *The Emerging Nonprofit Sector* (Manchester: Manchester University Press).

Salmon, J. (1993), 'The Manufacturing of New Human Resources in Wales: An Industrial District Perspective', in Institute of Welsh Affairs (ed.), *Welsh Economic Review Special Issue: Inward Investment in Wales* (Cardiff: Welsh Economy Research Unit), pp. 27–9.

Salmon, W. C. (1990), 'Rationality and Objectivity in Science *or* Tom Kuhn Meets Tom Bayes', in C. W. Savage (ed.), *Scientific Theories* (Minneapolis: University of Minnesota Press), pp. 175–204; reprinted in D. Papineau (ed.), *The Philosophy of Science* (Oxford: Oxford University Press, 1996), 256–89.

Samuel, Y. and Lewin-Epstein, N. (1979), 'The Occupational Situs as a Predictor of Work Values', *American Journal of Sociology*, 85: 625–39.

Sanyal, N. (1930), *Development of Indian Railways* (Calcutta: University Press).

Scott, A. (1997) (ed.), *The Limits of Globalization: Cases and Arguments* (London: Routledge).

Scott, H. (2002), 'Pru to Transfer Jobs to India', bbc online news, 30 September.

Scourfield, J., Evans, J., Shah, W. and Beynon, H. (2002), 'Responding to the Experiences of Minority Ethnic Children in Virtually All-White Communities', *Child and Family Social Work*, 7/3: 161–76.

Sheahen, A. (2003), 'The Negative Income Tax Experiment of the 1970s in the USA', from *www.basicincome.be*

Shteinbuka, I. (1995), 'Industrial Policy in Transition: The Case of Latvia', in M. M. Tykkyläinen (ed.), *Local and Regional Development during the 1990s Transition in Eastern Europe* (Aldershot: Avebury), p. 269.

Smale, W. (2002), 'Grants Reach a Record High', *Western Mail*, 10 April.

Smith, P. (1999), 'Credit for Bangladesh', *Economic Review*, 17/2: 16–19.

Smith, R., Arthur, L., Keenoy, T. and Anthony, P. D. (2001), 'Capital Anchoring and Co-operative Ownership: The Reality of the Operation of a Co-operative Enterprise in a Globalising Economy', Conference on Politics, Public Policy and the Employment Relationship, Sixteenth Employment Research Unit Annual Conference, Cardiff.

——, ——, —— and —— (2002), 'Tower Colliery: Back to the Future?', International Sociological Association, World Congress, Brisbane, Australia.

Snower, D. J. (1996), 'Evaluating Unemployment Policies: What do the Underlying Theories Tell Us?', *Oxford Review of Economic Policy*, 11/1: 110–35.

South Wales Echo (2002), 'Klan Man Jailed for Racial Harassment', 7 March.

Stroeken, J. (1996), 'A Case for Basic Income: The Dutch Social Security Debate is Hotting Up', *New Economy*, 3/3: 187–91.

Strömpl, J. (2000), 'The Transition in Estonian Society and its Impact on a Girls' Reformatory School', *European Journal of Social Work*, 3/1: 29–42.

Summers, M. (ed.) (1992), *Economic Alternatives for Eastern Europe* (London: New Economics Foundation).

Swedberg, R. (1996), *Economic Sociology* (Cheltenham: Elgar).

Tacq, J. (1997), *Multivariate Analysis Techniques in Social Science Research: From Problem to Analysis* (Thousand Oaks, Calif.: Sage).

Taylor, A. (2001), '"People's Company" in Water Deal', *Times*, 31 January.

Tewdwr-Jones, M. and Phelps, N. A. (1999), 'Unsustainable Behaviour? The Subordination of Local Governance in Creating Customised Spaces for Asian FDI', paper presented to the Regional Studies Association Conference, Bilbao, September.

Thomas, D. (1996), 'Winner or Loser in the New Europe? Regional Funding, Inward Investment and Prospects for the Welsh Economy', *European Urban and Regional Studies*, 3/3: 225–40.

—— (1999), 'The Welsh Economy, 1949–1999', *Transactions of the Honourable Society of Cymmorodorion*, NS 5: 161–81.

Thomas, J. J. (1992), *Informal Economic Acitivity* (Hemel Hempstead: Harvester Wheatsheaf).

Thomas, K. (1999), *The Oxford Book of Work* (Oxford: Oxford University Press).

Thomas, M. (1991), 'Colliery Closure and the Miner's Experience of Redundancy', *Contemporary Wales*, 4: 45–65.

Thompson, E. P. (1963), *The Making of the English Working Class* (Harmondsworth: Penguin).

Tickell, R. E. (1995), *The Vale of Nantgwilt: A Submerged Valley*; repr. from 1894 original (London: J. S. Virtue & Co.).

Tower Colliery (2000), *Tower Energy Services: Energy for the 21st Century* (Hirwaun: Tower Colliery).

Toynbee, P. (2003), *Hard Work: Life in Low-Pay Britain* (London: Bloomsbury).

Trainor, T. (2002), 'Conference to Tackle Racist Attitudes', *Western Mail* online, 21 January.

Treasury (2001), *Blue Book* (London: TSO).

Trigilia, C. (2002), *Economic Sociology: State, Market, and Society in Modern Capitalism* (Oxford: Blackwell).

Trosset, C. (1993), *Welshness Performed: Welsh Concepts of Person and Society* (Tucson: University of Arizona Press).

—— and Caulkins, D. (2001), 'Triangulation and Confirmation in the Study of Welsh Concepts of Personhood', *Journal of Anthropological Research*, 57/1: 61–81.

Turnbull, P. and Wass, V. (1999), 'Redundancy and the Paradox of Job Insecurity', ch. 4 of E. Heery and J. Salmon (eds), *The Insecure Workforce* (London: Routledge), pp. 57–77.

Tykkyläinen, M. (1995), *Local and Regional Development during the 1990s Transition in Eastern Europe* (Aldershot: Avebury, 1995).

Undy, R., Fosh, P., Morris, H., Smith, P. and Martin, R. (1996), *Managing the Unions: The Impact of Legislation on Trade Unions' Behaviour* (Oxford: Clarendon Press).

van Parijs, P. (1995), *Real Freedom for All* (Oxford: Clarendon Press).

Vincent, J. (1998), 'Voluntary Sector Comparisons in England, Scotland, Wales and Northern Ireland', ch. 10 in C. Pharoah and M. Smerdon (eds), *Dimensions of the Voluntary Sector* (West Malling: Charities Aid Foundation), pp. 81–6.

Visvanathan, S. (1997), *A Carnival for Science: Essays on Science, Technology and Development* (Delhi: Oxford University Press).

WAC (Welsh Affairs Select Committe) (1998), *Fourth Report: Investment in Industry in Wales*, HC821 (London: TSO).

Waddington, D., Dicks, B. and Critcher, C. (1992), '"It Feels like Somebody Close has Died": The Social Impact of Pit Closure', unpublished research paper, Sheffield Hallam University.

Wales European Taskforce (1999), *West Wales and the Valleys Objective 1: Single Programming Document for the Period 2000–2006* (Cardiff: Wales European Taskforce).

Wang, C. (1998), 'Productivity Spillovers from Foreign Direct Investment: Evidence from UK Industry Level Panel Data', paper presented at the Third Annual Postgraduate Economics Conference, Leeds, 13 November.

Wass, V. and Mainwaring, L. (1989), 'Economic and Social Consequences of Rationalization in the South Wales Coal Industry', *Contemporary Wales*, 3: 161–85.

Watkins, C. (1877), *Buried Alive! A Narrative of Suffering and Heroism, Being the Tale of the Rhondda Colliers as Related by Themselves* (London: Houlston & Sons).

Watson, R. (1997), *Rhondda Coal, Cardiff Gold: The Insoles of Llandaff, Coal Owners and Shippers* (Cardiff: Merton Priory Press).

Watson, S. (1991), 'Gilding the Smokestacks: The New Symbolic Representations of Deindustralized Regions', *Environment and Planning D: Society and Space*, 9: 59–70.

Weber, M. (1915), 'The Protestant Sects and the Spirit of Capitalism'; reprinted in Gerth, H. H. and Wright Mills, C. (eds), *From Max Weber: Essays in Sociology* (London: Routledge and Kegan Paul, 1948), pp. 267–301.

Webster, D. (2000), 'The Geographical Concentration of Labour-Market Disadvantage', *Oxford Review of Economy Policy*, 16/1: 114–28.

Welsh Assembly (2001), *Quinquennial Review of the Welsh Development Agency* (Cardiff: Welsh Assembly).

—— (2002a), *A Winning Wales: The National Economic Development Strategy of the Welsh Assembly Government* (Cardiff: Welsh Assembly).

—— (2002b), *Digest of Welsh Statistics* (Cardiff: Welsh Assembly).

—— (2003), *Digest of Welsh Local Area Statistics* (Cardiff: Welsh Assembly).

—— (2004), *Digest of Welsh Statistics* (Cardiff: Welsh Statistics Directorate).

Welsh Office (1998a), *Welsh Local Area Statistics 1998* (Cardiff: Welsh Office)

—— (1998b), *Digest of Welsh Statistics 1998* (Cardiff: Welsh Office).

—— (1998c), *Statistics for Assembly Constituency Areas 1998* (Cardiff: Welsh Office)

—— (1998d), *Pathway to Prosperity* (Cardiff: Welsh Office).

—— (1999), *Digest of Welsh Local Area Statistics* (Cardiff: Welsh Office).

Westergaard, J., Noble, I. and Walker, A. (1989), *After Redundancy: The Experience of Economic Insecurity* (Cambridge: Polity Press).

Western Mail (2001), 'Co-operation is the Best Way Forward', 2 October.

Williams, C. (1996), *Democratic Rhondda: Politics and Society 1885–1951* (Cardiff: University of Wales Press).

Williams, C. C. and Windebank, J. (1998), *Informal Employment in the Advanced Economies: Implications for Work and Welfare* (London: Routledge).

Williams, D A. and Smith, D. J. (1998), 'The Entry Mode Decisions of Multinational Enterprises and Regional Economic Development', in S. Hill and B. Morgan (eds), *Inward Investment, Business Finance, and Regional Development* (Basingstoke: Macmillan), pp. 65–79.

Williams, D. J. (2003), 'Engineering a Sustainable Future', presentation to the Welsh Economy Research Unit Eleventh Annual Conference: Sustainable Development in Wales: Theory, Practice and Measurement, Cardiff Business School, 14 May.

Williams, J. (1980), 'The Coal Industry, 1750–1914', ch. 4 in A. H. John and G. Williams (eds), *Glamorgan County History*, v. *Industrial Glamorgan* (Cardiff: University of Wales Press), pp. 155–210.

Williams, L. J. (1998), *Digest of Welsh Historical Statistics* (Cardiff: Welsh Office).

Williams, S. R. (1995), 'The True "Cymraes": Images of Women in Women's Nineteenth-Century Welsh Periodicals', in A. V. John (ed.), *Our Mothers' Land: Chapters in Welsh Women's History, 1830–1939* (Cardiff: University of Wales Press), pp. 69–91.

Williamson, D. (2003), 'The Case for Organic Dinners', *Western Mail*, 16 June, p. 7.

Wilson, J. and Musick, M. A. (1997), 'Work and Volunteering: The Long Arm of the Job', *Social Forces*, 76/1: 251–72.

Winckler, V. (1987), 'Women and Work in Contemporary Wales', *Contemporary Wales*, 1: 53–71.

Woolsey Biggart, N. (2002), *Readings in Economic Sociology* (Oxford: Blackwell).

Wylie, I. (2001), 'Underground Activists', *Fast Company*, 52: 50.

Young, S., Hood, N. and Peters, E. (1994), 'Targeting Policy as a Competitive Strategy for European Inward Investment Agencies', *European Urban and Regional Studies*, 1/2: 143–59.

Yunus, M. (1999), 'The Bank that Likes to Say Yes', *Scientific American*, November, 12–15.

Index